AMERICANS AT PLAY

AMERICANS AT PLAY

Demographics of Outdoor Recreation & Travel

New Strategist Publications, Inc.

Ithaca, New York

New Strategist Publications, Inc.

P.O. Box 242, Ithaca, NY 14851

607/273-0913

ISBN 1-885070-11-X

Printed in the United States of America

for Phil

Table of Contents

Chapter 6. Nature Observation

Chapter 7. Outdoor Team Sports

Chapter 8. Watersports

Chapter 9. Winter Sports

Tables

Chapter 3. Outdoor Family Activities

Chapter 4. Fishing and Hunting

Chapter 5. Individual Sports

Chapter 6. Nature Observation

Chapter 7. Outdoor Team Sports

Chapter 8. Watersports

Chapter 9. Winter Sports

Chapter 10. High School Sports Participation

Chapter 11. College Sports Participation

Chapter 12. Recreational Travel

Introduction

Time is a most-precious commodity today. How we spend our free time says something about who we are and what we value.

Americans at Play: The Demographics of Outdoor Recreation & Travel takes the resting pulse of the nation. It examines who participates in which sports, how the sports we watch affect participation, and how much we spend getting away from it all.

A frequent accusation made against modern American society is that too many of us use technology—television and computers—to insulate ourselves from others. But the millions of people who wholeheartedly and single-mindedly participate in the various recreational activities profiled in this book prove otherwise. This is a nation still very much full of passionate players.

What's the most-popular outdoor recreational activity in the United States today? Which sports are the hottest for people aged 40 to 49? How do the affluent like to play? You'll find the answers in Chapter 1, along with participation rankings by sex, race, education, and other demographic characteristics.

Chapter 2 shows you the money—how much the average household spends on recreation, participant sports, recreational lessons, and athletic gear. Average and indexed spending tables are included, as well as data describing market share by age, income, education, region, race, Hispanic origin, and household type. You will discover how much it costs to attend a major league sporting event, courtesy of *The Team Marketing Report*'s Fan Cost Index™.

Chapters 3 through 9 look at outdoor recreational activities in more detail. Each sport's profile includes who participates by age, income, sex, race, education, and household size. The profiles also reveal the hottest trends in each activity based on extensive interviews with experts. Together, the demographics and expert insight help you understand the trends in each sport.

Chapters 10 and 11 offer a glimpse into the future, revealing the sports popular among today's high school and college students, how they have changed, and how they might change in the future.

The final chapter gives you an overview of the demographics of pleasure travel, since travel is often part and parcel of recreational participation. This chapter tells you who travels, what they do when they travel, and how much they spend.

All told, *Americans at Play* examines about 60 of the most-popular outdoor recreational activities in depth. Most of the data on outdoor recreational participation are from the Forest Service's *1994-95 National Survey of Recreation and the Environment*. The spending data included in this book are from the Bureau of Labor Statistics' *1995 Consumer Expenditure Survey*. (For more about these surveys, see the section, "Behind the Numbers," on page 8.) Data from other sources are also included in the book, as needed. While *Americans at Play* attempts to be comprehensive about the demographics of outdoor recreation, no book on recreation in the United States can be truly complete because new recreational activities are invented every day.

One thing you won't find in this book is a depth of information on fans of professional sports. Information on the spectators of professional sports is included only when it relates to participation. One reason why professional sports fans are not examined in depth is the dearth of reliable and comparable public information about who watches or attends professional team sporting events. The few data professional teams are willing to reveal are of poor quality and incomparable with the data available from other teams. A spokesperson for Major League Baseball claimed she had never seen a demographic survey of baseball fans.

Attendance at Selected Spectator Sports, 1985 and 1993

(number of persons attending selected spectator sports, numerical and percent change in attendance, 1985 and 1993; ranked by numerical change)

	number attending (millions)		change, 1985-93	
	1993	1985	number (millions)	percent
Major League Baseball	71.2	47.7	23.5	49.2%
National Basketball Association	19.1	11.5	7.6	65.7
National Hockey League	17.2	12.8	4.4	34.3
NCAA—women's college basketball	4.2	2.1	2.1	102.4
NCAA—men's college basketball	28.5	26.6	1.4	7.1
National Football League	14.8	14.1	0.7	5.1
NCAA—college football	34.9	35.0	-0.1	-0.1

Source: Bureau of the Census, Statistical Abstract of the United States, 1996

The second and more-important reason why professional team sports take a back seat to participatory sports in *Americans at Play* is that participatory sports are becoming more important than spectator sports. In reality, most sports occur at the amateur level, away from player strikes and inflated salaries. While 71 million Americans attended a Major League Baseball game in 1993, the year of peak attendance,

Participation in Outdoor Recreational Activities, 1982-83 and 1994-95

(number of persons aged 16 or older participating in selected outdoor recreational activities, numerical and percent change in number of participants, 1982-83 and 1994-95; ranked by numerical change)

	number participating (millions)		change, 1982-83 to 1994-95	
	1994-95	1982-83	number (millions)	percent
Walking	133.6	93.6	40.0	42.7%
Bird watching	54.1	21.2	32.9	155.2
Sightseeing	113.4	81.3	32.1	39.5
Attending outdoor sports event	95.2	70.7	24.5	34.7
Hiking	47.7	24.7	23.0	93.1
Swimming (nonpool)	78.1	56.5	21.6	38.2
Picnicking	98.4	84.8	13.6	16.0
Motorboating	46.9	33.6	13.3	39.6
Swimming (pool)	88.5	76.0	12.5	16.4
Camping (developed area)	41.5	30.0	11.5	38.3
Camping (any)	53.7	42.4	11.3	26.7
Boating	60.1	49.5	10.6	21.4
Camping (primitive area)	28.0	17.7	10.3	58.2
Off-road driving	27.8	19.4	8.4	43.3
Outdoor team sports	49.5	42.4	7.1	16.7
Golf	29.6	23.0	6.6	28.7
Running, jogging	52.5	45.9	6.6	14.4
Backpacking	15.2	8.8	6.4	72.7
Downhill skiing	16.8	10.6	6.2	58.5
Sledding	20.4	17.7	2.7	15.3
Water-skiing	17.8	15.9	1.9	11.9
Snowmobiling	7.0	5.3	1.7	32.1
Cross-country skiing	6.6	5.3	1.3	24.5
Bicycling	57.4	56.5	0.9	1.6
Ice skating	10.4	10.6	-0.2	-1.9
Sailing	9.6	10.6	-1.0	-9.4
Horseback riding	14.2	15.9	-1.7	-10.7
Fishing	58.3	60.1	-1.8	-3.0
Hunting	18.8	21.2	-2.4	-11.3
Attending outdoor concert	41.5	44.2	-2.7	-6.1
Tennis	21.2	30.0	-8.8	-29.3

Source: USDA Forest Service, 1982-83 Nationwide Recreation Survey *and* 1994-95 National Survey on Recreation and the Environment

nearly twice as many took part in fitness walking for exercise or pleasure—134 million. While the number of people attending women's college basketball games doubled between 1985 and 1993, so did the number of bird watchers. More importantly, bird watchers outnumber those who attend professional basketball games by an enormous 35 million. Participatory sports are far more relevant to a greater number of Americans, and American businesses, than professional team sports.

Linking a product or service to a professional team sport can be a powerful marketing tool. But the lack of comparable data between, say, the National Hockey League and the National Basketball Association, raises questions about the efficiency of such an approach. Marketers must trust the numbers offered by the sport itself (not an objective source, by any means) or do their own research to see if the spectators of the sport are the consumers they want.

The mounting problems of professional team sports make participatory sports and recreational activities look even better as a way to reach consumers. This book is your guide to those consumers. Although each of the activities profiled in *Americans at Play* is as individual as a fingerprint, there are common threads to many of the

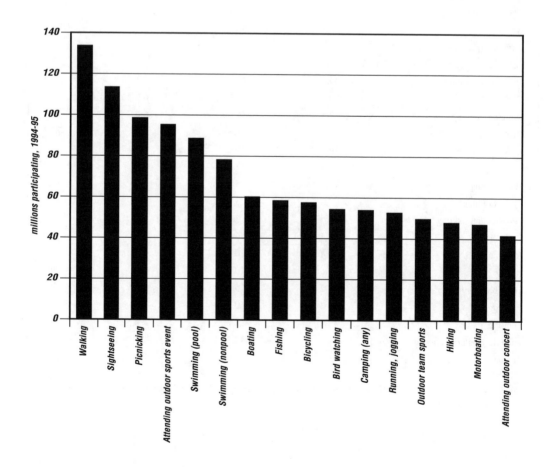

sports, noted by the many experts cited in the book. Here are the eight most-important trends in participatory sports and recreation.

Trend 1. Aging Boomers

The demographic profiles of participants in most sports and recreational activities show similar patterns by age. Participation is above average among people under age 50 and below average for those aged 50 or older. This is about to change. The oldest members of the baby-boom generation—the first to embrace sports and fitness as a lifestyle—are now entering their 50s. In the next decade, participation in sports and recreation will surge within the fiftysomething age group as it fills with boomers. This group will be one of the biggest growth markets for participatory sports.

Trend 2. Pioneering Women

Women will constitute a growing share of participants in most sports and recreational activities—thanks to the aging of generations of women who have benefited from Title IX. This law, which requires schools receiving federal funds to provide equal athletic opportunities for males and females, has been around for 25 years. While the

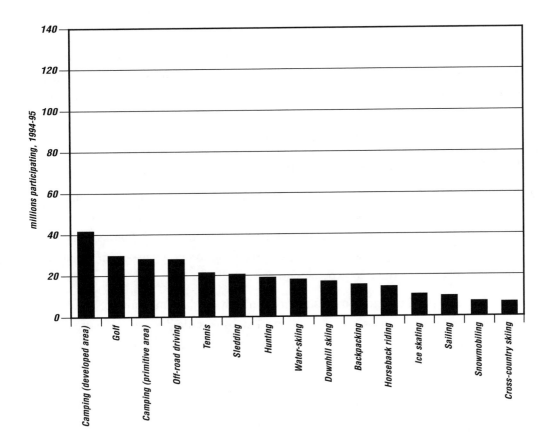

law hasn't always been enforced, compliance with Title IX has changed sports profoundly. Even so, the world of sports is only just beginning to feel the effects of Title IX. While most sports have changed to accommodate women, women are also changing sports. Terms like "saner," "smarter," "better" are bandied about when we discuss the impact women have had on sports. Even the concept of competition is changing, according to Mariah Burton Nelson, former basketball pro and author of several books on women's impact on athletics. She sees competition as a form of intimacy, of "seeking together." In what she terms the "Champion Model" of competition, your opponent is your source of inspiration—not your enemy.

The female sports consumer is avidly sought by businesses. Manufacturers are creating gear specifically designed for women—not just lighter and smaller versions of equipment designed for men. This will allow women to really flex their muscles and show what they can do.

Trend 3. Hybrid Sports

We're nowhere near the final recreational frontier. Although physical fitness is still a consideration for many active people, it's not the only reason to recreate today. Gyms and health clubs, viewed as fluorescent confinement by many, are trying to add excitement to routines. They are moving from working out to playing out.

The challenge, inside gyms and out, is to constantly come up with new ideas. This has spawned hybrid sports—such as in-line skating and snowboarding—which require different skills to master. The next winning combination is hard to predict. One possibility is "balf," a hybrid of baseball and golf. The increased interest in golf, especially among young people, might allow "balf" to flourish.

Trend 4. Be an Expert—or Just Look Like One

Be it for females or males, athletic gear has become more professional and high-tech. Manufacturing technology has improved to the point where equipment enhances rather than detracts from athletic performance. Retailing has improved, thanks to sports superstores, making highly specialized gear available to everyone—from amateurs who probably don't need it to experts who do.

Sports apparel has gone mainstream even as it has become more colorful and stylish. Once the province of Army/Navy surplus stores, today's sports clothing looks so good that children and adults are buying expensive garb just to wear it to the mall.

Trend 5. Shrinking Resources

Complaints about lack of space are common to almost every activity. Just when an increasing number of people are becoming interested in the outdoors, more of the nation is becoming urbanized and funding for parks and recreation is being cut. The result is that access to land and water is becoming scarce.

This creates a variety of problems. Fees have already been raised in national parks. Even higher fees and a more extensive reservation system will become necessary to control the crowds. This could create an "elite effect": those who can afford to do so may increasingly recreate on private land.

Some activities could be priced out of the reach of lower- and middle-class families, narrowing the participation base for some activities. Many organizations are concerned about this and have started outreach or community programs—especially in inner cities—to recruit the next generation of participants in their sport.

Shrinking resources also will necessitate more government regulation. Sports without strong advocacy groups could get lost in the competitive shuffle for land and water. The March/April 1997 issue of *National Parks*, for example, discusses a possible ban on personal watercraft (commonly known by Kawasaki's brand name, Jet Ski) in national parks in the United States. Personal watercraft are not the only participatory sports getting squeezed. Expect to see more regulation of a greater variety of sports in the future.

Trend 6. Sports for the Disabled

Advances in medical and other technologies are allowing the disabled to become more active than ever before. Consequently, there is a growing market of recreation consumers who have disabilities.

So far, this market has barely been tapped. Manufacturers are just waking up to the potential—particularly as active baby boomers age. Cannondale, the high-end bicycle manufacturer, has just made a foray into sport wheelchairs, for example—a market worth $400 million in annual sales, according to the company.

The Americans with Disabilities Act and the Individuals with Disabilities Education Act mandate equal access for people with disabilities. Their impact on the world of sports could be similar to that of Title IX. The success of the Special Olympics and Paraolympics show the potential of this niche. Therapeutic recreation, or the use of recreation to help heal the body and mind, is also a growing trend that will surge with the aging of the baby-boom generation.

Trend 7. The Olympic Effect

The summer and winter Olympic games create a sports feeding frenzy in the United States every two years. Nothing motivates Americans more to become active than seeing their country win in world competition.

The next Olympic winter event (and the last of this century) will take place in Japan in 1998. Debuting sports include women's ice hockey, curling, and possibly snowboarding. Whatever sports are new during an Olympic will be important recreationally during the Olympic year. If the United States does well in the sport, it will remain important for a long time thereafter.

Trend 8. Cycles

No sport remains hot forever. Like many things in our economy, the popularity of individual recreational activities is cyclical. Enthusiasts of sports that are on the way up think they can buck the odds and continue to grow forever, while devotees of sports that are on the way down believe fervently in the cycle theory because it means they're not on the way out. When a new challenge emerges, it's cool and cutting edge to try it. Some of those who try it become devoted fans, but most will move on to the next challenge. Watch out for sports that are overexposed—tried by many but adopted by few. When manufacturers begin to build a surplus of equipment, the downward spiral may have begun.

The United States was founded as much on hard play as on hard work. As our society diversifies, our differences will be reflected in our choice of activities. As the population ages, sports and recreation will adapt. As the world becomes smaller, the ways we play will take on a more global feel. Although Americans say they work too hard, they still have time to play hard, too. Here's how they play.

Behind the Numbers

• **National Survey on Recreation and the Environment**

Most of the data on outdoor recreational participation in *Americans at Play* are from the *1994-95 National Survey on Recreation and the Environment*. This survey provides the most reliable and comprehensive information about Americans' participation in outdoor recreation. Seven recreation surveys have been conducted over the years, the first in 1960; others were taken in 1965, 1970, 1972, 1977, 1982-83, and 1994-95. Because funding for these surveys has been hard to come by, the survey instrument and methodology have changed over the years, making many of the historical data incomparable with the most recent survey.

The 1994-95 survey was conducted by the United States Department of Agriculture's Forest Service and sponsored by a variety of government and private agencies, including the Sporting Goods Manufacturers Association. Survey researchers interviewed 17,220 Americans aged 16 or older from January 1994 through May 1995. Because of the large sample size, the results can be broken down by age, sex, household income, and other demographic characteristics. Survey researchers asked respondents which outdoor recreational activities they had participated in during the past 12 months. While the answers do not reveal the characteristics of the hard-core fans of various recreational pursuits, they do reveal the reach of each market.

For more information about the National Survey on Recreation and the Environment, contact H. Ken Cordell, project leader, United States Department of Agriculture Forest Service, Southern Research Station, Forestry Sciences Laboratory, Athens, Georgia 30602-2044; telephone (706) 546-2457.

- **Consumer Expenditure Survey**

The spending data in *Americans at Play* are from the Bureau of Labor Statistics' *1995 Consumer Expenditure Survey*. This is an ongoing nationwide survey of household spending, including everything from big-ticket items such as homes and cars to small purchases like athletic gear, admission to sporting events, and fees for recreational lessons. In taking the survey, researchers interview 25,000 U.S. households each year, collecting data on nearly 1,000 separate categories of products and services. For more information about the survey, contact the Bureau of Labor Statistics at (202) 606-6900.

The spending tables in the book show three types of spending figures for households: average annual, indexed, and market shares. The average spending figures are for all households in a segment—in other words, all households within a given income range—not just those who purchased the item. When examining average spending data, it is important to remember that by including both purchasers and non-purchasers in the calculation, the average spending amount is diluted, especially for infrequently purchased items. The average household, for example, spent $50.33 on athletic gear, game tables, and exercise equipment in 1995. This figure includes households who spent nothing on equipment as well as those who spent something. Since the number of households who spent something on athletic gear is smaller than the total number of households, the average spending figures underestimate the amount spent by purchasers.

More telling than the average spending figures are the indexes, which reveal the best customers for a product or service. The indexes compare the spending of each household segment with the spending of the average household. To compute the index, the average spending of households in each segment are divided by the average spending of all households. An index of 132 means that average spending by the segment is 32 percent above the all-household average (100 plus 32). An index of 68 means that spending by the segment is 32 percent below average (100 minus 32). Households with an index of 170 for athletic gear, for example, are a strong market for this product, because they spend 70 percent more than the average household.

The market share figures reveal which household segments dominate spending in a category. The figures are calculated by first multiplying the average spending of each household segment by the number of households in the segment. This figure is then divided by the total spending of all households on an item, which results in the percentage (or market share) of total spending on an item that is accounted for by each household segment. Market share figures make it easy to discern which household segments account for most of the spending on a particular product or service. In 1995, for example, householders aged 35 to 44 accounted for 45 percent of all household spending on recreational lessons, clearly dominating this category.

Market share figures can be misleading and should be used with caution. The household segment controlling the largest share of spending on an item may not be the segment most likely to purchase the item (i.e., the best customers). This is because market shares are greatly influenced by the number of households in a segment. Because the baby-boom generation is now in the 35-to-54 age group, for example, householders in that age group tend to dominate spending in most categories. But 35-to-54-year-olds are not necessarily the best customers (i.e., those with the greatest propensity to buy) of a product or service. To determine who the best customers are, use the indexes.

Because the participation and spending data in *Americans at Play* come from two different sources, they do not always match. For many recreational activities, no spending data are available. Some spending categories do not precisely match a specific recreational activity. The demographic breakouts are not exactly the same in the two surveys. But there are enough similarities in demographic breakouts and enough overlap in recreational categories to make it worthwhile to include the spending data in the book. The combination of participation rates and spending data reveals how Americans have fun.

Chapter 1

Rankings of Participation in Outdoor Recreational Activities

"Sports are war, minus the shooting," George Orwell once wrote. Sports played among even the best of friends still have that "go for the throat" feel to them. Even when recreating alone, we compete against ourselves.

There's no less competition among participatory sports, each vying to be America's favorite. In this competition, there are clear winners and losers. Some participatory sports and recreational activities are much more popular than others.

At the top of the list are walking, sightseeing, picnicking, attending an outdoor sports event, and swimming. More than one-third of Americans aged 16 or older took part in each of these activities in 1994-95. The top five are popular because they are not physically demanding, are relatively inexpensive, don't necessitate learning new skills, and don't require much preparation to enjoy.

"Family values" may be a political catch phrase, but it's a very real consideration in recreation today. Family activities rank high overall—sightseeing is second, picnicking third. Boating, fishing, and camping all rank among the top 20 outdoor sport and recreational activities. With millions of baby boomers now raising children, it's no wonder family-oriented activities are so popular.

Twenty-five percent of Americans aged 16 or older participated in outdoor team sports in 1994-95, and volleyball was the most popular. Many team sports are dominated by young adults. Middle-aged Americans are too busy to take part, while many older Americans find team sports too strenuous. The lack of broad appeal diminishes their overall popularity.

Some of the least-popular activities are those that receive the most ink, such as snowboarding and kayaking. These are today's cool sports, getting a lift in the public's imagination—even though fewer than 1 percent of the population aged 16 or older participate in each of them. In a few years, they are likely to be replaced in the public's mind by newer, cooler sports.

An examination of the rankings on the following pages is certain to surprise many. It is more than a little revealing to see, for example, that fish viewing is more popular than downhill skiing, or that horseback riding is more popular than riding a personal watercraft. The rankings change by age, income, sex, race, and education in both expected and surprising ways.

Participation in Outdoor Recreational Activities: Total Population

(percent of persons aged 16 or older who have participated in selected recreational activities at least once in the past 12 months, 1994-95; ranked by percentage participating)

	percent	number (millions)		percent	number (millions)
Walking	66.7%	133.6	Saltwater fishing	9.5%	19.0
Sightseeing	56.6	113.4	Hunting (any)	9.4	18.8
Picnicking	49.1	98.4	Water-skiing	8.9	17.8
Attending outdoor sports event	47.5	95.2	Downhill skiing	8.4	16.8
Swimming (pool)	44.2	88.5	Backpacking	7.6	15.2
Swimming (nonpool)	39.0	78.1	Floating, rafting	7.6	15.2
Wildlife viewing	31.2	62.5	Snorkeling	7.2	14.4
Boating (any)	30.0	60.1	Big game hunting	7.1	14.2
Fishing (any)	29.1	58.3	Horseback riding	7.1	14.2
Bicycling	28.6	57.4	Football	6.8	13.6
Studying nature near water	27.6	55.3	Baseball	6.8	13.6
Bird watching	27.0	54.1	Canoeing	6.6	13.2
Camping (any)	26.8	53.7	Small-game hunting	6.5	13.0
Running, jogging	26.2	52.5	Ice skating	5.2	10.4
Outdoor team sports	24.7	49.5	Sailing	4.8	9.6
Freshwater fishing	24.4	48.9	Soccer	4.7	9.4
Hiking	23.8	47.7	Caving	4.7	9.4
Motorboating	23.4	46.9	Personal watercraft riding	4.7	9.4
Camping (developed area)	20.7	41.5	Mountain climbing	4.5	9.0
Attending outdoor concert	20.7	41.5	Rowing	4.2	8.4
Golf	14.8	29.6	Rock climbing	3.7	7.4
Volleyball	14.4	28.8	Snowmobiling	3.5	7.0
Camping (primitive area)	14.0	28.0	Cross-country skiing	3.3	6.6
Off-road driving	13.9	27.8	Orienteering	2.4	4.8
Fish viewing	13.7	27.4	Migratory-bird hunting	2.1	4.2
Softball	13.1	26.2	Surfing	1.3	2.6
Basketball	12.8	25.6	Windsurfing	1.1	2.2
Tennis	10.6	21.2	Snowboarding	0.8	1.6
Sledding	10.2	20.4	Kayaking	0.7	1.4

Source: USDA Forest Service, 1994-95 National Survey of Recreation and the Environment

Rankings of Participation in Outdoor Recreational Activities:

by Age

Young adults are more likely to take part in most sport and recreational activities than older Americans. While 61 percent of people aged 16 to 24 swim in a pool in a year's time, for example, the proportion drops to 55 percent among 25-to-29-year-olds and continues to fall steadily to a low of 22 percent among Americans aged 60 or older.

Some activities decline more steeply with age than others—particularly those that are physically demanding such as running. Fifty percent of 16-to-24-year-olds participate in running, compared to just 8 percent of those aged 60 or older. Some activities are more popular among older than younger Americans, such as walking and bird watching.

While participation in many activities declines with age, many activities appear among the top ten in all age groups. These include walking, swimming, picnicking, hiking, bicycling, and freshwater fishing.

Ranking of Participation in Outdoor Recreational Activities: Ages 16 to 24

(percent of persons aged 16 to 24 who have participated in selected outdoor recreational activities at least once in the past 12 months, 1994-95; ranked by percent participating)

1. Walking	68.2%		24. Baseball	14.1%
2. Swimming (pool)	60.6		25. Soccer	13.2
3. Swimming (nonpool)	51.3		26. Horseback riding	12.4
4. Running, jogging	50.4		27. Saltwater fishing	11.8
5. Picnicking	45.1		28. Canoeing	11.7
6. Bicycling	37.8		29. Personal watercraft riding	10.4
7. Hiking	31.5		30. Snorkeling	10.4
8. Basketball	31.0		31. Ice skating	9.9
9. Freshwater fishing	30.3		32. Big-game hunting	9.7
10. Volleyball	28.0		33. Small-game hunting	9.5
11. Motorboating	27.8		34. Rock climbing	8.3
12. Camping (developed areas)	27.6		35. Mountain climbing	8.2
13. Camping (primitive areas)	22.7		36. Caving	7.9
14. Tennis	21.4		37. Sailing	6.3
15. Football	20.6		38. Rowing	5.9
16. Softball	20.4		39. Snowmobiling	5.9
17. Water-skiing	17.7		40. Orienteering	4.1
18. Bird watching	16.4		41. Surfing	3.7
19. Floating, rafting	15.8		42. Cross-country skiing	3.5
20. Sledding	15.7		43. Migratory-bird hunting	3.0
21. Downhill skiing	15.5		44. Kayaking	2.7
22. Golf	15.3		45. Windsurfing	1.7
23. Backpacking	14.3		46. Snowboarding	1.5

Source: USDA Forest Service, 1994-95 National Survey on Recreation and the Environment

Ranking of Participation in Outdoor Recreational Activities: Ages 25 to 29

(percent of persons aged 25 to 29 who have participated in selected outdoor recreational activities at least once in the past 12 months, 1994-95; ranked by percent participating)

1. Walking	72.5%	
2. Swimming (pool)	54.7	
3. Picnicking	54.2	
4. Swimming (nonpool)	49.5	
5. Bicycling	36.3	
6. Running, jogging	33.3	
7. Hiking	30.2	
8. Motorboating	30.2	
9. Freshwater fishing	27.9	
10. Camping (developed area)	25.5	
11. Volleyball	23.2	
12. Softball	22.6	
13. Bird watching	21.2	
14. Camping (primitive area)	19.9	
15. Golf	19.0	
16. Basketball	18.7	
17. Water-skiing	15.8	
18. Downhill skiing	14.3	
19. Sledding	13.0	
20. Saltwater fishing	12.4	
21. Tennis	12.2	
22. Backpacking	11.9	
23. Floating, rafting	11.9	

24. Football	11.6%
25. Snorkeling	10.7
26. Horseback riding	10.2
27. Big-game hunting	9.7
28. Canoeing	9.3
29. Small-game hunting	9.2
30. Baseball	8.1
31. Personal watercraft riding	8.1
32. Caving	7.0
33. Mountain climbing	6.3
34. Ice skating	6.2
35. Sailing	6.2
36. Soccer	6.0
37. Rock climbing	5.5
38. Snowmobiling	5.4
39. Rowing	4.5
40. Cross-country skiing	3.5
41. Orienteering	3.3
42. Migratory-bird hunting	2.2
43. Surfing	1.9
44. Kayaking	1.8
45. Windsurfing	1.7
46. Snowboarding	1.1

Source: USDA Forest Service, 1994-95 National Survey on Recreation and the Environment

Ranking of Participation in Outdoor Recreational Activities: Ages 30 to 39

(percent of persons aged 30 to 39 who have participated in selected outdoor recreational activities at least once in the past 12 months, 1994-95; ranked by percent participating)

1.	Walking	74.7%	24. Big-game hunting	8.7%
2.	Picnicking	59.8	25. Floating, rafting	8.4
3.	Swimming (pool)	53.0	26. Backpacking	8.3
4.	Swimming (nonpool)	48.2	27. Canoeing	8.2
5.	Bicycling	37.4	28. Baseball	8.0
6.	Hiking	29.5	29. Small-game hunting	7.4
7.	Freshwater fishing	28.9	30. Ice skating	6.7
8.	Bird watching	28.4	31. Football	6.2
9.	Running, jogging	28.4	32. Personal watercraft riding	5.5
10.	Motorboating	27.7	33. Caving	5.3
11.	Camping (developed area)	26.0	34. Mountain climbing	5.3
12.	Volleyball	17.8	35. Sailing	5.1
13.	Golf	17.7	36. Soccer	5.0
14.	Softball	17.7	37. Snowmobiling	4.7
15.	Camping (primitive area)	16.6	38. Rowing	4.3
16.	Sledding	15.7	39. Rock climbing	3.9
17.	Basketball	14.1	40. Cross-country skiing	3.7
18.	Tennis	11.7	41. Orienteering	2.7
19.	Water-skiing	10.7	42. Migratory-bird hunting	2.6
20.	Saltwater fishing	10.1	43. Windsurfing	1.4
21.	Downhill skiing	9.9	44. Kayaking	1.3
22.	Snorkeling	9.5	45. Surfing	1.2
23.	Horseback riding	8.8	46. Snowboarding	0.9

Source: USDA Forest Service, 1994-95 National Survey on Recreation and the Environment

Ranking of Participation in Outdoor Recreational Activities: Ages 40 to 49

(percent of persons aged 40 to 49 who have participated in selected outdoor recreational activities at least once in the past 12 months, 1994-95; ranked by percent participating)

1. Walking	72.0%	24. Water-skiing	7.1%
2. Picnicking	55.4	25. Backpacking	7.0
3. Swimming (pool)	44.8	26. Big-game hunting	6.9
4. Swimming (nonpool)	42.4	27. Floating, rafting	6.3
5. Bird watching	33.8	28. Baseball	6.1
6. Bicycling	30.6	29. Small-game hunting	6.0
7. Hiking	27.0	30. Ice skating	5.6
8. Freshwater fishing	26.7	31. Sailing	5.3
9. Motorboating	24.2	32. Rowing	4.5
10. Running, jogging	23.3	33. Cross-country skiing	4.4
11. Camping (developed area)	22.6	34. Caving	4.3
12. Golf	15.4	35. Mountain climbing	3.7
13. Camping (primitive area)	13.8	36. Personal watercraft riding	3.3
14. Softball	12.1	37. Snowmobiling	3.0
15. Volleyball	11.3	38. Soccer	3.0
16. Sledding	10.5	39. Rock climbing	2.9
17. Saltwater fishing	10.4	40. Orienteering	2.4
18. Tennis	9.7	41. Football	2.3
19. Basketball	8.7	42. Migratory-bird hunting	2.2
20. Snorkeling	8.1	43. Kayaking	1.4
21. Downhill skiing	8.0	44. Snowboarding	0.9
22. Canoeing	7.4	45. Windsurfing	0.9
23. Horseback riding	7.2	46. Surfing	0.5

Source: USDA Forest Service, 1994-95 National Survey on Recreation and the Environment

Ranking of Participation in Outdoor Recreational Activities Ages 50 to 59

(percent of persons aged 50 to 59 who have participated in selected outdoor recreational activities at least once in the past 12 months, 1994-95; ranked by percent participating)

1.	Walking	65.5%	24. Sledding	4.4%
2.	Picnicking	47.7	25. Horseback riding	4.3
3.	Swimming (pool)	34.8	26. Cross-country skiing	4.0
4.	Bird watching	32.8	27. Rowing	4.0
5.	Swimming (nonpool)	30.5	28. Downhill skiing	3.9
6.	Bicycling	22.0	29. Baseball	3.8
7.	Motorboating	21.1	30. Sailing	3.7
8.	Freshwater fishing	20.2	31. Water-skiing	3.6
9.	Hiking	18.1	32. Floating, rafting	3.3
10.	Running, jogging	17.2	33. Caving	2.9
11.	Camping (developed area)	15.6	34. Ice skating	2.5
12.	Golf	12.0	35. Mountain climbing	2.3
13.	Camping (primitive area)	9.2	36. Snowmobiling	2.1
14.	Saltwater fishing	8.3	37. Migratory-bird hunting	2.0
15.	Volleyball	6.9	38. Personal watercraft riding	1.8
16.	Big-game hunting	6.6	39. Rock climbing	1.8
17.	Small-game hunting	6.4	40. Orienteering	1.5
18.	Softball	6.3	41. Soccer	1.5
19.	Tennis	6.1	42. Football	1.1
20.	Canoeing	4.9	43. Kayaking	0.9
21.	Basketball	4.7	44. Snowboarding	0.6
22.	Snorkeling	4.7	45. Windsurfing	0.6
23.	Backpacking	4.5	46. Surfing	0.5

Source: USDA Forest Service, 1994-95 National Survey on Recreation and the Environment

Ranking of Participation in Outdoor Recreational Activities: Ages 60 or Older

(percent of persons aged 60 or older who have participated in selected outdoor recreational activities at least once in the past 12 months, 1994-95; ranked by percent participating)

1. Walking	51.8%	24. Caving	1.6%
2. Picnicking	35.1	25. Volleyball	1.6
3. Bird watching	28.9	26. Backpacking	1.5
4. Swimming (pool)	21.8	27. Floating, rafting	1.4
5. Swimming (nonpool)	16.7	28. Snorkeling	1.4
6. Freshwater fishing	13.9	29. Cross-country skiing	1.2
7. Motorboating	13.3	30. Horseback riding	1.2
8. Bicycling	10.7	31. Baseball	1.1
9. Golf	10.3	32. Basketball	1.1
10. Hiking	9.6	33. Downhill skiing	1.0
11. Camping (developed area)	9.0	34. Migratory-bird hunting	1.0
12. Running, jogging	8.0	35. Orienteering	0.9
13. Saltwater fishing	5.4	36. Ice skating	0.8
14. Camping (primitive area)	4.3	37. Snowmobiling	0.8
15. Tennis	3.1	38. Water-skiing	0.8
16. Sailing	2.8	39. Rock climbing	0.7
17. Rowing	2.7	40. Personal watercraft riding	0.4
18. Big-game hunting	2.6	41. Windsurfing	0.4
19. Small-game hunting	2.3	42. Football	0.3
20. Canoeing	1.9	43. Surfing	0.3
21. Softball	1.9	44. Kayaking	0.2
22. Sledding	1.8	45. Snowboarding	0.1
23. Mountain climbing	1.7	46. Soccer	0.1

Source: USDA Forest Service, 1994-95 National Survey on Recreation and the Environment

Rankings of Participation in Outdoor Recreational Activities:

by Household Income

Households with incomes of $100,000 or more have higher rates of participation in activities that require expensive equipment or travel. The participation gap between affluent and middle-income households is greatest for golf, downhill skiing, swimming, running, snorkeling, tennis, bicycling, and motorboating. The affluent are less likely than those with middle incomes to hunt for big game, camp, and play a variety of team sports such as football, baseball, basketball, volleyball, and softball.

Nevertheless, the 10 most-popular outdoor sport and recreational activities among affluent households are identical to those of middle-income households, with two exceptions. Freshwater fishing ranks 7th among middle-income households, with 28 percent participating, but it ranks 11th among the affluent, with a smaller 24 percent taking part. Conversely, golf ranks 9th among the affluent, with 30 percent golfing in a year, but 15th among middle-income households, with half as many participating.

Comparison of Participation in Outdoor Recreational Activities:
High- vs. Middle-Income Households

(percent of persons living in households with incomes of $100,000 or more or in households with incomes between $25,000 and $49,999 who have participated in selected outdoor recreational activities at least once in the past 12 months, 1994-95; ranked by percentage point difference)

	household income		
	$100,000 or more	**$25,000- $49,999**	**percentage point difference**
1. Golf	30.0%	14.5%	15.5
2. Downhill skiing	20.7	7.8	12.9
3. Swimming (nonpool)	54.7	42.3	12.4
4. Running, jogging	38.1	26.4	11.7
5. Snorkeling	17.6	6.1	11.5
6. Swimming (pool)	59.6	48.1	11.5
7. Tennis	19.2	10.0	9.2
8. Bicycling	39.1	31.1	8.0
9. Motorboating	33.8	25.8	8.0
10. Hiking	32.8	26.2	6.6
11. Canoeing	9.9	4.2	5.7
12. Sailing	9.9	4.2	5.7
13. Saltwater fishing	15.6	10.1	5.5
14. Water-skiing	14.8	9.4	5.4
15. Personal watercraft riding	10.0	4.7	5.3
16. Floating, rafting	11.7	7.9	3.8
17. Horseback riding	11.2	7.4	3.8
18. Cross-country skiing	6.2	3.2	3.0
19. Rowing	7.2	4.3	2.9
20. Walking	74.8	71.9	2.9
21. Backpacking	10.1	7.8	2.3
22. Ice skating	7.7	5.4	2.3
23. Soccer	6.6	4.4	2.2
24. Windsurfing	3.0	0.9	2.1

(continued)

(continued from previous page)

	household income		
	$100,000 or more	**$25,000- $49,999**	**percentage point difference**
25. Kayaking	3.1%	1.3%	1.8
26. Mountain climbing	6.1	4.6	1.5
27. Rock climbing	5.1	3.6	1.5
28. Migratory-bird hunting	3.6	2.3	1.3
29. Sledding	12.2	11.4	0.8
30. Bird watching	29.3	28.6	0.7
31. Orienteering	3.1	2.6	0.5
32. Caving	5.1	5.1	0.0
33. Snowboarding	0.9	1.0	-0.1
34. Surfing	0.9	1.0	-0.1
35. Football	6.6	6.8	-0.2
36. Snowmobiling	4.3	4.5	-0.2
37. Baseball	6.4	7.3	-0.9
38. Basketball	11.8	13.2	-1.4
39. Camping (primitive area)	14.1	16.3	-2.2
40. Small-game hunting	5.6	8.0	-2.4
41. Big-game hunting	5.9	8.9	-3.0
42. Picnicking	51.8	55.5	-3.7
43. Freshwater fishing	23.6	27.5	-3.9
44. Volleyball	12.2	16.7	-4.5
45. Softball	10.4	15.2	-4.8
46. Camping (developed area)	19.6	24.4	-4.8

Source: USDA Forest Service, 1994-95 National Survey on Recreation and the Environment

Ranking of Participation in Outdoor Activities: Affluent Households

(percent of persons aged 16 or older living in households with incomes of $100,000 or more who have participated in selected outdoor recreational activities at least once in the past 12 months, 1994-95; ranked by percent participating)

1.	Walking	74.8%	24.	Softball	10.4%
2.	Swimming (pool)	59.6	25.	Backpacking	10.1
3.	Swimming (nonpool)	54.7	26.	Personal watercraft riding	10.0
4.	Picnicking	51.8	27.	Canoeing	9.9
5.	Bicycling	39.1	28.	Sailing	9.9
6.	Running, jogging	38.1	29.	Ice skating	7.7
7.	Motorboating	33.8	30.	Rowing	7.2
8.	Hiking	32.8	31.	Football	6.6
9.	Golf	30.0	32.	Soccer	6.6
10.	Bird watching	29.3	33.	Baseball	6.4
11.	Freshwater fishing	23.6	34.	Cross-country skiing	6.2
12.	Downhill skiing	20.7	35.	Mountain climbing	6.1
13.	Camping (developed area)	19.6	36.	Big-game hunting	5.9
14.	Tennis	19.2	37.	Small-game hunting	5.6
15.	Snorkeling	17.6	38.	Caving	5.1
16.	Saltwater fishing	15.6	39.	Rock climbing	5.1
17.	Water-skiing	14.8	40.	Snowmobiling	4.3
18.	Camping (primitive area)	14.1	41.	Migratory-bird hunting	3.6
19.	Sledding	12.2	42.	Kayaking	3.1
20.	Volleyball	12.2	43.	Orienteering	3.1
21.	Basketball	11.8	44.	Windsurfing	3.0
22.	Floating, rafting	11.7	45.	Snowboarding	0.9
23.	Horseback riding	11.2	46.	Surfing	0.9

Source: USDA Forest Service, 1994-95 National Survey on Recreation and the Environment

Ranking of Participation in Outdoor Recreational Activities: Middle-Income Households

(percent of persons aged 16 or older living in households with incomes between $25,000 and $49,999 who have participated in selected outdoor recreational activities at least once in the past 12 months, 1994-95; ranked by percent participating)

1.	Walking	71.9%	24.	Backpacking	7.8%
2.	Picnicking	55.5	25.	Downhill skiing	7.8
3.	Swimming (pool)	48.1	26.	Horseback riding	7.4
4.	Swimming (nonpool)	42.3	27.	Baseball	7.3
5.	Bicycling	31.1	28.	Football	6.8
6.	Bird watching	28.6	29.	Snorkeling	6.1
7.	Freshwater fishing	27.5	30.	Ice skating	5.4
8.	Running, jogging	26.4	31.	Caving	5.1
9.	Hiking	26.2	32.	Personal watercraft riding	4.7
10.	Motorboating	25.8	33.	Mountain climbing	4.6
11.	Camping (developed area)	24.4	34.	Snowmobiling	4.5
12.	Volleyball	16.7	35.	Soccer	4.4
13.	Camping (primitive area)	16.3	36.	Rowing	4.3
14.	Softball	15.2	37.	Canoeing	4.2
15.	Golf	14.5	38.	Sailing	4.2
16.	Basketball	13.2	39.	Rock climbing	3.6
17.	Sledding	11.4	40.	Cross-country skiing	3.2
18.	Saltwater fishing	10.1	41.	Orienteering	2.6
19.	Tennis	10.0	42.	Migratory-bird hunting	2.3
20.	Water-skiing	9.4	43.	Kayaking	1.3
21.	Big-game hunting	8.9	44.	Snowboarding	1.0
22.	Small-game hunting	8.0	45.	Surfing	1.0
23.	Floating, rafting	7.9	46.	Windsurfing	0.9

Source: USDA Forest Service, 1994-95 National Survey on Recreation and the Environment

Rankings of Participation in Outdoor Recreational Activities:

by Sex

The gender gap is still alive and well in outdoor sports and recreation. Men have higher participation rates than women in most activities. The gap is greatest for freshwater fishing (32 percent of men versus 17 percent of women), golf (22 versus 8 percent), basketball (19 versus 7 percent), big-game hunting (13 versus 2 percent), small-game hunting (12 versus 1 percent), and running (32 versus 21 percent). Women's participation is greater than men's in only five activities: ice skating, horseback riding, walking, picnicking, and bird watching.

Despite the gender gap, the 10 most-popular activities among men and women are almost identical. Camping in a developed area ranks 10th among women, but just misses the top 10 list among men—although men are slightly more likely to camp in developed areas than women (23 versus 19 percent). Freshwater fishing ranks 5th among men, but 11th among women.

Women's participation in a variety of sport and recreational activities is rising as younger, more-active generations of women replace less-active older women. This will reduce the gender gap in the years ahead.

Comparison of Participation in Recreational Activities: Men vs. Women

(percent of men and women aged 16 or older who have participated in selected outdoor recreational activities at least once in the past 12 months, 1994-95; ranked by percentage point difference)

	men	women	percentage point difference
1. Freshwater fishing	32.3%	17.2%	15.1
2. Golf	22.4	7.8	14.6
3. Basketball	18.5	7.4	11.1
4. Big-game hunting	12.7	2.0	10.7
5. Small-game hunting	12.1	1.4	10.7
6. Running, jogging	31.6	21.1	10.5
7. Camping (primitive area)	19.0	9.1	9.9
8. Football	11.9	2.0	9.9
9. Motorboating	27.4	19.9	7.5
10. Saltwater fishing	13.3	5.9	7.4
11. Swimming (nonpool)	42.8	35.6	7.2
12. Hiking	27.1	20.9	6.2
13. Softball	16.2	10.1	6.1
14. Baseball	9.7	4.0	5.7
15. Backpacking	10.2	5.1	5.1
16. Water-skiing	11.5	6.6	4.9
17. Bicycling	31.0	26.5	4.5
18. Volleyball	16.6	12.2	4.4
19. Camping (developed area)	22.9	18.7	4.2
20. Canoeing	9.1	5.1	4.0
21. Downhill skiing	10.5	6.5	4.0
22. Migratory-bird hunting	4.1	0.4	3.7
23. Snorkeling	9.1	5.5	3.6
24. Soccer	6.2	3.4	2.8

(continued)

(continued from previous page)

	men	women	percentage point difference
25. Rock climbing	5.1%	2.5%	2.6
26. Mountain climbing	5.8	3.3	2.5
27. Swimming (pool)	45.6	43.1	2.5
28. Personal watercraft riding	6.0	3.6	2.4
29. Orienteering	3.6	1.3	2.3
30. Snowmobiling	4.7	2.5	2.2
31. Floating, rafting	8.7	6.6	2.1
32. Tennis	11.7	9.6	2.1
33. Caving	5.7	3.8	1.9
34. Surfing	2.2	0.5	1.7
35. Rowing	5.0	3.5	1.5
36. Sledding	10.8	9.7	1.1
37. Sailing	5.2	4.3	0.9
38. Kayaking	1.8	0.9	0.9
39. Cross-country skiing	3.5	3.0	0.5
40. Windsurfing	1.3	0.9	0.4
41. Snowboarding	1.0	0.7	0.3
42. Ice skating	5.2	5.3	-0.1
43. Horseback riding	7.0	7.3	-0.3
44. Walking	65.1	68.5	-3.4
45. Picnicking	47.1	51.0	-3.9
46. Bird watching	24.7	29.2	-4.5

Source: USDA Forest Service, 1994-95 National Survey on Recreation and the Environment

Ranking of Participation in Outdoor Recreational Activities: Men

(percent of men aged 16 or older who have participated in selected recreational outdoor activities at least once in the past 12 months, 1994-95; ranked by percent participating)

1. Walking	65.1%		24. Downhill skiing	10.5%
2. Picnicking	47.1		25. Backpacking	10.2
3. Swimming (pool)	45.6		26. Baseball	9.7
4. Swimming (nonpool)	42.8		27. Canoeing	9.1
5. Freshwater fishing	32.3		28. Snorkeling	9.1
6. Running, jogging	31.6		29. Floating, rafting	8.7
7. Bicycling	31.0		30. Horseback riding	7.0
8. Motorboating	27.4		31. Soccer	6.2
9. Hiking	27.1		32. Personal watercraft riding	6.0
10. Bird watching	24.7		33. Mountain climbing	5.8
11. Camping (developed area)	22.9		34. Caving	5.7
12. Golf	22.4		35. Ice skating	5.2
13. Camping (primitive area)	19.0		36. Sailing	5.2
14. Basketball	18.5		37. Rock climbing	5.1
15. Volleyball	16.6		38. Rowing	5.0
16. Softball	16.2		39. Snowmobiling	4.7
17. Saltwater fishing	13.3		40. Migratory-bird hunting	4.1
18. Big-game hunting	12.7		41. Orienteering	3.6
19. Small-game hunting	12.1		42. Cross-country skiing	3.5
20. Football	11.9		43. Surfing	2.2
21. Tennis	11.7		44. Kayaking	1.8
22. Water-skiing	11.5		45. Windsurfing	1.3
23. Sledding	10.8		46. Snowboarding	1.0

Source: USDA Forest Service, 1994-95 National Survey on Recreation and the Environment

Ranking of Participation in Outdoor Recreational Activities: Women

(percent of women aged 16 or older who have participated in selected outdoor recreational activities at least once in the past 12 months, 1994-95; ranked by percent participating)

1.	Walking	68.5%	24. Snorkeling	5.5%
2.	Picnicking	51.0	25. Ice skating	5.3
3.	Swimming (pool)	43.1	26. Backpacking	5.1
4.	Swimming (nonpool)	35.6	27. Canoeing	5.1
5.	Bird watching	29.2	28. Sailing	4.3
6.	Bicycling	26.5	29. Baseball	4.0
7.	Running, jogging	21.1	30. Caving	3.8
8.	Hiking	20.9	31. Personal watercraft riding	3.6
9.	Motorboating	19.9	32. Rowing	3.5
10.	Camping (developed area)	18.7	33. Soccer	3.4
11.	Freshwater fishing	17.2	34. Mountain climbing	3.3
12.	Volleyball	12.2	35. Cross-country skiing	3.0
13.	Softball	10.1	36. Rock climbing	2.5
14.	Sledding	9.7	37. Snowmobiling	2.5
15.	Tennis	9.6	38. Big-game hunting	2.0
16.	Camping (primitive area)	9.1	39. Football	2.0
17.	Golf	7.8	40. Small-game hunting	1.4
18.	Basketball	7.4	41. Orienteering	1.3
19.	Horseback riding	7.3	42. Kayaking	0.9
20.	Floating, rafting	6.6	43. Windsurfing	0.9
21.	Water-skiing	6.6	44. Snowboarding	0.7
22.	Downhill skiing	6.5	45. Surfing	0.5
23.	Saltwater fishing	5.9	46. Migratory-bird hunting	0.4

Source: USDA Forest Service, 1994-95 National Survey on Recreation and the Environment

Rankings of Participation in Outdoor Recreational Activities:

by Race and Hispanic Origin

Outdoor sports and recreation are dominated by whites. Blacks have higher participation rates than whites in only seven activities: volleyball, softball, baseball, team handball, football, running, and basketball. People of "other" race, a category that includes Asians and Hispanics in the survey, participate more than whites in 14 activities, including kayaking, surfing, orienteering, and saltwater fishing.

Behind the white–black participation gap are the higher incomes of whites, which allow them to take part more often in activities that require expensive equipment or travel. The biggest gap between white and black participation, for example, is in motorboating, which is relatively expensive. Twenty-seven percent of whites go motorboating in a year, versus only 7 percent of blacks.

Income differences also account for the gap between whites and "others." Again, motorboating shows the biggest gap. Many of the activities more popular among "others" than among whites can be explained by place of residence. A large proportion of Asians and Hispanics live in Florida, California, and Hawaii—coastal states. Thus, they are more likely than whites to take part in activities such as kayaking, surfing, and saltwater fishing. In addition, because the Hispanic population includes a larger proportion of young adults, their participation in more physically demanding activities often surpasses that of whites—such as mountain climbing, snowboarding, and team sports such as baseball and basketball.

Comparison of Participation in Outdoor Recreational Activities: Whites vs. Blacks

(percent of whites and blacks aged 16 or older who have participated in selected outdoor recreational activities at least once in the past 12 months, 1994-95; ranked by percentage point difference)

	whites	blacks	percentage point difference
1. Swimming (nonpool)	42.6%	16.8%	25.8
2. Motorboating	26.5	7.0	19.5
3. Hiking	26.0	8.1	17.9
4. Swimming (pool)	47.0	29.1	17.9
5. Camping (developed area)	22.9	6.3	16.6
6. Walking	69.0	55.8	13.2
7. Golf	16.9	4.1	12.8
8. Camping (primitive area)	15.5	4.2	11.3
9. Freshwater fishing	26.3	15.0	11.3
10. Picnicking	50.3	40.5	9.8
11. Water-skiing	10.3	1.1	9.2
12. Bicycling	29.9	21.2	8.7
13. Sledding	11.5	3.2	8.3
14. Bird watching	28.4	20.5	7.9
15. Floating, rafting	8.6	1.7	6.9
16. Downhill skiing	9.3	2.7	6.6
17. Canoeing	7.9	1.6	6.3
18. Big-game hunting	8.1	1.9	6.2
19. Backpacking	8.2	3.0	5.2
20. Snorkeling	7.8	3.0	4.8
21. Ice skating	5.9	1.7	4.2
22. Small-game hunting	7.2	3.1	4.1
23. Personal watercraft riding	5.3	1.3	4.0
24. Horseback riding	7.6	3.7	3.9

(continued)

(continued from previous page)

	whites	blacks	percentage point difference
25. Rock climbing	4.2%	0.4%	3.8
26. Cross-country skiing	3.8	0.4	3.4
27. Caving	5.1	1.7	3.4
28. Sailing	5.2	2.0	3.2
29. Tennis	10.8	7.8	3.0
30. Snowmobiling	4.0	1.0	3.0
31. Mountain climbing	4.8	1.9	2.9
32. Rowing	4.6	2.3	2.3
33. Migratory-bird hunting	2.5	0.3	2.2
34. Saltwater fishing	9.6	7.4	2.2
35. Kayaking	1.4	0.2	1.2
36. Soccer	4.7	3.6	1.1
37. Surfing	1.4	0.5	0.9
38. Orienteering	2.4	1.7	0.7
39. Snowboarding	0.8	0.5	0.3
40. Windsurfing	1.1	1.1	0.0
41. Volleyball	14.1	16.2	-2.1
42. Softball	12.9	15.8	-2.9
43. Baseball	6.3	9.5	-3.2
44. Football	6.1	10.1	-4.0
45. Running, jogging	24.9	31.9	-7.0
46. Basketball	11.4	21.9	-10.5

Source: USDA Forest Service, 1994-95 National Survey on Recreation and the Environment

Comparison of Participation in Outdoor Recreational Activities: Whites vs. "Other"

(percent of whites and others aged 16 or older who have participated in selected outdoor recreational activities at least once in the past 12 months, 1994-95; ranked by percentage point difference)

	whites	other	percentage point difference
1. Motorboating	26.5%	13.9%	12.6
2. Swimming (pool)	47.0	36.1	10.9
3. Swimming (nonpool)	42.6	32.2	10.4
4. Walking	69.0	58.6	10.4
5. Golf	16.9	7.1	9.8
6. Freshwater fishing	26.3	16.8	9.5
7. Bird watching	28.4	21.4	7.0
8. Sledding	11.5	5.9	5.6
9. Water-skiing	10.3	5.3	5.0
10. Camping (developed area)	22.9	18.2	4.7
11. Big-game hunting	8.1	3.8	4.3
12. Bicycling	29.9	26.2	3.7
13. Floating, rafting	8.6	4.9	3.7
14. Ice skating	5.9	2.6	3.3
15. Camping (primitive area)	15.5	12.3	3.2
16. Small-game hunting	7.2	4.1	3.1
17. Hiking	26.0	23.1	2.9
18. Softball	12.9	10.2	2.7
19. Canoeing	7.9	5.2	2.7
20. Downhill skiing	9.3	7.1	2.2
21. Cross-country skiing	3.8	1.7	2.1
22. Snowmobiling	4.0	2.1	1.9
23. Personal watercraft riding	5.3	3.6	1.7
24. Sailing	5.2	3.7	1.5

(continued)

(continued from previous page)

	whites	other	percentage point difference
25. Rowing	4.6%	3.2%	1.4
26. Migratory-bird hunting	2.5	1.2	1.3
27. Picnicking	50.3	49.1	1.2
28. Horseback riding	7.6	6.5	1.1
29. Rock climbing	4.2	3.3	0.9
30. Backpacking	8.2	7.5	0.7
31. Windsurfing	1.1	0.8	0.3
32. Caving	5.1	4.8	0.3
33. Snorkeling	7.8	7.5	0.3
34. Volleyball	14.1	14.2	-0.1
35. Mountain climbing	4.8	4.9	-0.1
36. Snowboarding	0.8	1.0	-0.2
37. Kayaking	1.4	1.8	-0.4
38. Surfing	1.4	2.0	-0.6
39. Orienteering	2.4	3.3	-0.9
40. Saltwater fishing	9.6	10.8	-1.2
41. Baseball	6.3	7.8	-1.5
42. Basketball	11.4	13.4	-2.0
43. Tennis	10.8	12.9	-2.1
44. Soccer	4.7	7.1	-2.4
45. Football	6.1	9.5	-3.4
46. Running, jogging	24.9	31.7	-6.8

Note: Persons of "other" race include Asians, American Indians, and Hispanics.
Source: USDA Forest Service, 1994-95 National Survey on Recreation and the Environment

Ranking of Participation in Outdoor Recreational Activities: Whites

(percent of whites aged 16 or older who have participated in selected outdoor recreational activities at least once in the past 12 months, 1994-95; ranked by percent participating)

1. Walking	69.0%		24. Big-game hunting	8.1%
2. Picnicking	50.3		25. Canoeing	7.9
3. Swimming (pool)	47.0		26. Snorkeling	7.8
4. Swimming (nonpool)	42.6		27. Horseback riding	7.6
5. Bicycling	29.9		28. Small-game hunting	7.2
6. Bird watching	28.4		29. Baseball	6.3
7. Motorboating	26.5		30. Football	6.1
8. Freshwater fishing	26.3		31. Ice skating	5.9
9. Hiking	26.0		32. Personal watercraft riding	5.3
10. Running, jogging	24.9		33. Sailing	5.2
11. Camping (developed area)	22.9		34. Caving	5.1
12. Golf	16.9		35. Mountain climbing	4.8
13. Camping (primitive area)	15.5		36. Soccer	4.7
14. Volleyball	14.1		37. Rowing	4.6
15. Softball	12.9		38. Rock climbing	4.2
16. Sledding	11.5		39. Snowmobiling	4.0
17. Basketball	11.4		40. Cross-country skiing	3.8
18. Tennis	10.8		41. Migratory-bird hunting	2.5
19. Water-skiing	10.3		42. Orienteering	2.4
20. Saltwater fishing	9.6		43. Kayaking	1.4
21. Downhill skiing	9.3		44. Surfing	1.4
22. Floating, rafting	8.6		45. Windsurfing	1.1
23. Backpacking	8.2		46. Snowboarding	0.8

Source: USDA Forest Service, 1994-95 National Survey on Recreation and the Environment

Ranking of Participation in Outdoor Recreational Activities: Blacks

(percent of blacks aged 16 or older who have participated in selected outdoor recreational activities at least once in the past 12 months, 1994-95; ranked by percent participating)

1.	Walking	55.8%	24. Small-game hunting	3.1%
2.	Picnicking	40.5	25. Backpacking	3.0
3.	Running, jogging	31.9	26. Snorkeling	3.0
4.	Swimming (pool)	29.1	27. Downhill skiing	2.7
5.	Basketball	21.9	28. Rowing	2.3
6.	Bicycling	21.2	29. Sailing	2.0
7.	Bird watching	20.5	30. Big-game hunting	1.9
8.	Swimming (nonpool)	16.8	31. Mountain climbing	1.9
9.	Volleyball	16.2	32. Caving	1.7
10.	Softball	15.8	33. Floating, rafting	1.7
11.	Freshwater fishing	15.0	34. Ice skating	1.7
12.	Football	10.1	35. Orienteering	1.7
13.	Baseball	9.5	36. Canoeing	1.6
14.	Hiking	8.1	37. Personal watercraft riding	1.3
15.	Tennis	7.8	38. Water-skiing	1.1
16.	Saltwater fishing	7.4	39. Windsurfing	1.1
17.	Motorboating	7.0	40. Snowmobiling	1.0
18.	Camping (developed area)	6.3	41. Snowboarding	0.5
19.	Camping (primitive area)	4.2	42. Surfing	0.5
20.	Golf	4.1	43. Cross-country skiing	0.4
21.	Horseback riding	3.7	44. Rock climbing	0.4
22.	Soccer	3.6	45. Migratory-bird hunting	0.3
23.	Sledding	3.2	46. Kayaking	0.2

Source: USDA Forest Service, 1994-95 National Survey on Recreation and the Environment

Ranking of Participation in Outdoor Recreational Activities: "Other"

(percent of persons of "other" race aged 16 or older who have participated in selected outdoor recreational activities at least once in the past 12 months, 1994-95; ranked by percent participating)

1. Walking	58.6%
2. Picnicking	49.1
3. Swimming (pool)	36.1
4. Swimming (nonpool)	32.2
5. Running, jogging	31.7
6. Bicycling	26.2
7. Hiking	23.1
8. Bird watching	21.4
9. Camping (developed area)	18.2
10. Freshwater fishing	16.8
11. Volleyball	14.2
12. Motorboating	13.9
13. Basketball	13.4
14. Tennis	12.9
15. Camping (primitive area)	12.3
16. Saltwater fishing	10.8
17. Softball	10.2
18. Football	9.5
19. Baseball	7.8
20. Backpacking	7.5
21. Snorkeling	7.5
22. Downhill skiing	7.1
23. Golf	7.1

24. Soccer	7.1%
25. Horseback riding	6.5
26. Sledding	5.9
27. Canoeing	5.2
28. Floating, rafting	4.9
29. Mountain climbing	4.9
30. Caving	4.8
31. Small-game hunting	4.1
32. Big-game hunting	3.8
33. Sailing	3.7
34. Personal watercraft riding	3.6
35. Water-skiing	5.3
36. Orienteering	3.3
37. Rock climbing	3.3
38. Rowing	3.2
39. Ice skating	2.6
40. Snowmobiling	2.1
41. Surfing	2.0
42. Kayaking	1.8
43. Cross-country skiing	1.7
44. Migratory-bird hunting	1.2
45. Snowboarding	1.0
46. Windsurfing	0.8

Note: Persons of "other" race include Asians, American Indians, and Hispanics.
Source: USDA Forest Service, 1994-95 National Survey on Recreation and the Environment

Rankings of Participation in
Outdoor Recreational Activities:

by Education

Education influences sport and recreation participation in several ways. First, income rises steadily with education, allowing better-educated people to participate more in activities that require expensive equipment or travel. Second, being in college exposes young adults to sport and recreational activities in which they would not otherwise take part; many continue to participate in those activities throughout their lives. A third factor is age. The college educated are, in general, younger than those with less education because educational levels in our society have been rising. Therefore, the college educated (i.e., younger adults) are more likely to take part in a variety of physically demanding sports than those with less education (i.e., older adults).

The college educated are significantly more likely than high school graduates to take part in activities such as hiking, golfing, bicycling, downhill skiing, tennis, sailing, canoeing, and rowing. Those who went no further than high school are more likely to hunt and fish than the college educated. They are also more likely to play a variety of team sports such as baseball, basketball, football, softball, team handball, and volleyball.

Comparison of Participation in Outdoor Recreational Activities: College vs. High School

(percent of persons aged 16 or older with a college degree and with a high school degree only who have participated in selected outdoor recreational activities at least once in the past 12 months, 1994-95; ranked by percentage point difference)

	college graduates	high school graduates	percentage point difference
1. Walking	75.8%	61.2%	14.6
2. Hiking	31.1	17.6	13.5
3. Swimming (pool)	50.9	38.2	12.7
4. Swimming (nonpool)	45.7	33.8	11.9
5. Golf	21.3	10.4	10.9
6. Picnicking	56.3	45.9	10.4
7. Bicycling	34.3	24.1	10.2
8. Running, jogging	30.5	20.5	10.0
9. Downhill skiing	12.6	4.5	8.1
10. Tennis	14.8	6.8	8.0
11. Bird watching	32.5	25.1	7.4
12. Snorkeling	10.9	4.5	6.4
13. Sailing	8.3	2.3	6.0
14. Cross-country skiing	6.2	1.5	4.7
15. Backpacking	9.6	5.5	4.1
16. Motorboating	25.9	21.9	4.0
17. Canoeing	8.9	5.3	3.6
18. Sledding	11.6	8.3	3.3
19. Ice skating	6.6	3.7	2.9
20. Water-skiing	9.7	7.3	2.4
21. Horseback riding	7.7	6.0	1.7
22. Rowing	5.3	3.7	1.6
23. Mountain climbing	4.9	3.6	1.3
24. Windsurfing	1.8	0.6	1.2

(continued)

(continued from previous page)

	college graduates	high school graduates	percentage point difference
25. Orienteering	3.0%	1.8%	1.2
26. Soccer	4.6	3.5	1.1
27. Kayaking	1.9	1.0	0.9
28. Saltwater fishing	9.9	9.1	0.8
29. Floating, rafting	7.6	6.8	0.8
30. Rock climbing	4.0	3.3	0.7
31. Camping (developed area)	20.4	19.7	0.7
32. Surfing	1.6	1.0	0.6
33. Personal watercraft riding	4.5	4.0	0.5
34. Caving	4.5	4.1	0.4
35. Migratory-bird hunting	2.3	1.9	0.4
36. Snowboarding	0.7	0.8	-0.1
37. Volleyball	13.3	13.5	-0.2
38. Softball	12.2	12.8	-0.6
39. Snowmobiling	2.9	3.8	-0.9
40. Camping (primitive area)	13.0	14.0	-1.0
41. Football	4.5	6.7	-2.2
42. Basketball	10.2	12.4	-2.2
43. Small-game hunting	5.0	7.3	-2.3
44. Baseball	4.6	7.4	-2.8
45. Big-game hunting	4.6	8.6	-4.0
46. Freshwater fishing	21.3	26.1	-4.8

Source: USDA Forest Service, 1994-95 National Survey on Recreation and the Environment

Ranking of Participation in Outdoor Recreational Activities: College Graduates

(percent of persons aged 16 or older with a college degree who have participated in selected outdoor recreational activities at least once in the past 12 months, 1994-95; ranked by percent participating)

1.	Walking	75.8%	24.	Canoeing	8.9%
2.	Picnicking	56.3	25.	Sailing	8.3
3.	Swimming (pool)	50.9	26.	Horseback riding	7.7
4.	Swimming (nonpool)	45.7	27.	Floating, rafting	7.6
5.	Bicycling	34.3	28.	Ice skating	6.6
6.	Bird watching	32.5	29.	Cross-country skiing	6.2
7.	Hiking	31.1	30.	Rowing	5.3
8.	Running, jogging	30.5	31.	Small-game hunting	5.0
9.	Motorboating	25.9	32.	Mountain climbing	4.9
10.	Freshwater fishing	21.3	33.	Baseball	4.6
11.	Golf	21.3	34.	Big-game hunting	4.6
12.	Camping (developed area)	20.4	35.	Soccer	4.6
13.	Tennis	14.8	36.	Caving	4.5
14.	Volleyball	13.3	37.	Football	4.5
15.	Camping (primitive area)	13.0	38.	Personal watercraft riding	4.5
16.	Downhill skiing	12.6	39.	Rock climbing	4.0
17.	Softball	12.2	40.	Orienteering	3.0
18.	Sledding	11.6	41.	Snowmobiling	2.9
19.	Snorkeling	10.9	42.	Migratory-bird hunting	2.3
20.	Basketball	10.2	43.	Kayaking	1.9
21.	Saltwater fishing	9.9	44.	Windsurfing	1.8
22.	Water-skiing	9.7	45.	Surfing	1.6
23.	Backpacking	9.6	46.	Snowboarding	0.7

Source: USDA Forest Service, 1994-95 National Survey on Recreation and the Environment

Ranking of Participation in Outdoor Recreational Activities: High School Graduates

(percent of persons aged 16 or older with a high school degree only who have participated in selected outdoor recreational activities at least once in the past 12 months, 1994-95; ranked by percent participating)

1.	Walking	61.2%	24. Tennis	6.8%
2.	Picnicking	45.9	25. Football	6.7
3.	Swimming (pool)	38.2	26. Horseback riding	6.0
4.	Swimming (nonpool)	33.8	27. Backpacking	5.5
5.	Freshwater fishing	26.1	28. Canoeing	5.3
6.	Bird watching	25.1	29. Downhill skiing	4.5
7.	Bicycling	24.1	30. Snorkeling	4.5
8.	Motorboating	21.9	31. Caving	4.1
9.	Running, jogging	20.5	32. Personal watercraft riding	4.0
10.	Camping (developed area)	19.7	33. Snowmobiling	3.8
11.	Hiking	17.6	34. Ice skating	3.7
12.	Camping (primitive area)	14.0	35. Rowing	3.7
13.	Volleyball	13.5	36. Mountain climbing	3.6
14.	Softball	12.8	37. Soccer	3.5
15.	Basketball	12.4	38. Rock climbing	3.3
16.	Golf	10.4	39. Sailing	2.3
17.	Saltwater fishing	9.1	40. Migratory-bird hunting	1.9
18.	Big-game hunting	8.6	41. Orienteering	1.8
19.	Sledding	8.3	42. Cross-country skiing	1.5
20.	Baseball	7.4	43. Kayaking	1.0
21.	Small-game hunting	7.3	44. Surfing	1.0
22.	Water-skiing	7.3	45. Snowboarding	0.8
23.	Floating, rafting	6.8	46. Windsurfing	0.6

Source: USDA Forest Service, 1994-95 National Survey on Recreation and the Environment

Chapter 2

Spending on Entertainment, Sports, and Recreation

Playing is serious business in the United States—so serious that it was included in the Declaration of Independence as a self-evident truth. Americans have the right to pursue happiness—in other words, to play.

In pursuit of happiness, we spend a lot of money. The average household spent $1,612 on all forms of entertainment in 1995, according to the Bureau of Labor Statistics' Consumer Expenditure Survey. The Commerce Department estimates that personal consumption expenditures on all types of recreation amounted to $370 billion in 1994—or 8 percent of total personal consumption expenditures. Since 1970, spending on recreation has quadrupled, even after adjusting for inflation. The rapid growth of the recreation industry is likely to continue, according to government projections. Employment in recreation is projected to grow at an annual rate of 3.3 percent between now and 2005, according to the Bureau of Labor Statistics, making it one of the fastest-growing industries.

Behind these high-flying numbers is the increasing involvement of the American public in a broad range of recreational activities. Our rising standard of living and educational level explain our growing penchant for outdoor fun. The recreational lifestyle has permeated every facet of our lives and has even come to symbolize the American way of life. Sportswear, for example, is now accepted as everyday dress—worn not only on weekends but also to the office and even to church. The athletic shoe market alone generated revenues of $11.4 billion in 1995. Athletic shoes account for the largest share of the shoe market—38 percent in 1995. Yet only 28 percent of athletic shoes are bought for athletic uses. Most are worn to work, school, or casually.

With the aging of the active, adventurous baby boomers into their peak earning years, spending on recreation should climb significantly in the next decade. Not only will boomers boost spending on recreation, but their children are entering their teens—the age of peak participation in many outdoor recreational activities. Their burgeoning numbers will add to recreational spending, and they will encourage their parents to do—and spend—even more.

Spending

Entertainment

Spending on all forms of entertainment is well above average for householders aged 35 to 54. This broad expenditure category includes not only all types of sports equipment, but also recreational vehicles, boats, fees for participant sports, and the cost of attending sporting events. The entertainment category also includes spending on movie and theater tickets, the purchase of television sets, stereos, and other entertainment items not covered in this book.

Entertainment spending is greatly influenced by income. In 1995, households with incomes of $70,000 or more spent over twice as much on entertainment as the average household (with an index of 224). Those with annual incomes below $20,000 spent only half as much as the average household on entertainment (with an index of 47). Households with incomes of $40,000 or more accounted for 58 percent of all spending on entertainment.

Entertainment spending rises with education. The college educated, in fact, control over one-third of all spending on entertainment. By household type, entertainment spending is greatest among households with children aged 6 to 17. Interestingly, however, married couples without children at home control a larger share of spending on entertainment (24 versus 22 percent) because they are much more numerous than couples with school-aged children.

Households in the West spend considerably more on entertainment than those in any other region. Nevertheless, their share of entertainment spending is surpassed by the share controlled by households in the South because the South is much more populous.

Spending on Entertainment, 1995

(average annual, indexed, and market share of spending by consumer units on entertainment, by selected demographic characteristics, 1995; index definition: 100 is the average; an index of 132 means that spending by consumer units in the segment is 32 percent above average; an index of 68 means spending by consumer units in the segment is 32 percent below average)

	average	index	market share
Average consumer unit	**$1,612.09**	**100**	**100.0%**
Age			
Under age 25	1,081.45	67	4.6
Aged 25 to 34	1,682.23	104	19.8
Aged 35 to 44	1,950.78	121	27.5
Aged 45 to 54	2,137.90	133	24.0
Aged 55 to 64	1,576.78	98	12.0
Aged 65 or older	928.66	58	12.2
Income			
Under $20,000	797.03	47	17.5
$20,000 to $29,999	1,215.57	72	10.9
$30,000 to $39,999	1,762.69	104	13.3
$40,000 to $49,999	1,922.50	114	11.2
$50,000 to $69,999	2,507.58	149	18.5
$70,000 or more	3,776.46	224	28.4
Race			
White and "other"	1,701.03	106	93.6
Black	925.35	57	6.5
Hispanic origin			
Non-Hispanic	1,658.90	103	94.9
Hispanic	1,059.90	66	5.1
Education			
Not a high school graduate	768.65	48	10.0
High school graduate only	1,371.11	85	27.2
Some college	1,810.44	112	25.7
College graduate	2,453.00	152	36.9

(continued)

(continued from previous page)

	average	index	market share
Household type			
Married couples, total	$2,076.81	129	67.5%
Married couple only	1,829.81	114	24.3
Married couple with children	2,319.43	144	39.0
Oldest child under age 6	1,979.64	123	6.6
Oldest child aged 6 to 17	2,501.05	155	22.1
Oldest child aged 18 or older	2,221.89	138	10.3
Single parent with children under 18	1,081.74	67	4.4
Single person	992.14	62	17.4
Region			
Northeast	1,543.65	96	19.2
Midwest	1,602.26	99	24.9
South	1,459.44	91	30.8
West	1,938.75	120	25.1

Source: Bureau of Labor Statistics, 1995 Consumer Expenditure Survey; *calculations by New Strategist*

Spending

Participant Sports

The pattern of spending on participant sports (such as greens fees for golfing, admissions to swimming pools, etc.) is similar to the spending patterns on all entertainment, with one important exception: Those spending the most on participant sports are older.

Spending on participant sports is well above average for householders ranging in age from 35 to 64—particularly when the spending occurs on out-of-town trips. In fact, the biggest spenders on participant sports on out-of-town trips are people aged 55 to 64. Because they travel more than younger adults, people aged 55 to 64 spend 69 percent more than the average household in this category. Nevertheless, the largest share of spending on participant sports while on out-of-town trips is controlled by householders aged 35 to 44, simply because there are more households in this age group than in the older one.

Spending on participant sports is much greater among the affluent than among other households. Over half the spending on participant sports is controlled by households with incomes of $50,000 or more.

Whites and non-Hispanics spend more on participant sports than blacks or Hispanics, and college graduates spend more than those with less education.

By household type, married couples with children aged 6 to 17 spend the most on participant sports in their home town, but married couples without children at home (many of them empty nesters) spend the most on this category while out of town. Couples without children at home account for 39 percent of all spending on participant sports while on trips.

Spending on Participant Sports, 1995

(average annual, indexed, and market share of spending by consumer units on participant sports, by selected demographic characteristics, 1995; index definition: 100 is the average; an index of 132 means that spending by consumer units in the segment is 32 percent above average; an index of 68 means spending by consumer units in the segment is 32 percent below average)

	total		in home town			on out-of-town trips		
	average	*index*	*average*	*index*	*market share*	*average*	*index*	*market share*
Average consumer unit	**$95.80**	**100**	**$66.55**	**100**	**100.0%**	**$29.25**	**100**	**100.0%**
Age								
Under age 25	47.70	50	32.82	49	3.4	14.88	51	3.5
Aged 25 to 34	93.92	98	67.68	102	19.2	26.24	90	17.0
Aged 35 to 44	108.43	113	75.59	114	25.8	32.84	112	25.5
Aged 45 to 54	113.54	119	83.58	126	22.7	29.96	102	18.5
Aged 55 to 64	109.41	114	60.12	90	11.1	49.29	169	20.7
Aged 65 or older	76.41	80	55.90	84	17.8	20.51	70	14.8
Income								
Under $20,000	31.15	33	24.06	35	12.9	7.09	25	9.4
$20,000 to $29,999	59.75	62	48.95	70	10.7	10.80	39	5.9
$30,000 to $39,999	106.05	111	72.51	104	13.3	33.54	120	15.3
$40,000 to $49,999	112.75	118	81.87	118	11.6	30.88	111	10.9
$50,000 to $69,999	165.39	173	121.32	175	21.7	44.07	158	19.6
$70,000 or more	248.79	260	163.19	235	29.8	85.60	306	38.9
Race								
White and "other"	105.51	110	73.11	110	97.4	32.40	111	98.2
Black	19.79	21	15.20	23	2.6	4.59	16	1.8
Hispanic origin								
Non-Hispanic	100.82	105	69.74	105	96.6	31.08	106	98.0
Hispanic	36.16	38	28.63	43	3.3	7.53	26	2.0
Education								
Not a high school graduate	30.28	32	21.96	33	6.9	8.32	28	5.9
High school graduate only	67.75	71	50.54	76	24.3	17.21	59	18.8
Some college	96.47	101	71.02	107	24.4	25.45	87	19.9
College graduate	188.59	197	121.86	183	44.4	66.73	228	55.3

(continued)

(continued from previous page)

	total		in home town			on out-of-town trips		
	average	*index*	*average*	*index*	*market share*	*average*	*index*	*market share*
Household type								
Married couples, total	$130.09	136	$88.57	133	69.8%	$41.52	142	74.4%
Married couple only	142.30	149	89.35	134	28.7	52.95	181	38.7
Married couple w/ children	126.89	132	91.86	138	37.4	35.03	120	32.5
Oldest child under 6	92.68	97	73.74	111	6.0	18.94	65	3.5
Oldest child 6 to 17	146.36	153	106.58	160	22.8	39.78	136	19.4
Oldest child 18 or older	114.46	119	76.88	116	8.6	37.58	128	9.6
Single parent w/ children <18	32.61	34	24.73	37	2.4	7.88	27	1.8
Single person	63.87	67	44.17	66	18.7	19.70	67	19.0
Region								
Northeast	85.19	89	57.50	86	17.3	27.69	95	18.9
Midwest	106.36	111	75.94	114	28.6	30.42	104	26.1
South	80.02	84	57.01	86	29.2	23.01	79	26.8
West	119.03	124	79.51	119	24.9	39.52	135	28.2

Note: The average spending figures are extremely low because both purchasers and non-purchasers are included in the calculation. While the average spending figures do not show how much buyers of participant sports spend, the patterns revealed by the index and market share figures do show who is most likely to spend on participant sports and how much spending is controlled by each demographic segment.
Source: Bureau of Labor Statistics, 1995 Consumer Expenditure Survey; calculations by New Strategist

Spending

Recreational Lessons

Spending on fees for recreational lessons is dominated by married couples with children aged 6 to 17, who control 56 percent of all spending in this category. This household type spends nearly four times as much as the average household on recreational lessons as they send their children to swimming classes and sign them up for horseback riding lessons.

By age, the 35-to-44 age group spends the most on recreational lessons because they are the ones most likely to have children aged 6 to 17 at home. Income has an enormous effect on spending in this category. Householders with incomes of $70,000 or more spent an average of $213 on lessons in 1995, versus the much lower $58 spent by the average household. Affluent households control 45 percent of all spending in this category.

College graduates spend twice as much as the average household on recreational lessons, controlling 53 percent of the market. Spending in this category is well above average in both the Northeast and Midwest.

Spending on recreational lessons could climb in the future due to increased regulation of outdoor activities. Recreational organizations are beginning to offer lessons to meet or sidestep regulations. An example is the personal watercraft safety program, "Ride Smart from the Start," offered by the National Recreation and Parks Association.

Spending on Fees for Recreational Lessons, 1995

(average annual, indexed, and market share of spending by consumer units on recreational lessons, by selected demographic characteristics, 1995; index definition: 100 is the average; an index of 132 means that spending by consumer units in the segment is 32 percent above average; an index of 68 means spending by consumer units in the segment is 32 percent below average)

	average	*index*	*market share*
Average consumer unit	**$57.91**	**100**	**100.0%**
Age			
Under age 25	4.53	8	0.5
Aged 25 to 34	51.02	88	16.7
Aged 35 to 44	113.99	197	44.8
Aged 45 to 54	89.37	154	27.9
Aged 55 to 64	26.64	46	5.6
Aged 65 or older	12.20	21	4.4
Income			
Under $20,000	13.28	22	8.2
$20,000 to $29,999	20.92	35	5.3
$30,000 to $39,999	45.86	76	9.8
$40,000 to $49,999	49.95	83	8.2
$50,000 to $69,999	113.65	189	23.6
$70,000 or more	212.68	354	45.0
Race			
White and "other"	63.20	109	96.8
Black	16.47	28	3.2
Hispanic origin			
Non-Hispanic	59.96	104	95.5
Hispanic	33.59	58	4.5
Education			
Not a high school graduate	6.50	11	2.3
High school graduate only	39.52	68	21.9
Some college	57.48	99	22.7
College graduate	126.84	219	53.1

(continued)

(continued from previous page)

Household type	average	index	market share
Married couples, total	$89.93	155	81.4%
Married couple only	19.30	33	7.1
Married couple with children	150.75	260	70.6
Oldest child under age 6	63.13	109	5.9
Oldest child aged 6 to 17	227.79	393	56.0
Oldest child aged 18 or older	67.26	116	8.7
Single parent with children under 18	41.51	72	4.7
Single person	19.44	34	9.5
Region			
Northeast	79.50	137	27.5
Midwest	53.83	93	23.3
South	40.60	70	23.9
West	70.35	121	25.3

Note: The average spending figures are extremely low because both purchasers and non-purchasers are included in the calculation. While the average spending figures do not show how much buyers of recreational lessons spend, the patterns revealed by the index and market share figures do show who is most likely to spend on recreational lessons and how much spending is controlled by each demographic segment.
Source: Bureau of Labor Statistics, 1995 Consumer Expenditure Survey; *calculations by New Strategist*

Spending

Social, Recreation, and Civic Club Memberships

Spending on social, recreation, and civic club memberships is well above average for householders in two age groups: 45 to 54, and 65 or older. The largest share of spending (26 percent) is controlled by householders aged 65 or older. This spending buys memberships in organizations such as pool and tennis clubs, country clubs, and golf clubs. A large share of spending in this category is not for recreational purposes, however.

Not surprisingly, the affluent spend the most on club memberships. People with incomes of $70,000 or more spend nearly three times as much as the average household, accounting for over one-third of all spending in this category. College graduates dominate spending on club memberships, accounting for 57 percent of the market. Other big spenders include married couples without children at home and people living in the West.

In a study of people who work out at health clubs, the National Sporting Goods Association (NSGA) of Mount Prospect, Illinois, found a different profile from those who spend on club memberships overall. More than 70 percent of health club users are aged 18 to 44, for example, and only 5 percent are aged 65 or older. The NSGA reports that 22 million people worked out at health clubs in 1995.

The Sporting Goods Manufacturers Association reports a slightly smaller number of people who work out at health clubs—19 million in 1995. It also finds 12 million people who worked out using home gyms. Those who work out at home also tend to belong to health clubs.

Spending on Social, Recreation, and Civic Club Memberships, 1995

(average annual, indexed, and market share of spending by consumer units on social, recreation, and civic club memberships, by selected demographic characteristics, 1995; index definition: 100 is the average; an index of 132 means that spending by consumer units in the segment is 32 percent above average; an index of 68 means spending by consumer units in the segment is 32 percent below average)

	average	index	market share
Average consumer unit	$80.67	100	100.0%
Age			
Under age 25	33.82	42	2.9
Aged 25 to 34	58.26	72	13.7
Aged 35 to 44	74.58	92	21.0
Aged 45 to 54	108.77	135	24.4
Aged 55 to 64	78.68	98	12.0
Aged 65 or older	99.63	124	26.1
Income			
Under $20,000	42.73	53	19.7
$20,000 to $29,999	38.10	47	7.2
$30,000 to $39,999	77.13	96	12.2
$40,000 to $49,999	72.77	90	8.9
$50,000 to $69,999	91.84	114	14.2
$70,000 or more	240.24	298	37.8
Race			
White and "other"	88.55	110	97.3
Black	19.03	24	2.7
Hispanic origin			
Non-Hispanic	84.73	105	96.9
Hispanic	32.50	40	3.1
Education			
Not a high school graduate	14.23	18	3.7
High school graduate only	41.52	51	16.5
Some college	81.49	101	23.1
College graduate	188.80	234	56.8

(continued)

(continued from previous page)

	average	index	market share
Household type			
Married couples, total	$117.56	146	76.4%
Married couple only	144.96	180	38.4
Married couple with children	103.63	128	34.8
Oldest child under age 6	75.25	93	5.0
Oldest child aged 6 to 17	112.19	139	19.8
Oldest child aged 18 or older	107.77	134	10.0
Single parent with children under 18	19.79	25	1.6
Single person	46.09	57	16.1
Region			
Northeast	69.23	86	17.2
Midwest	62.21	77	19.4
South	77.73	96	32.8
West	118.70	147	30.7

Note: The average spending figures are extremely low because both purchasers and non-purchasers are included in the calculation. While the average spending figures do not show how much buyers of social, recreation, and civic club memberships spend, the patterns revealed by the index and market share figures do show who is most likely to spend on social, recreation, and civic club memberships and how much spending is controlled by each demographic segment.
Source: Bureau of Labor Statistics, 1995 Consumer Expenditure Survey; calculations by New Strategist

Spending

Athletic Gear, Game Tables, and Exercise Equipment

Many types of consumers spend on athletic gear, game tables, and exercise equipment. No single household segment dominates spending in this category.

Spending on athletic gear, game tables, and exercise equipment is above average for householders ranging in age from 25 to 64. It is above average for both households with mid-level and households with affluent incomes. It is above average for all types of married couples, as well as for college graduates and for those with some college. The broad appeal of this category accounts for the enormous success of sporting goods superstores, which can now be found in most of the nation's metropolitan areas.

Interestingly, married couples without children at home (many of them empty nesters) account for a significant 29-percent share of this market, surpassing the 25 - percent share accounted for by couples with children aged 6 to 17. As boomers age, spending by empty nesters on these products is likely to rise as the sports participation of older Americans grows.

Spending on athletic gear is closely monitored by the sports industry. Between now and 2003, manufacturers expect outdoor gear to enjoy the fastest growth, according to *Worldwide Sporting Goods Outlook* by the World Federation Sporting Goods Industry and Kurt Salmon Associates. This projection mirrors the growing participation of Americans in outdoor sports and recreation. Other categories of athletic gear examined by the report are licensed team wear, golf and tennis apparel, fitness gear, team uniforms, swimming gear, and ski gear. Licensed team wear—which is second only to outdoor gear in projected growth—is authorized clothing carrying the name of a sports team. The health of this category is closely tied to the public's perception of spectator sports. The Sporting Goods Manufacturers Association, which tracks sales of licensed products, expects licensed merchandise to remain strong because of stepped-up marketing by the major leagues. Another positive factor for this category is the growth in women's professional sports, which should boost sales of licensed products to girls and women.

Spending on Athletic Gear, Game Tables, and Exercise Equipment, 1995

(average annual, indexed, and market share of spending by consumer units on athletic gear, game tables, and exercise equipment, by selected demographic characteristics, 1995; index definition: 100 is the average; an index of 132 means that spending by consumer units in the segment is 32 percent above average; an index of 68 means spending by consumer units in the segment is 32 percent below average)

	average	*indexed*	*market share*
Average consumer unit	**$50.33**	**100**	**100.0%**
Age			
Under age 25	37.73	75	5.1
Aged 25 to 34	50.86	101	19.1
Aged 35 to 44	68.46	136	30.9
Aged 45 to 54	62.76	125	22.6
Aged 55 to 64	54.84	109	13.4
Aged 65 or older	21.14	42	8.9
Income			
Under $20,000	16.49	32	12.0
$20,000 to $29,999	23.36	46	6.9
$30,000 to $39,999	59.86	117	15.0
$40,000 to $49,999	63.70	125	12.2
$50,000 to $69,999	96.11	188	23.4
$70,000 or more	122.74	240	30.5
Race			
White and "other"	54.96	109	96.8
Black	14.10	28	3.2
Hispanic origin			
Non-Hispanic	52.60	105	96.4
Hispanic	23.35	46	3.6
Education			
Not a high school graduate	22.18	44	9.2
High school graduate only	36.77	73	23.4
Some college	57.88	115	26.3
College graduate	85.34	170	41.1

(continued)

(continued from previous page)

Household type	average	index	market share
Married couples, total	$71.73	143	74.7%
Married couple only	69.12	137	29.4
Married couple with children	78.23	155	42.1
Oldest child under age 6	77.18	153	8.3
Oldest child aged 6 to 17	87.37	174	24.7
Oldest child aged 18 or older	61.60	122	9.2
Single parent with children under 18	31.74	63	4.1
Single person	24.17	48	13.6
Region			
Northeast	45.56	91	18.1
Midwest	53.67	107	26.8
South	45.88	91	31.0
West	58.15	116	24.1

Note: The average spending figures are extremely low because both purchasers and non-purchasers are included in the calculation. While the average spending figures do not show how much buyers of athletic gear, game tables, and exercise equipment spend, the patterns revealed by the index and market share figures do show who is most likely to spend on athletic gear, game tables, and exercise equipment and how much spending is controlled by each demographic segment.
Source: Bureau of Labor Statistics, 1995 Consumer Expenditure Survey; calculations by New Strategist

Spending

Admissions to Sporting Events

The biggest spenders on admissions to sporting events are, by far, the affluent. House-holders aged 45 to 54, who are in their peak earning years, spend the most on admissions to sporting events—42 percent more than the average household. This age group is especially likely to spend big on sporting events while on out-of-town trips, controlling the largest share (28 percent) of that market. Americans aged 55 to 64 spend less than average on sporting events in their home town, but they spend above average on sporting events while they are on out-of-town trips. Altogether, householders aged 45 or older control 58 percent of spending on out-of-town sporting events.

Households with annual incomes below $40,000 spend less than average on admissions to sports events. Spending is well above average for households with incomes of $50,000 or more. The most-affluent households control 46 percent of spending on admissions to hometown sporting events. The high level of expenditures by the affluent can be explained in part by their purchase of season tickets and more-expensive seats.

Whites spend more than blacks or Hispanics on admissions to sporting events. Married couples with children aged 18 or older at home spend more than any other household type in this category. Behind this high level of spending is admission to college sports events.

Southerners spend more than householders in other regions on admissions to sporting events—11 percent more than average. Most of this spending occurs in their home towns. Southerners control 41 percent of spending on admissions to hometown sports events. Westerners spend the most on out-of-town sports events.

Spending on Admissions to Sporting Events, 1995

(average annual, indexed, and market share of spending by consumer units on sporting events, by selected demographic characteristics, 1995; index definition: 100 is the average; an index of 132 means that spending by consumer units in the segment is 32 percent above average; an index of 68 means spending by consumer units in the segment is 32 percent below average)

	total		in home town			on out-of-town trips		
	average	*index*	*average*	*index*	*market share*	*average*	*index*	*market share*
Average consumer unit	**$42.21**	**100**	**$28.71**	**100**	**100.0%**	**$13.50**	**100**	**100.0%**
Age								
Under age 25	24.98	59	19.84	69	4.7	5.14	38	2.6
Aged 25 to 34	42.07	100	30.43	106	20.1	11.64	86	16.3
Aged 35 to 44	49.73	118	35.81	125	28.4	13.92	103	23.5
Aged 45 to 54	59.93	142	39.04	136	24.6	20.89	155	28.0
Aged 55 to 64	40.34	96	25.14	88	10.7	15.20	113	13.8
Aged 65 or older	25.73	61	15.62	54	11.5	10.11	75	15.8
Income								
Under $20,000	15.59	37	10.25	33	12.1	5.34	38	13.9
$20,000 to $29,999	20.98	50	13.67	43	6.6	7.31	51	7.8
$30,000 to $39,999	35.98	85	23.72	75	9.6	12.26	86	11.0
$40,000 to $49,999	45.40	108	28.30	90	8.8	17.10	120	11.8
$50,000 to $69,999	71.58	170	45.82	145	18.1	25.76	181	22.5
$70,000 or more	148.78	352	111.67	354	44.9	37.11	260	33.0
Race								
White and "other"	45.48	108	30.88	108	95.4	14.60	108	95.9
Black	16.62	39	11.74	41	4.6	4.88	36	4.1
Hispanic origin								
Non-Hispanic	44.34	105	30.37	106	97.6	13.97	103	95.4
Hispanic	16.95	40	9.02	31	2.4	7.93	59	4.6
Education								
Not a high school graduate	11.03	26	4.70	16	3.4	6.33	47	9.8
High school graduate only	32.93	78	21.99	77	24.5	10.94	81	26.0
Some college	44.11	105	29.39	102	23.4	14.72	109	24.9
College graduate	79.50	188	57.60	201	48.7	21.90	162	39.3

(continued)

(continued from previous page)

	total		in home town			on out-of-town trips		
	average	index	average	index	market share	average	index	market share
Household type								
Married couples, total	$52.93	125	$33.96	118	62.0%	$18.97	141	73.7%
Married couple only	49.94	118	29.77	104	22.2	20.17	149	32.0
Married couple w/ children	58.74	139	40.04	139	37.8	18.70	139	37.5
Oldest child under 6	36.89	87	25.95	90	4.9	10.94	81	4.4
Oldest child 6 to 17	56.94	135	37.89	132	18.8	19.05	141	20.1
Oldest child 18 or older	77.87	184	54.26	189	14.2	23.61	175	13.1
Single parent w/ children <18	19.72	47	13.58	47	3.1	6.14	45	3.0
Single person	31.62	75	24.27	85	23.9	7.35	54	15.4
Region								
Northeast	33.58	80	19.88	69	13.9	13.70	101	20.3
Midwest	39.54	94	27.04	94	23.6	12.50	93	23.2
South	46.93	111	34.40	120	40.8	12.53	93	31.6
West	45.98	109	29.89	104	21.7	16.09	119	24.8

Note: The average spending figures are extremely low because both purchasers and non-purchasers are included in the calculation. While the average spending figures do not show how much buyers of admissions to sporting events spend, the patterns revealed by the index and market share figures do show who is most likely to pay to see sporting events and how much spending is controlled by each demographic segment.
Source: Bureau of Labor Statistics, 1995 Consumer Expenditure Survey; calculations by New Strategist

Spending

The Fan Cost Index™

Deciding to attend a sporting event is not strictly a matter of finances, according to Sean Brenner, editor of *Team Marketing Report*, a trade publication for the sports marketing industry. Brenner compiles the Fan Cost Index™ each year, which compares the expense of attending professional games. In 1997, baseball was the best bargain, costing less than pro-basketball, football, or hockey. But lower cost won't entice people to a baseball game if they're not already fans.

The decision to go to a professional game is determined by a variety of factors, including what is available in the local area, Brenner says. The politics of a sport influence attendance, for example. "Strikes, labor disputes…the fans have no control over these things, and they influence their taste for the game," Brenner notes. Events in the major leagues affect minor league and amateur sports, although the direction is not always predictable. A strike, for example, might turn fans off completely, or it could benefit the minor leagues because fans flock to their games instead.

Another important factor that determines which sporting event people attend is how well a team is doing. "There's high demand for tickets to see the hottest and most- successful teams," Brenner says. Losing is generally bad for ticket sales, but "fans of some teams are fans of the image, of the mystique of the stadium."

Looking towards the future, Brenner believes competition for fans will intensify. "There are more professional leagues, more teams," he says. New sports are crowding the field. Women's professional leagues could become powerful competitors as well. "They could experience huge growth," Brenner says.

Average Ticket Price and Fan Cost Index™, 1991 to 1997

(average ticket price and Fan Cost Index™ for selected spectator sports, 1991 to 1997; the Fan Cost Index™ is the sum of the cost of four average-price tickets, four small soft drinks, two small beers, four hot dogs, parking for one car, two game programs, and two souvenir caps)

	average ticket price (dollars)	percent change in price from preceding year	Fan Cost Index™	percent change in Fan Cost Index™ from preceding year
Major League Baseball				
1997	$11.98	7.1%	105.63	3.0%
1996	11.19	6.1	102.58	5.9
1995	10.55	1.0	96.83	1.1
1994	10.45	8.9	95.80	5.5
1993	9.60	3.2	90.84	5.3
1992	9.30	7.6	86.24	11.4
1991	8.64	-	77.40	-
National Basketball Association				
1996-97	34.08	8.0	203.38	6.3
1995-96	31.56	10.2	191.31	8.0
1994-95	28.63	5.6	177.12	5.0
1993-94	27.12	7.8	168.68	6.6
1992-93	25.16	8.3	158.17	9.8
1991-92	23.24	-	144.10	-
National Football League				
1996	35.74	6.6	208.45	4.7
1995	33.52	9.7	199.09	9.0
1994	30.56	6.6	182.72	5.4
1993	28.68	5.5	173.33	6.2
1992	27.19	7.8	163.19	7.6
1991	25.21	-	151.55	-
National Hockey League				
1996-97	38.34	10.3	220.72	8.5
1995-96	34.75	6.1	203.46	5.4
1994-95	32.75	-	193.10	-

Note: No National Hockey League surveys were conducted prior to 1994-95.
Source: All information ©Team Marketing Report, Chicago Illinois. Reprinted with permission.

Chapter 3

Outdoor Family Activities

Who participates:
- *young and middle-aged Americans*
- *middle- and high-income householders*
- *households with preschoolers*

Outdoor family activity trends:
- *a heyday for family activities*
- *upscale picnics and games*

Nearly two in three people aged 16 or older gathered with family and friends out-doors and away from home in the past 12 months. A majority of nearly every demo-graphic segment took part in such outdoor gatherings, including 70 percent of 25-to-29-year-olds, over half of those with household incomes of $15,000 or more, over 60 percent of both men and women, most whites and most blacks, and 70 percent of households with preschoolers.

Picnicking is also popular with millions of Americans. Forty-nine percent of people aged 16 or older picnicked in the past 12 months. Participation in picnicking does not vary much by demographic segment. Those least likely to do so are Ameri-cans aged 60 or older, those with household incomes below $15,000, those who do not have a high school diploma, and people who live alone. Those most likely to picnic are the middle-aged, people with at least some college, and people with preschoolers at home.

Yard games—such as horseshoes, croquet, Frisbee, or lawn darts—are most popu-lar among adults under age 40. While 37 percent of all Americans take part in yard games each year, the figure is at least 44 percent among people under age 40. Men are more likely to play than women (41 versus 33 percent), and whites are more likely than blacks and "others" (primarily Asians and Hispanics). People who live with pre-schoolers are more likely to play yard games than people without young children at home (46 versus 35 percent).

The Future of Outdoor Family Activities

With the enormous baby-boom generation now raising children, family activities are in their heyday. Boomers are leaving their mark on picnicking and other family activities, as they have on everything else. Family activities are going upscale. Gathering with friends and family no longer necessarily means hot dogs and hamburgers. Many are opting for gourmet fare, with hotels and specialty restaurants getting involved.

"The humble picnic is becoming a hot and potentially lucrative attraction in high-end travel," says *The Wall Street Journal* (May 23, 1997). "For the price of a four-star dinner, hotels and gourmet shops are arranging almost everything but the ants."

Yard games are also going upscale, with specialty retailers such as L.L. Bean offering high-quality croquet sets and other family games.

As boomers age, family activities will continue to be important—especially since so many children live at home well into their 20s. When grandchildren come along, there will be more excuses and opportunities for family gatherings, picnics, and yard games.

Participation in Outdoor Family Activities

(percent of persons aged 16 or older who participated in outdoor family activities at least once in the past year, by selected demographic characteristics, 1994-95)

	gathering with family and friends outdoors	picnicking	yard games
Total	**61.8%**	**49.1%**	**36.9%**
Age			
Aged 16 to 24	68.1	45.1	43.6
Aged 25 to 29	70.2	54.2	46.4
Aged 30 to 39	69.2	59.8	47.1
Aged 40 to 49	65.4	55.4	39.4
Aged 50 to 59	59.5	47.7	31.3
Aged 60 or older	44.1	35.1	16.8
Income			
Under $15,000	43.7	35.8	22.5
$15,000 to $24,999	57.4	46.7	32.2
$25,000 to $49,999	68.1	55.5	41.8
$50,000 to $74,999	70.7	56.6	45.4
$75,000 to $99,999	70.1	56.3	44.1
$100,000 or more	71.9	51.8	39.2
Sex			
Men	63.8	47.1	41.0
Women	60.2	51.0	32.9
Race and Hispanic origin			
White	63.2	50.3	39.2
Black	56.0	40.5	26.3
Other, including Hispanic	56.2	49.1	24.9
Education			
Not a high school graduate	48.1	32.5	28.0
High school graduate	59.5	45.9	35.6
Some college	65.5	53.1	40.5
College graduate	67.2	56.3	38.5
Number of persons in household			
One	50.1	38.5	25.1
Two	59.6	46.6	32.0
Three	66.2	52.9	41.4
Four	69.2	55.6	46.2
Five or more	66.8	55.5	44.4

(continued)

(continued from previous page)

	gathering with family and friends outdoors	picnicking	yard games
Number of persons aged 16 or older in household			
One	54.1%	42.7%	28.3%
Two	64.4	52.6	38.3
Three or more	64.4	48.2	41.1
Number of persons under age 6 in household			
None	59.9	46.6	34.5
One or more	69.6	59.2	45.6

Source: USDA Forest Service, 1994-95 National Survey on Recreation and the Environment

Fishing and Hunting

Fishing and hunting used to be a matter of survival. Today, they are a matter of recreation. Fishing is an integral part of many cultures, causing it to have widespread appeal in the United States. Hunting is less popular, although with nearly 19 million participants, it's far from extinct. In recent years, hunting has been on the decline, however. As the nation diversifies and women gain greater influence on recreation, hunting's narrow appeal to white men may reduce its popularity even further.

Fishing is a popular activity in every demographic group. Anglers (a gender-neutral term for people who fish) are much more likely to cast their bait in freshwater than saltwater. Hunters are about equally likely to hunt big and small game, while fewer people hunt migratory birds.

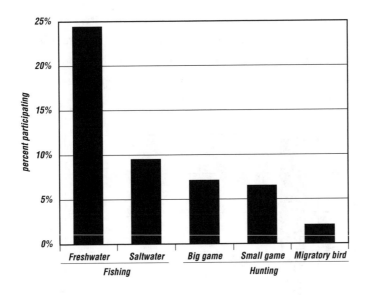

Fishing

Who fishes:
- *all age groups*
- *all income groups*

Fishing trends:
- *better technology*
- *concerns about overfishing*
- *competition with commercial fishing*

Fishing is one of the most-popular recreational activities in the United States. Nearly three in ten Americans aged 16 or older went fishing in the past 12 months. Freshwater fishing is far more popular than saltwater fishing, with one in four Americans having been freshwater fishing in the past year versus only 10 percent who have been saltwater fishing.

Fishing is popular across most demographic categories. Unlike many recreational activities, fishing appeals almost equally to middle-aged and young adults. Even among the oldest Americans, fishing remains a highly popular activity. Seventeen percent of people aged 60 or older went fishing at least once in the past year, with 14 percent involved in freshwater fishing and 5 percent in saltwater fishing.

The popularity of freshwater fishing varies little by income. In contrast, participation in saltwater fishing rises steadily with income. Behind this pattern is the need for people living inland to travel to the coast to fish in saltwater—which makes it more expensive. In addition, some forms of saltwater fishing require ocean-faring vessels, which are costly to buy or rent. Sixteen percent of people with household incomes of $100,000 or more have been saltwater fishing in the past year, versus fewer than 10 percent of those with incomes below $25,000.

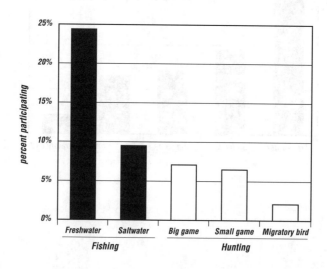

Men are much more likely than women to fish, with 38 percent of men having done so in the past year. But a substantial 21 percent of women also participate in fishing. Similarly, while whites are more likely to fish than blacks and Hispanics, many blacks and Hispanics fish. The differences by race are much less distinct for saltwater than for freshwater fishing. In fact, people of "other" race—primarily Asians and Hispanics—are more likely to saltwater-fish than whites.

Participation in fishing does not vary much by education. It is more popular among people living in larger households and in households including young children. Behind this pattern is the appeal of fishing as a family activity.

The Future of Freshwater Fishing

"Every day is a Saturday when you're fishing," says Scott Richardson, outdoors journalist and columnist for the *Illinois Panatagraph* newspaper.

People are introduced to freshwater fishing through their families. "It's a 'come along with me' kind of activity," Richardson says. "Someone usually shows you how to do it." Besides the fun of catching fish, freshwater fishing provides an excuse to be outside, to bond with friends or family, and to exercise "good old American competitiveness," Richardson says.

Fishing can be inexpensive, which accounts for its popularity. There is so much information available about fishing that anglers can become as educated as they like about the sport. The volume of information has resulted in a more sophisticated and knowledgeable group of participants. Technological advances in the sport are also making it easier to find and catch fish.

The growing success of those who fish is straining certain species and has raised concerns about overfishing. Richardson says there are no greater conservationists than people who fish. "We understand that it's all built around the resource," says Richardson. "When fishermen pay for their annual license, a portion goes into stocking programs and generating our own resource." There has been "real cooperation" between anglers and conservationists, he says.

In the future, the growth of freshwater fishing could be threatened by competition with other activities for water and for leisure time. Another problem is Mother Nature herself. Catastrophic floods in various parts of the country mean high water, season after season. Because of this impediment, there could be a generation of kids that never really "catches the fishing bug. You break the chain," says Richardson. When parents don't teach their kids to fish, there could be a "decrease in participation over time."

The Future of Saltwater Fishing

"Historically, people had to fish to survive, " says Tom Ohaus, charter boat captain of Angling Unlimited in Sitka, Alaska. Today, people get introduced to saltwater fishing through their families.

"Children want to fish," Ohaus says. Some people never stop fishing as they grow up, others return to it to relive childhood memories. The appeal of saltwater fishing varies from person to person. "Kids like to hook the fish, feel it tug, and catch it," Ohaus says. For other people, "the environment matters more than the fishing... They like to be outside." Still others are in it for the competition. They "want their fish to be bigger than their friend's," says Ohaus.

Saltwater fishing is more expensive than freshwater fishing because ocean-faring vessels cost more than those designed for the average lake or river. Travel is usually involved in saltwater fishing as well. "Freshwater fishing is more the average guy's sport," Ohaus says.

GPS technology and navigational systems, as well as better sounding equipment, are making it much easier to find and catch fish. "There isn't much luck to it" anymore, he says.

Improved technology has raised concerns about overfishing the oceans, which are less controlled than freshwater lakes and rivers. These concerns are heightened because saltwater fishing is much more commercial than freshwater fishing. "When you're catching salmon and halibut, there's an enormous emphasis on what you can kill," Ohaus explains. In contrast, freshwater fishing is often catch-and-release.

Ohaus sees an approaching crisis, with saltwater fish species being dangerously depleted. He also sees increased conflict between business and sport fishing. "Creating limits is very important," he says. "A less-consumptive approach is necessary."

Participation in Fishing

(percent of persons aged 16 or older who participated in fishing at least once in the past year, by selected demographic characteristics, 1994-95)

	total	fishing	
		freshwater	*saltwater*
Total	**29.1%**	**24.4%**	**9.5%**
Age			
Aged 16 to 24	35.4	30.3	11.8
Aged 25 to 29	34.3	27.9	12.4
Aged 30 to 39	33.9	28.9	10.1
Aged 40 to 49	31.5	26.7	10.4
Aged 50 to 59	24.9	20.2	8.3
Aged 60 or older	17.1	13.9	5.4
Income			
Under $15,000	20.3	16.1	5.3
$15,000 to $24,999	26.6	22.9	6.6
$25,000 to $49,999	32.2	27.5	10.1
$50,000 to $74,999	33.9	28.4	11.6
$75,000 to $99,999	33.7	27.7	14.2
$100,000 or more	32.1	23.6	15.6
Sex			
Men	37.8	32.3	13.3
Women	21.1	17.2	5.9
Race and Hispanic origin			
White	30.9	26.3	9.6
Black	19.6	15.0	7.4
Other, including Hispanic	23.7	16.8	10.8
Education			
Not a high school graduate	27.5	23.4	7.6
High school graduate	30.7	26.1	9.1
Some college	31.2	26.4	10.3
College graduate	26.3	21.3	9.9
Number of persons in household			
One	20.4	16.3	6.9
Two	26.3	22.1	8.9
Three	32.3	26.6	11.3
Four	36.1	31.4	10.5
Five or more	33.4	28.4	10.5

(continued)

(continued from previous page)

| | total | fishing | |
		freshwater	saltwater
Number of persons aged			
16 or older in household			
One	22.9%	18.6%	7.2%
Two	30.8	26.1	10.0
Three or more	31.8	26.8	10.6
Number of persons under			
age 6 in household			
None	27.9	23.3	9.2
One or more	34.0	28.9	10.6

Source: USDA Forest Service, 1994-95 National Survey on Recreation and the Environment

Hunting

Who hunts:
- *men*
- *whites*
- *high school graduates*

Hunting trends:
- *more women*
- *land-use issues*

Hunting is a far-less-popular recreational activity than fishing. Only 9 percent of Americans aged 16 or older have been hunting in the past year. Hunting for big game is about equal in popularity to small-game hunting, with 7 percent of people aged 16 or older participating in each of these activities. Only 2 percent hunt for migratory birds.

While hunting is more popular among young adults than among older Americans, participation declines only gradually with age. The participation rate is highest among 16-to-24-year-olds, at 13 percent. Participation drops to 4 percent among people aged 60 or older.

Hunting is most popular among people with middle incomes. Over 10 percent of those living in households with incomes of $25,000 to $99,999 have been hunting in the past 12 months, versus just 8 percent of those in the most-affluent households. This pattern is true for both big-game and small-game hunting. In contrast, migratory-bird hunting rises with income, to a peak of nearly 4 percent among those with household incomes of $75,000 or more.

Men are far more likely to hunt than women. Seventeen percent of men have gone hunting in the past 12 months, versus only 3 percent of women. Unlike many recreational activities, hunting is less popular among college graduates than among

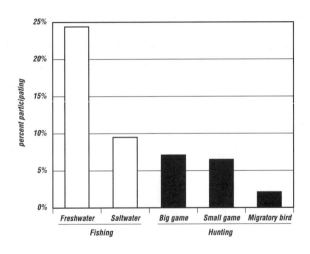

those with less education. Only 7 percent of college graduates have been hunting in the past 12 months, versus 11 percent of those with a high school diploma or less. Migratory-bird hunting does not follow this pattern, however, with the college educated slightly more likely to participate than those with less education.

Hunting is most popular among people who live in larger households. Behind this pattern is the greater involvement of 16-to-24-year-olds in hunting, many of whom are teenagers still living at home.

The Future of Hunting

"It takes a hunter to make a hunter," explains Mark Damian Duda, president and executive director of Responsive Management, a Virginia-based natural resource research organization.

Because there is a lot to learn, "people will give it up if there's nobody to teach them," explains Diana Rupp, conservation news editor of *Sports Afield*. For most people, a family member is the teacher.

"Nationwide, hunting and fishing are declining slightly. It's directly due to urbanization and a lack of free time. For hunting, access is the number one issue," says Duda.

Rupp agrees. "Land-use conflicts happen more and more, although hunting usually happens at a time of year when nothing else does." If the trend continues, hunting may become more of "a pay thing" on private land, says Rupp.

Access is not the only issue facing hunters. They also have a serious case of bad press, according to Rupp. But, she explains, "the vast majority of hunters are in the sport because they like being outdoors. Hunting enables a person to really be in the animal's world."

"Hunters are the biggest conservation group around," says Steve Patnode, owner and president of Outdoors On-Line. "As a whole, hunters and fishers spend the most on protecting habitat. More wildlife is displaced by agriculture than by hunters."

Although hunting is still dominated by white men, women are making in-roads into the sport. "Women hunters are much more serious than men," Rupp has found. "They spend more hours in the field." As a result, she says, women's conservation and outdoor groups are springing up. "Becoming an outdoors woman" workshops are held in 47 states, she says. Hunting magazines are also trying to include more pictures of women hunters. Riding this wave, manufacturers are designing more gear for women.

Minorities, on the other hand, have remained a very small percentage of the hunting community. Duda doesn't see that changing in the future. Hunting is a cultural tradition and is not part of the black and Hispanic communities.

"Hunting can use a new look," concludes Rupp. "I'm hoping we can make hunting more palatable." The increased female presence will help change the image from a "macho bloodfest to more of a family sport," she says.

Participation in Hunting

(percent of persons aged 16 or older who participated in hunting at least once in the past year, by selected demographic characteristics, 1994-95)

	total	big game	small game	migratory bird
			hunting	
Total	**9.4%**	**7.1%**	**6.5%**	**2.1%**
Age				
Aged 16 to 24	13.4	9.7	9.5	3.0
Aged 25 to 29	12.2	9.7	9.2	2.2
Aged 30 to 39	11.1	8.7	7.4	2.6
Aged 40 to 49	9.1	6.9	6.0	2.2
Aged 50 to 59	9.0	6.6	6.4	2.0
Aged 60 or older	3.8	2.6	2.3	1.0
Income				
Under $15,000	4.4	3.1	2.8	0.7
$15,000 to $24,999	9.6	7.4	6.8	1.4
$25,000 to $49,999	11.6	8.9	8.0	2.3
$50,000 to $74,999	10.8	8.1	7.1	2.6
$75,000 to $99,999	10.5	7.3	8.3	3.7
$100,000 or more	8.0	5.9	5.6	3.6
Sex				
Men	16.8	12.7	12.1	4.1
Women	2.7	2.0	1.4	0.4
Race and Hispanic origin				
White	10.6	8.1	7.2	2.5
Black	3.4	1.9	3.1	0.3
Other, including Hispanic	5.7	3.8	4.1	1.2
Education				
Not a high school graduate	10.8	7.7	7.4	1.9
High school graduate	10.8	8.6	7.3	1.9
Some college	10.0	7.8	6.8	2.3
College graduate	7.0	4.6	5.0	2.3
Number of persons in household				
One	6.9	5.1	4.8	2.0
Two	8.4	6.0	5.4	2.0
Three	11.5	8.7	8.2	2.5
Four	10.8	8.4	7.4	2.3
Five or more	10.8	8.6	7.7	1.9

(continued)

(continued from previous page)

| | total | hunting | | |
		big game	small game	migratory bird
Number of persons aged				
16 or older in household				
One	7.2%	5.4%	4.9%	1.9%
Two	9.9	7.4	6.6	2.1
Three or more	10.9	8.2	8.0	2.3
Number of persons under				
age 6 in household				
None	8.9	6.6	6.0	2.2
One or more	11.5	9.3	8.3	1.9

Source: USDA Forest Service, 1994-95 National Survey on Recreation and the Environment

Spending on Fishing and Hunting Equipment

No single demographic group dominates spending on fishing and hunting equipment, reflecting the broad appeal of fishing in particular. Spending is above average among householders aged 25 to 34, as well as among those aged 45 to 64. Spending peaks in the 45-to-54 age group, at 51 percent above average.

The most-affluent households spend nearly twice as much as the average household on hunting and fishing equipment. Together, households with incomes of $50,000 or more account for nearly half the spending in this market.

In contrast to their spending patterns for most sports and recreational activities, spending by college graduates on hunting and fishing equipment is below average. People who went no further than high school, and those with a few years of college, spend the most. Together, these two educational segments control two-thirds of all spending in this category.

By household type, married couples with children aged 18 or older spend the most on hunting and fishing equipment—more than twice as much as the average household. Spending in this category is much higher than average in the Midwest, and far below average in the Northeast and South.

Spending on Fishing and Hunting Equipment, 1995

(average annual, indexed, and market share of spending by consumer units on hunting and fishing equipment, by selected demographic characteristics, 1995; index definition: 100 is the average; an index of 132 means that spending by consumer units in the segment is 32 percent above average; an index of 68 means spending by consumer units in the segment is 32 percent below average)

	average	index	market share
Average consumer unit	$17.00	100	100.0%
Age			
Under age 25	10.04	59	4.1
Aged 25 to 34	20.72	122	23.1
Aged 35 to 44	16.18	95	21.7
Aged 45 to 54	25.69	151	27.3
Aged 55 to 64	19.90	117	14.3
Aged 65 or older	7.70	45	9.6
Income			
Under $20,000	6.08	34	12.7
$20,000 to $29,999	13.07	73	11.1
$30,000 to $39,999	17.17	96	12.3
$40,000 to $49,999	28.31	158	15.6
$50,000 to $69,999	33.35	187	23.2
$70,000 or more	35.40	198	25.1
Race			
White and "other"	19.14	113	99.8
Black	0.24	1	0.2
Hispanic origin			
Non-Hispanic	18.00	106	97.7
Hispanic	5.17	30	2.4
Education			
Not a high school graduate	14.29	84	17.6
High school graduate only	19.95	117	37.6
Some college	19.81	117	26.6
College graduate	12.81	75	18.3

(continued)

(continued from previous page)

	average	index	market share
Household type			
Married couples, total	$21.67	127	66.8%
Married couple only	16.05	94	20.2
Married couple with children	26.23	154	41.8
Oldest child under age 6	18.49	109	5.9
Oldest child aged 6 to 17	24.04	141	20.1
Oldest child aged 18 or older	35.97	212	15.8
Single parent with children under 18	4.70	28	1.8
Single person	11.95	70	19.8
Region			
Northeast	10.57	62	12.4
Midwest	29.58	174	43.7
South	11.22	66	22.5
West	17.49	103	21.4

Note: The average spending figures are extremely low because both purchasers and non-purchasers are included in the calculation. While the average spending figures do not show how much buyers of fishing and hunting equipment spend, the patterns revealed by the index and market share figures do show who is most likely to spend on fishing and hunting equipment and how much spending is controlled by each demographic segment.
Source: Bureau of Labor Statistics, 1995 Consumer Expenditure Survey; calculations by New Strategist

Chapter 5

Individual Sports

Among the many types of individual sports, those that do not require a lot of equipment—such as walking, running, bicycling, and hiking—enjoy the highest rates of participation in all demographic segments. Elite sports such as golf and tennis rank second in popularity.

Some individual sports capture a disproportionate amount of media attention compared to the number of people participating in them. These so-called "extreme" sports—such as mountain climbing—appeal to a tiny minority of adults. Rising rates of participation in tamer sports may partly explain the "extreme" sport hype. As more Americans hike, bicycle, and take part in other outdoor sports, the sports ideal is shifting from baseball and football players to rock climbers, snowboarders, and other envelope-pushing athletes.

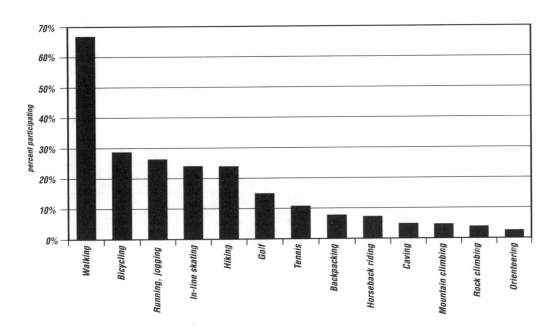

Backpacking

Who backpacks:
- *young adults*
- *men*

Backpacking Trends:
- *specialized gear*
- *access restrictions*

Nearly 8 percent of Americans aged 16 or older participate in backpacking at least once during a 12-month period. Young adults are most likely to backpack, with 14 percent of those aged 16 to 24 and 12 percent of 25-to-29-year-olds having done so in the past year. Participation drops with age, to fewer than 2 percent of people aged 60 or older.

Backpacking does not vary much by household income. Between 8 and 10 percent of people in households with incomes of $25,000 or more have been backpacking in the past 12 months. Behind this pattern is the involvement of young adults—typically with low incomes—in the sport.

Men are twice as likely as women to be backpackers, 10 versus 5 percent. Whites are more than twice as likely as blacks to backpack, 8 versus 3 percent. The college educated are most likely to backpack, with 10 percent having done so in the past year. People without a high school diploma are more likely to backpack than those with a high school degree because of age differences in the two groups. Many of those with-

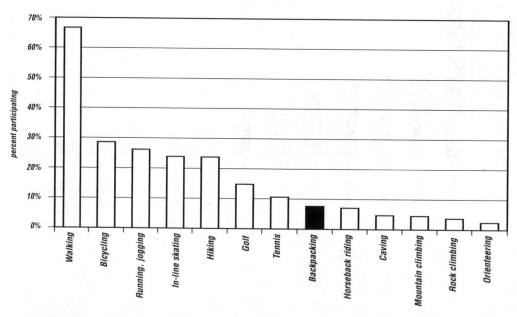

out a high school diploma are teenagers still in high school—the age group most likely to backpack. In contrast, a large share of high school graduates are older Americans—the age group least likely to backpack.

Participation in backpacking does not vary by the presence of young children in the home. It is more common in households with three or more adults, however. Many of these households are married couples with backpacking teenagers.

Backpacking's Future

Backpackers start young, and many do not like it at first, says Susan Bruton, an instructor for the Colorado Outward Bound School. "It's hard," Bruton explains.

Parents often provide a child with his or her first backpacking experience, but kids get hooked as teenagers. People get hooked for a variety of reasons, Bruton says, depending on the age group. Teenagers become enthralled after seeing backpackers in movies, on MTV Sports, or even in Nike advertisements. Adults and teens alike can be attracted to backpacking as an achievement—such as backpacking along the Appalachian Trail. People also enjoy backpacking for the same reason they enjoy other outdoor sports—the need to get away from it all.

A major change in backpacking is the improvement in gear technology. Although better gear has reduced the misery factor, that comfort has come at a cost. Bruton says gear prices haven't hit their ceiling yet. "It used to be that gear was available in army green. Now you've got bright colors and it's bought by people who aren't even going out and using it. It's a real status thing," she notes.

Beyond appearances, gear is now lighter and custom fitted. Women can buy gear designed for them. Better gear is making the sport easier because of its specialization. "You can get a pack designed especially for carrying rock climbing gear for a fly fisherman," Bruton says.

Backpackers often take part in other sports while they are on the trails, for example, rock climbing, mountaineering, fly fishing, or back country skiing. People who are into photography are also often backpackers, Bruton has noticed.

In the future, look for more backpacking programs tailored to the needs of older people, more specialized and expensive gear, and more government regulation of open spaces, Bruton says. "Because there are more individuals out there, the Forest Service will need to regulate land use," she explains. This could result in more permits being required, reducing the spontaneity of the sport enjoyed by backpackers today.

Participation in Backpacking

(percent of persons aged 16 or older who participated in backpacking at least once in the past year, by selected demographic characteristics, 1994-95)

Total	**7.6%**
Age	
Aged 16 to 24	14.3
Aged 25 to 29	11.9
Aged 30 to 39	8.3
Aged 40 to 49	7.0
Aged 50 to 59	4.5
Aged 60 or older	1.5
Income	
Under $15,000	5.3
$15,000 to $24,999	6.4
$25,000 to $49,999	7.8
$50,000 to $74,999	9.9
$75,000 to $99,999	8.7
$100,000 or more	10.1
Sex	
Men	10.2
Women	5.1
Race and Hispanic origin	
White	8.2
Black	3.0
Other, including Hispanic	7.5
Education	
Not a high school graduate	7.4
High school graduate	5.5
Some college	7.9
College graduate	9.6
Number of persons in household	
One	6.0
Two	6.4
Three	10.0
Four	7.6
Five or more	9.3

(continued)

(continued from previous page)

**Number of persons aged
16 or older in household**

One	6.5%
Two	6.9
Three or more	10.1

**Number of persons under
age 6 in household**

None	7.6
One or more	7.5

Source: USDA Forest Service, 1994-95 National Survey on Recreation and the Environment

Bicycling

Who bicycles:
- *people under age 60*
- *college-educated householders*

Bicycling trends:
- *urban cruisers*
- *older cyclists*

Bicycling is one of America's most-popular sports. Twenty-nine percent of people aged 16 or older have bicycled at least once in the past year. Participation is highest among people under age 40—more than one-third of them have cycled in the past year. But even among those aged 50 or older, bicycling is popular. Twenty-two percent of people aged 50 to 59 have bicycled in the past year, as have 11 percent of those aged 60 or older.

Bicycling is popular in every demographic segment. While participation increases with income, peaking at 39 percent among people with household incomes of $100,000 or more, it is above 30 percent among those with household incomes all the way down to $25,000. Even among those with the lowest incomes, under $15,000 per year, 18 percent are cyclists.

Bicycling is multicultural. Whites are only slightly more likely than blacks to have bicycled in the past year—29 versus 21 percent. Among "others" (primarily Asians and Hispanics), 26 percent have been cycling in the past year. Men are only slightly more likely to be cyclists than women, 31 versus 27 percent.

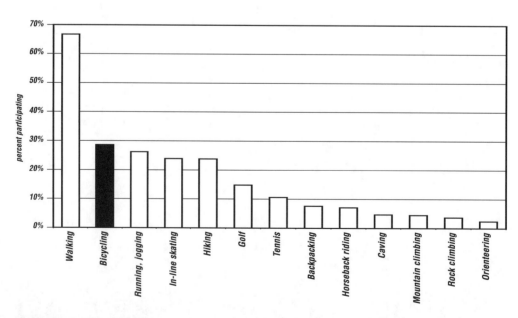

Among college graduates, 34 percent are cyclists. This share compares with 24 percent of people who went no further than high school.

Children are a catalyst for bicycling. Families with children under age 6 are more likely to cycle than those without young children at home—34 versus 27 percent. Households with four or more people (most are families with children) are more likely to cycle than smaller households.

Spending on Bicycles

The biggest spenders on bicycles, by far, are married couples with children aged 6 to 17. These families spend more than twice as much as the average household on bicycles, accounting for 31 percent of all spending in this market. Married couples without children at home spend only half as much as the average household on bicycles, controlling only 11 percent of the market.

By age, householders in the 35-to-44 age group spend the most on bicycles because they are the ones likely to have children aged 6 to 17. Householders in this age group spend 66 percent more than the average household on bicycles.

Although whites spend more than blacks on bicycles, the gap between Hispanics and non-Hispanics is not as wide. Non-Hispanics spend about an average amount on bicycles, while Hispanics spend 7 percent less than average.

Spending rises with income. Households with incomes of $40,000 or more spend above average on bicycles.

The South is the only region with below-average spending on bicycles. Southern households spend 20 percent less than the average household on bicycles. Households in the West spend the most on bicycles—30 percent more than average.

Bicycling's Future

"People get into cycling for fitness—they do it on weekends, maybe at lunch. They start to discover that it's an easy thing to use instead of a car. Then it becomes a sort of religious devotion to the bike," says Geoff Drake, editor of *Bicycling Magazine*.

Right now, mountain biking is hot, ranked third among equipment-related sports activities by the Sporting Goods Manufacturing Association in 1994. But, says Drake, "we knew all along that most mountain bikes were sold to people who never used them off-road." Apparently, cyclists want the features of mountain bikes—their style, stability, and comfort—whether they take them off-road or not.

Because of this trend, Drake predicts that the future of cycling lies in a new type of bike that is yet to have a standard industry name. He describes these bikes as "urban commuter vehicles, cruiser bikes, city bikes. They're more practical for people to use as transportation or to ride on a bike path." The riding position is upright, and the tires are smooth.

As a result, watch for this trend: the cycling commuter. Bicycles are cheaper, more environmentally sound, and in some urban areas faster than a car. And for employees who commute by bicycle and arrive sweaty at the office, some companies are providing showers.

Another trend is the older cycler. "The neat thing about bicycling is that it's low-impact. It's a gentle sport, a lot like swimming in that respect," says Drake. He adds that a lot of former runners with "trashed knees" turn to cycling.

"The problem is that, in this country, bicycles are still relegated to the position of a toy," says Drake. The growing millions of cyclists in the United States might just change that.

Participation in Bicycling

(percent of persons aged 16 or older who participated in bicycling at least once in the past year, by selected demographic characteristics, 1994-95)

Total	**28.6%**
Age	
Aged 16 to 24	37.8
Aged 25 to 29	36.3
Aged 30 to 39	37.4
Aged 40 to 49	30.6
Aged 50 to 59	22.0
Aged 60 or older	10.7
Income	
Under $15,000	18.0
$15,000 to $24,999	21.8
$25,000 to $49,999	31.1
$50,000 to $74,999	35.9
$75,000 to $99,999	37.0
$100,000 or more	39.1
Sex	
Men	31.0
Women	26.5
Race and Hispanic origin	
White	29.9
Black	21.2
Other, including Hispanic	26.2
Education	
Not a high school graduate	23.5
High school graduate	24.1
Some college	30.3
College graduate	34.3
Number of persons in household	
One	20.3
Two	24.1
Three	32.1
Four	36.4
Five or more	35.6

(continued)

(continued from previous page)

**Number of persons aged
16 or older in household**

One	23.1%
Two	29.5
Three or more	32.7

**Number of persons under
age 6 in household**

None	27.0
One or more	33.9

Source: USDA Forest Service, 1994-95 National Survey on Recreation and the Environment

Spending on Bicycles, 1995

(average annual, indexed, and market share of spending by consumer units on bicycles, by selected demographic characteristics, 1995; index definition: 100 is the average; an index of 132 means that spending by consumer units in the segment is 32 percent above average; an index of 68 means spending by consumer units in the segment is 32 percent below average)

	average	index	market share
Average consumer unit	**$12.59**	**100**	**100.0%**
Age			
Under age 25	18.39	146	10.0
Aged 25 to 34	16.17	128	24.3
Aged 35 to 44	20.92	166	37.8
Aged 45 to 54	10.26	81	14.7
Aged 55 to 64	6.38	51	6.2
Aged 65 or older	4.10	33	6.9
Income			
Under $20,000	5.58	42	15.6
$20,000 to $29,999	12.64	96	14.5
$30,000 to $39,999	12.54	95	12.1
$40,000 to $49,999	15.89	120	11.8
$50,000 to $69,999	23.70	179	22.3
$70,000 or more	24.67	186	23.7
Race			
White and "other"	13.25	105	93.3
Black	7.39	59	6.6
Hispanic origin			
Non-Hispanic	12.66	101	92.7
Hispanic	11.75	93	7.3
Education			
Not a high school graduate	3.35	27	5.6
High school graduate only	12.71	101	32.3
Some college	16.23	129	29.5
College graduate	16.94	135	32.6

(continued)

(continued from previous page)

	average	index	market share
Household type			
Married couples, total	$14.35	114	59.7%
Married couple only	6.38	51	10.8
Married couple with children	21.03	167	45.3
Oldest child under age 6	13.30	106	5.7
Oldest child aged 6 to 17	27.76	220	31.4
Oldest child aged 18 or older	13.80	110	8.2
Single parent with children under 18	13.19	105	6.8
Single person	5.72	45	12.8
Region			
Northeast	12.78	102	20.3
Midwest	12.73	101	25.4
South	10.08	80	27.3
West	16.32	130	27.0

Note: The average spending figures are extremely low because both purchasers and non-purchasers are included in the calculation. While the average spending figures do not show how much buyers of bicycles spend, the patterns revealed by the index and market share figures do show who is most likely to spend on bicycles and how much spending is controlled by each demographic segment.
Source: Bureau of Labor Statistics, 1995 Consumer Expenditure Survey; calculations by New Strategist

Caving

Who caves: • *all demographic segments*

Caving trends: • *educational programs*
• *environmental awareness*
• *one-of-a-kind experiences*

There are two types of caving, which helps explain why caving is about equally popular among all demographic groups. Wild caving involves exploring and mapping undeveloped caves. It requires great skill and physical prowess. The second type of caving is touring showcase caves with a group. Many more people visit showcase caves than take part in wild caving.

Overall, about 5 percent of Americans have been caving in the past 12 months. Those most likely to have been caving are young adults. Eight percent of 16-to-24-year-olds and 7 percent of 25-to-29-year-olds have been caving in the past year. Many of these young cavers are exploring uncharted caves. The likelihood of caving falls with age, to 4 percent of people in their 40s, 3 percent of those in their 50s, and 2 percent of people in their 60s. Many older cavers are visiting showcase caves.

Caving shows little variation by household income or education. Men are slightly more likely to participate in caving than women—6 versus 4 percent. Whites and "others" (primarily Asians and Hispanics) are more likely to cave than blacks.

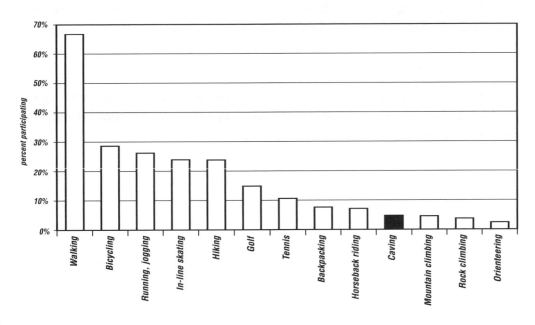

The more adults live in a household, the higher is the likelihood that household members participate in caving. That larger households are more likely to contain young adults—who are most likely to participate in caving—accounts for this pattern.

Caving's Future

People visit caves "because they enjoy nature, for the education, for an adventure, to come into a cool place on a summer day," says Anne Molosky, vice-president and general manager of Lincoln Caverns in Pennsylvania.

The business of showcase caving has changed in the past 20 years. Caves were once considered roadside attractions, says Molosky, with all of the accompanying bells and whistles. While some caves are still like that today, many have turned to a more natural and educational approach. This trend is driven by growing environmental concerns, Molosky observes.

A tour of the natural formations of a showcase cave can excite an interest in wild caving, Molosky says. But, as with rock climbing and mountaineering, the caving community encourages beginners to get appropriate training. A clumsy or careless caver can ruin thousands of years of Mother Nature's work. Molosky sees her role in running a showcase cave as the first line of defense for the cave environment. "People need to understand what a fragile environment they are entering. It's more than just an adventure, and it's more than just a sport."

Molosky says more older people are visiting caves. She attributes this to the improved physical fitness of older people and the new emphasis on walking for exercise. She also thinks more grandparents are taking their grandchildren to showcase caves.

The continuing interest in the environment and the proliferation of adventure sports bode well for the future of showcase caves and wild caving. On the showcase front, caves will try to distinguish themselves by offering unique programs. Lincoln Caverns, for example, offers a sluice where visitors can pan for gems.

The growing interest in bats has boosted the popularity of caving as well. "Bats are becoming more and more popular," Molosky says. "We do a lot with bat education. It has really helped business."

Participation in Caving

(percent of persons aged 16 or older who participated in caving at least once in the past year, by selected demographic characteristics, 1994-95)

Total	**4.7%**
Age	
Aged 16 to 24	7.9
Aged 25 to 29	7.0
Aged 30 to 39	5.3
Aged 40 to 49	4.3
Aged 50 to 59	2.9
Aged 60 or older	1.6
Income	
Under $15,000	3.3
$15,000 to $24,999	4.0
$25,000 to $49,999	5.1
$50,000 to $74,999	5.5
$75,000 to $99,999	5.2
$100,000 or more	5.1
Sex	
Men	5.7
Women	3.8
Race and Hispanic origin	
White	5.1
Black	1.7
Other, including Hispanic	4.8
Education	
Not a high school graduate	5.1
High school graduate	4.1
Some college	5.5
College graduate	4.5
Number of persons in household	
One	2.6
Two	4.6
Three	5.9
Four	5.2
Five or more	5.5

(continued)

(continued from previous page)

**Number of persons aged
16 or older in household**

One	3.5%
Two	4.8
Three or more	5.8

**Number of persons under
age 6 in household**

None	4.7
One or more	4.8

Source: USDA Forest Service, 1994-95 National Survey on Recreation and the Environment

Golf

Who golfs:
- *high-income households*
- *men*
- *whites*
- *highly educated*

Golfing trends:
- *broadening demographics*
- *environmental concerns*

Golf is one of the most-popular recreational activities among older Americans. Ten percent of people aged 60 or older have golfed at least once in the past 12 months. The proportion is even higher among younger adults, with 19 percent of people aged 25 to 29 having played golf in the past year.

Traditionally, golf has been a sport dominated by affluent white men. While the demographics of golfers are changing, those characteristics are still evident. Thirty percent of people with household incomes of $100,000 or more played golf in the past year, a share at least three times greater than that of golfers in households with incomes of $25,000 or less. Twenty-two percent of men have golfed recently, versus only 8 percent of women. Among whites, 17 percent played golf in the past 12 months, versus only 4 percent of blacks and 7 percent of "others" (primarily Asians and Hispanics).

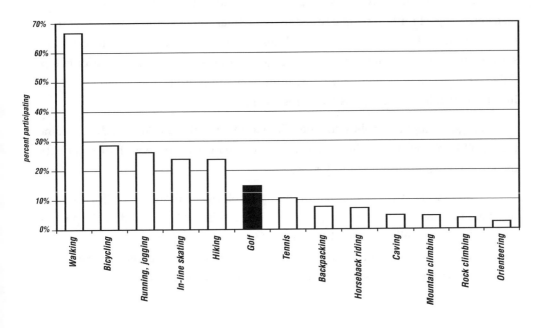

College graduates are twice as likely to play golf as are those who went no further than high school. Twenty percent of college graduates have played in the past 12 months versus only 10 percent of high school graduates.

Golf spectators are the same people as those who enjoy playing golf, and they share many of the same characteristics—affluent middle-aged and older men. There are some important differences between spectators at Professional Golfers Association (PGA) events and those who watch PGA golf on television, however.

Three in four spectators at PGA events are men, while the male share drops to two-thirds among PGA television viewers. Golf spectators at live events are younger than those who watch on television. People attending the PGA Tour have a median age of 39, versus a median age of 47 for those watching PGA games on television. For the Senior PGA Tour, those attending live events have a median age of 44, while those watching on television have an even older median of 53.

People attending live PGA events have much higher incomes than those watching games on television. In part, this is because televised PGA games attract so many retirees with lower incomes. One-fourth of those watching PGA events on television are retirees, as are one-third of those watching televised Senior PGA Tour games. Only 7 to 14 percent of spectators at live events are retired. The median income of those watching golf on television is $43,000 to $45,000. For those attending a live event, median household income is considerably higher—$65,000.

The Future of Golf

Golf is a sport in transition. Historically it is the game of "presidents, corporations, fat cats, and old guys in funny pants," explains Jim Frank, editor of *Golf* magazine. Then, an astounding 44 million people tuned in to the final round of the Masters golf tournament in Augusta, Georgia, to witness Tiger Woods' history-making victory. All of a sudden, the stodgy, duller-than-watching-grass-grow sport of golf has become hip. Other signs of change include the rising number of public golf courses and new clothing styles. Plaids and pompons are losing their grip.

Yet golf remains a hobby for the affluent, making it a marketer's dream come true. Golf is fast becoming the expressway to the wallets of those with discretionary income—young adults and empty nesters.

"The explosion that came with the impact of Tiger Woods," says Jon Podany, director of business development at the PGA Tour, "will not be ignored by the powers that be." Golf is well positioned to benefit from its discovery by the masses. As a spectator sport, it avoids the pitfalls of team sports—there are no teams, no team owners, and no salaried players. Professional golfers play on commission.

The attention the sport is receiving is bringing entrepreneurs out of the wood-work. Golfers are being targeted by an increasing array of products, from cigars to furniture to clothes. The exposure is increasing the demand for golf facilities, driving ranges, and even for a faster game. Podany predicts the emergence of three- and four-hole courses.

Golf is "addictive," Frank explains. "You can never get the perfect shot. You'll never master this game."

"Golf becomes a lifestyle. People put pictures of golf courses on their walls, they watch it on television, hang out at the club, talk about it with their friends, and play on the weekends," he continues. "There's also a travel aspect because, in most of the country, golf is not a year-round activity. But there's always some place in the world where it's golf weather."

There will be more golf-related activities in the future, as golf capitalizes on the sea of people swept in by Tiger Woods' celebrity, Podany says. Golf developers will try to make tournaments more fan- and kid-friendly. Tourist attractions like the World Golf Village in Florida, which will house a Hall of Fame, among other things, will give avid golfers another place to visit on their vacations.

Golf will remain more than just a game. Besides improvements in golf clubs and carts, other factors will affect the future of the sport. One of them is environmental concerns. Golf courses are frequently blamed for being land- and water-greedy and ecologically unsound because of the application of chemicals to keep courses green. The sport is beginning to look into ways to improve environmentally.

Some critics also maintain that by following prescribed rules, courses have become too tame. Combined with environmental concerns, this criticism could lead to the emergence of nontraditional, nonmanicured courses different from those seen on television today.

Despite these concerns, the bottom line is that golf is looking good. "Golf is a lifelong sport, it's not hard on you physically, and there's just no such thing as an ugly golf course," Frank concludes.

Participation in Golf

(percent of persons aged 16 or older who participated in golfing at least once in the past year, by selected demographic characteristics, 1994-95)

Total	**14.8%**
Age	
Aged 16 to 24	15.3
Aged 25 to 29	19.0
Aged 30 to 39	17.7
Aged 40 to 49	15.4
Aged 50 to 59	12.0
Aged 60 or older	10.3
Income	
Under $15,000	5.7
$15,000 to $24,999	9.5
$25,000 to $49,999	14.5
$50,000 to $74,999	22.6
$75,000 to $99,999	24.6
$100,000 or more	30.0
Sex	
Men	22.4
Women	7.8
Race and Hispanic origin	
White	16.9
Black	4.1
Other, including Hispanic	7.1
Education	
Not a high school graduate	9.2
High school graduate	10.4
Some college	15.6
College graduate	21.3
Number of persons in household	
One	12.4
Two	15.9
Three	16.3
Four	15.0
Five or more	13.1

(continued)

(continued from previous page)

Number of persons aged 16 or older in household	
One	12.1%
Two	16.2
Three or more	14.4

Number of persons under age 6 in household	
None	15.0
One or more	14.2

Source: USDA Forest Service, 1994-95 National Survey on Recreation and the Environment

Characteristics of Golf Spectators: PGA Tour and Senior PGA Tour

(percent distribution of golf spectators for the PGA and Senior PGA tours, by selected demographic characteristics, 1995)

	PGA Tour	Senior PGA Tour
Total	100%	100%
Sex		
Male	76	74
Female	24	26
Marital status		
Married	68	81
Single	32	19
Age		
Aged 18 to 24	7	5
Aged 25 to 34	30	22
Aged 35 to 44	27	24
Aged 45 to 54	21	24
Aged 55 to 64	9	15
Aged 65 or older	5	10
Median Age	39	44
Household income		
Under $50,0000	28	25
$50,000 to $74,999	24	28
$75,000 to $99,999	18	19
$100,000 or more	24	22
Median household income	$65,000	$65,000
Occupation		
Professionals, managers	55%	52%
Sales, clerical	14	14
Blue collar	6	6
Other	5	4
Retired	7	14
Self-employed	13	10

Source: Irwin Research 1995 On-Site Survey, Fall 1995 MRI, National Golf Foundation 1995 Report; *reprinted by permission of the PGA Tour*

Characteristics of Golf Television Viewers: PGA Tour and Senior PGA Tour

(percent distribution of golf television viewers for the PGA and Senior PGA Tours, by selected demographic characteristics, 1995)

	PGA Tour	Senior PGA Tour
Total	100%	100%
Sex		
Male	65	65
Female	35	35
Marital status		
Married	69	71
Single	16	12
Age		
Aged 18 to 24	8	6
Aged 25 to 34	18	15
Aged 35 to 44	20	14
Aged 45 to 59	24	28
Aged 60 or older	30	38
Median age	47	53
Household income		
Under $25,000	23	26
$25,000 to $49,999	32	33
$50,000 to $99,999	35	32
$100,000 or more	10	10
Median household income	$45,233	$42,939
Occupation		
Professionals, managers	24%	22%
Sales, clerical	18	16
Blue collar	8	6
Other	14	12
Retired	26	33
Self-employed	11	11

Source: Irwin Research 1995 On-Site Study, Fall 1995 MRI, National Golf Foundation 1995 Report*; reprinted by permission of the PGA Tour*

Hiking

Who hikes:
- *people under age 50*
- *the college educated*

Hiking trends:
- *improved equipment*
- *trail conservation*

Twenty-four percent of Americans have hiked in the past 12 months. Although the likelihood of hiking declines with age, the drop is gradual. Among 16-to-24-year-olds, 32 percent have hiked in the past year. This proportion falls by just 5 percentage points, to 27 percent, among people in their 40s. Even among people in their 60s, a relatively large share—nearly 10 percent—have hiked in the past 12 months.

Hiking is popular at most income levels. Participation is above average for households with incomes of $25,000 or more. More men than women are hikers—27 percent of men and 21 percent of women. Many more whites than blacks take part in hiking—26 percent of whites versus 8 percent of blacks. Behind this difference is the fact that many blacks live in urban areas with limited hiking opportunities.

Hiking participation rises with household size because of age differences between small and large households. Households with only one or two people are likely to be headed by older Americans, who are least likely to hike, while households with

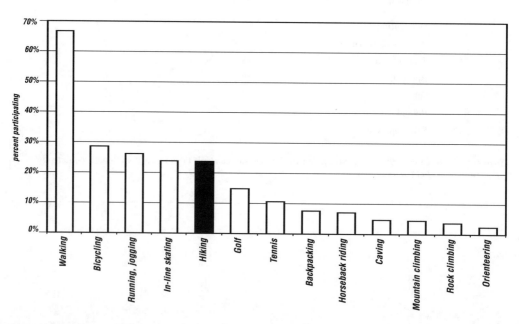

three or more people are more likely to include young and middle-aged adults, who are most likely to hike.

The Future of Hiking

"People are drawn to outdoor recreation because of the sense of accomplishment and adventure it provides, and simply because it's outdoors," says Rob Burbank, public information officer for the Appalachian Mountain Club. Hiking is one of the easiest ways to enjoy being outdoors. It is especially appealing because it can be as challenging or as easy as you want it to be.

Hiking is benefiting from the increasing quality of equipment. The development of Gore-Tex™, a "breathing" waterproof fabric, is an example of improved equipment, says Burbank, as are new types of socks that wick away moisture. As equipment improves, hiking is becoming more enjoyable and more people want to participate.

Although a large variety of hiking equipment is available, according to Burbank, one of the great things about hiking is that "you don't need all sorts of high-tech gear to get into the outdoors." People have been enjoying the outdoors without the fancy equipment for generations, he points out. Like car camping, hiking can serve as an entry point for other outdoor recreational activities. "Many people are introduced to the outdoors with their family. Then they may become more interested in a technical challenge, like rock climbing."

For serious hikers, trail conservation is an important issue. The Appalachian Mountain Club's adopt-a-trail program has been a sellout, says Burbank, with people really "juiced" about it. Combining outdoor recreation with resource management is another important trend. People will pay for the privilege of staying at a camp and then do the hard work of clearing fallen trees from trails, among other things. Burbank says participants in these programs are "tired, bug bitten, but happy."

Participation in Hiking

(percent of persons aged 16 or older who participated in hiking at least once in the past year, by selected demographic characteristics, 1994-95)

Total	**23.8%**
Age	
Aged 16 to 24	31.5
Aged 25 to 29	30.2
Aged 30 to 39	29.5
Aged 40 to 49	27.0
Aged 50 to 59	18.1
Aged 60 or older	9.6
Income	
Under $15,000	16.2
$15,000 to $24,999	18.1
$25,000 to $49,999	26.2
$50,000 to $74,999	30.7
$75,000 to $99,999	30.5
$100,000 or more	32.8
Sex	
Men	27.1
Women	20.9
Race and Hispanic origin	
White	26.0
Black	8.1
Other, including Hispanic	23.1
Education	
Not a high school graduate	18.4
High school graduate	17.6
Some college	25.8
College graduate	31.1
Number of persons in household	
One	18.4
Two	22.1
Three	26.0
Four	26.0
Five or more	28.6

(continued)

(continued from previous page)

Number of persons aged
16 or older in household

One	19.7%
Two	24.3
Three or more	27.4

Number of persons under
age 6 in household

None	23.4
One or more	25.6

Source: USDA Forest Service, 1994-95 National Survey on Recreation and the Environment

Horseback Riding

Who rides horses:
- *people under age 50*
- *high-income households*
- *households with children*

Horseback riding trends:
- *more older riders*

Horseback riding is a popular leisure-time activity for millions of Americans. Seven percent of the population aged 16 or older rode a horse in the past 12 months. Horseback riding is most popular among young adults. Twelve percent of people aged 16 to 24 have been riding recently, as have 10 percent of those aged 25 to 29. One factor behind the higher level of participation among young adults is their greater opportunity to ride horses while at college. Participation in horseback riding remains above average up to age 50, then falls to 4 percent among people aged 50 to 59 and to just 1 percent among those aged 60 or older.

Horseback riding is an activity that appeals to households with relatively high incomes, which can afford its expense. The popularity of riding is well above average for households with incomes of $50,000 or more, about average for those with incomes between $25,000 and $49,999, and below average for those with incomes below $25,000.

Men and women are equally likely to have been horseback riding in the past 12 months. Whites are about twice as likely as blacks to ride horses, 8 versus 4 percent.

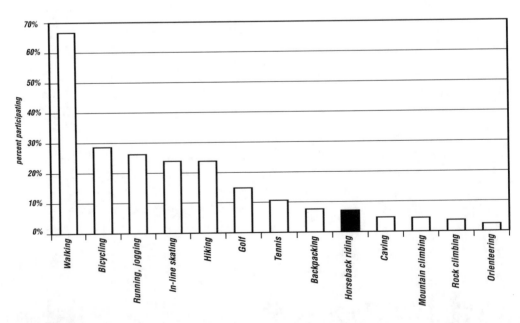

People living in households with children under age 6 are more likely to ride horses than those living in households without young children. Behind this pattern are families which take up horseback riding because their children are interested in the activity.

The Future of Horseback Riding

There's more to horseback riding than just sitting on a horse. There are many types of riding, or disciplines, ranging from the elite Olympic style to Western, saddle seat, and hunter seat. While some people ride competitively, many more are pleasure riders.

Horseback riding is a classic, low-tech sport in a high-tech world. The primary piece of equipment (the horse) and the venue (outdoors) are all provided by Mother Nature.

Horseback riders usually start when they are young. The initial childhood exposure may come from attending a horse show or reading a book or magazine about horses. Media coverage brings a steady flow of new horse enthusiasts to the sport. High-profile horseback riding accidents—such as actor Christopher Reeve's—can heighten safety concerns among parents. But in general, riding garners favorable media attention. It is being used increasingly as a form of physical therapy for the disabled.

"The American Horse Show Association (AHSA) membership is an extremely strong market for all kinds of quality, luxury products," proclaims the media guide of the national governing body for equestrian sport. The AHSA media guide notes that its 63,000 members spent an estimated $1.8 billion maintaining and showing their horses in 1995.

Riding faces many of the same problems as other sports, such as land-use constraints and a shrinking amount of free time among its followers. As boomers age and gain more leisure time, however, look for a surge in older riders. Horseback riding's rich tradition points to long-term stability for the sport.

Participation in Horseback Riding

(percent of persons aged 16 or older who participated in horseback riding at least once in the past year, by selected demographic characteristics, 1994-95)

Total	**7.1%**
Age	
Aged 16 to 24	12.4
Aged 25 to 29	10.2
Aged 30 to 39	8.8
Aged 40 to 49	7.2
Aged 50 to 59	4.3
Aged 60 or older	1.2
Income	
Under $15,000	3.7
$15,000 to $24,999	5.5
$25,000 to $49,999	7.4
$50,000 to $74,999	9.6
$75,000 to $99,999	9.9
$100,000 or more	11.2
Sex	
Men	7.0
Women	7.3
Race and Hispanic origin	
White	7.6
Black	3.7
Other, including Hispanic	6.5
Education	
Not a high school graduate	7.5
High school graduate	6.0
Some college	7.5
College graduate	7.7
Number of persons in household	
One	5.2
Two	4.9
Three	8.5
Four	9.4
Five or more	9.9

(continued)

(continued from previous page)

**Number of persons aged
16 or older in household**

One 5.8%

Two 6.8

Three or more 9.2

**Number of persons under
age 6 in household**

None 6.6

One or more 9.3

Source: USDA Forest Service, 1994-95 National Survey on Recreation and the Environment

In-Line Skating

Who in-line skates:

In-line skating trends:

- **children and young adults**

- **more older skaters**
- **becoming more mainstream**

Nearly 24 million people aged 7 or older participated in in-line skating more than once in 1995, according to the National Sporting Goods Association of Mount Prospect, Illinois. The participation data for this sport were not collected by the National Survey on Recreation and the Environment. Consequently, they are not comparable with those of other sports in this book.

A 62 percent majority of in-line skaters were under age 18. Among adults aged 18 or older, 9 million take part in in-line skating—about the same number as participate in sailing, soccer, or mountain climbing. Most adult participants are under age 35, with only 4 percent of in-line skaters aged 45 or older. Women account for half the in-line skaters.

The Future of In-Line Skating

In-line skating is the second-fastest-growing sport worldwide, according to the *1997 World Wide Sporting Goods Outlook Survey* by the World Federation Sporting Goods Industry and Kurt Salmon Associates.

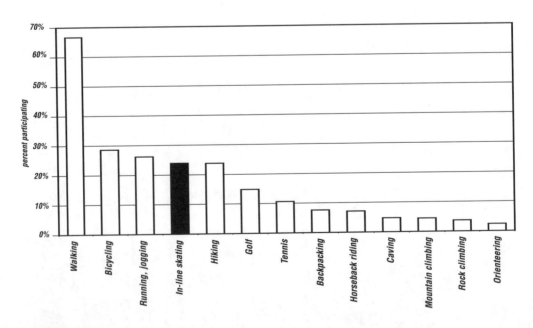

It attracts a young crowd, according to Gilbert Clark, executive director of the International In-Line Skate Association. But, he says, "we see it spreading upwards." Because of the recreational and fitness value of in-line skating, Clark believes, older people will become converts. "The problem today is that many people didn't do it as young kids. In another ten years, there will be enough people skating that it will be like bicycling," he predicts.

In-line skating is an urban phenomenon because that is where the pavement is. But today, except in the most-rural locations, "you can literally just go out your front door and skate," he says. "It is a truly modern sport—there are just as many women as men. Although minorities are underrepresented, that is changing."

In-line skating is moving beyond pure recreation and fitness and becoming practical. Skates are being used by some people to commute to work. "It's easier than a bike. There's no bike to put away," says Clark." Manufacturers are developing skates that can be snapped onto shoes. "It has the potential to expand," predicts Clark. There are also hybrids emerging from this already-hybrid activity—in-line hockey, in-line basketball, and in-line figure skating are some examples.

As do many other sports, in-line skating faces increased regulation. Aggressive skaters, like skateboarders, require designated places to practice their sport. Because of this requirement, Clark predicts, "skate parks will become a fixture in the community." Another plus, according to Clark, is the increasing number of bike paths around the country that can be used by in-line skaters.

"Skating will become very mainstream," Clark concludes.

Participation in In-Line Skating

(total number and percent distribution of persons aged 7 or older who participated in in-line skating more than once in 1995, by sex and age)

Total (millions)	**23.9**
Sex (percent)	
Male	49.7%
Female	50.3
Age (percent)	
Aged 7 to 11	33.6
Aged 12 to 17	28.6
Aged 18 to 24	12.6
Aged 25 to 34	13.5
Aged 35 to 44	7.8
Aged 45 to 54	2.1
Aged 55 to 64	0.7
Aged 65 to 74	0.4
Aged 75 or older	0.8

Source: 1995 Sports Participation Survey, *National Sporting Goods Association, Mt. Prospect, Illinois*

Mountain Climbing

Who climbs mountains:
- *young adults*
- *men*

Mountain climbing trends:
- *roadside climbing*
- *becoming more mainstream*

Just 4.5 percent of Americans aged 16 or older have been mountain climbing in the past 12 months. This sport is defined by the National Survey of Recreation and the Environment as "technical climbing that involves use of specialized equipment as well as challenges of weather and altitude, where the goal is to reach a summit." Because the sport is physically demanding, it is most appealing to young adults. The proportion of people who have been mountain climbing at least once in the past year is highest among 16-to-24-year-olds, at 8.2 percent. It remains above average for those aged 25 to 39.

Because climbing equipment is expensive and the sport usually involves travel, participation is above average for those living in households with incomes of $50,000 or more. It is below average for those living in households with incomes under $25,000.

Men are more likely than women to climb mountains, 6 versus 3 percent. Whites and "others" (primarily Asians and Hispanics) are more likely than blacks to enjoy mountain climbing.

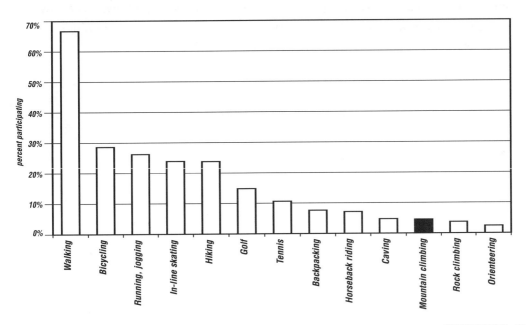

There is little variation in mountain climbing participation by presence of young children in the home. But people living in households with three or more adults are much more likely to participate in mountain climbing (6 percent) than those living in smaller households.

The Future of Mountain Climbing

Mountain climbers, like rock climbers, are tolerant of newcomers as long as "they're not yahoos, stay out of the way, and don't cause accidents," says Jed Williamson, president of Sterling College in Vermont, editor of *Accidents in North America Mountaineering*, immediate past president of the American Alpine Club, and chairman of its safety committee. His mountain climbing expeditions include Mount McKinley and Mount Everest from the Tibetan side.

Williamson explains that in mountaineering it's not a matter of elitism or purism but safety, "especially when an amateur is above you and about to drop a water bottle on your head."

Climbing gyms have brought more newcomers into the sport. This has fueled growth at "roadside" climbing spots, Williamson observes—where you park your car and walk a short distance to climb—rather than growth in back-country climbing.

"In my generation [twenty years ago], we were all a bunch of geeks. We wanted to do something outside the mainstream," says Williamson. "But now there is a new generation of climbers. People actually train to climb now. The way we used to train for climbing was to climb. They engage in it like they go to a health club."

Today's climbers "are more in tune to the here and now, to the general culture than we were." Mountain climbing was once the counterculture. "Now, you'll see a guy finish a climb and say he's got to go home to watch the Super Bowl." The newer generation has its own style. "It never would have occurred to me to wear a Walkman™ when climbing," he says.

Participation in Mountain Climbing

(percent of persons aged 16 or older who participated in mountain climbing at least once in the past year, by selected demographic characteristics, 1994-95)

Total	**4.5%**
Age	
Aged 16 to 24	8.2
Aged 25 to 29	6.3
Aged 30 to 39	5.3
Aged 40 to 49	3.7
Aged 50 to 59	2.3
Aged 60 or older	1.7
Income	
Under $15,000	2.8
$15,000 to $24,999	3.9
$25,000 to $49,999	4.6
$50,000 to $74,999	5.9
$75,000 to $99,999	6.1
$100,000 or more	6.7
Sex	
Men	5.8
Women	3.3
Race and Hispanic origin	
White	4.8
Black	1.9
Other, including Hispanic	4.9
Education	
Not a high school graduate	4.7
High school graduate	3.6
Some college	5.0
College graduate	4.9
Number of persons in household	
One	3.6
Two	4.2
Three	4.9
Four	4.3
Five or more	6.1

(continued)

(continued from previous page)

**Number of persons aged
16 or older in household**

One	3.9%
Two	4.3
Three or more	5.6

**Number of persons under
age 6 in household**

None	4.5
One or more	4.5

Source: USDA Forest Service, 1994-95 National Survey on Recreation and the Environment

Orienteering

Who orienteers:
- *young adults*
- *men*
- *college graduates*

Orienteering trends:
- *inclusion in educational curriculums*
- *potential Olympic sport*
- *ski orienteering*

Orienteering is going into an unpopulated area with topographical maps and a compass and looking for preset markers. Orienteering is far from America's favorite sport, but more than just a handful of people participate. Nearly 5 million Americans were involved in orienteering in 1995. Young adults are most likely to participate. Four percent of people aged 16 to 24 took part in orienteering in the past 12 months. Participation is below average among people aged 50 or older.

Participation in orienteering does not vary much by household income, but is above average among those living in households with incomes of $25,000 or more. Men are four times as likely to be involved in orienteering than women, 4 versus 1 percent. People of "other" race (mostly Asians and Hispanics) are more involved in orienteering than whites or blacks.

Two educational groups are most involved in orienteering—those without a high school diploma and college graduates. At the one end are high school students who get involved in orienteering through their physical education class or a local group.

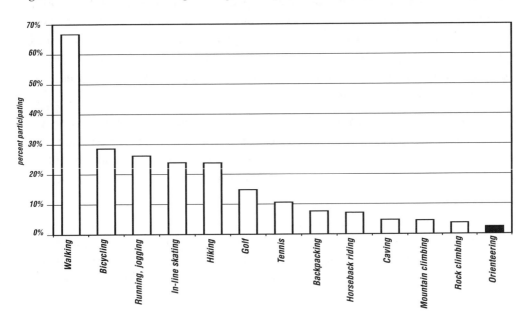

At the other end are highly educated people who enjoy the challenging puzzle of orienteering.

The likelihood of orienteering participation increases with household size. Behind this pattern is the involvement of teens in the sport.

The Future of Orienteering

"Orienteering does have a funny name," says Jon Nash, director of public relations and marketing for the United States Orienteering Federation. "Some people have suggested changing it. But it does work in other countries, so I don't think we'll change it."

Traditionally, orienteering is a race, where the orienteers must find markers in a certain amount of time. There are many types of orienteering, including ski orienteering, trail orienteering (for those inclined to stay on the beaten path), and even mountain bike orienteering. People who want to participate in orienteering without the time pressure of a race are called "wayfarers" or "mapwalkers." There's even an Australian overnight variation called rogaineing after the acronym for Rugged Outdoor Group Activity Involving Navigation and Endurance.

Orienteering appeals to "people who like to solve things," says Nash. Fans of "engineering problems and complex computations, crossword puzzles," for example. "People who like to read whodunits, who like riddles, who watch *Jeopardy*" would appreciate the mental component of the sport. Although it seems like a contradiction, Nash says, another appealing feature of orienteering is that it's a "solitary pursuit you can share. You can get that competition with others, but in an individual way." Another benefit of orienteering is its cost—basically nothing. "All you need is a compass, and you can rent one for fifty cents," he says.

Nash sees a bright future for the sport because of trends such as the environmental movement. Orienteering doesn't harm the environment, according to Nash. Another positive trend for orienteering is the general increase in family activities, since families can participate together in orienteering. There is also growth on the educational front, with orienteering being used in physical education as well as in science, art, and history classes.

There are a few downsides. Participants are vulnerable to wildlife-borne diseases such as rabies and Lyme disease. Access is also an issue. Not every environmental group shares Nash's assessment that orienteering is environmentally harmless. And orienteering is volunteer intensive—people are needed to map out courses, set up checkpoints, and so on.

Growing media coverage from diverse sources (Nash cites *Modern Bride* and *Cooking Light* as examples) is piquing interest and boosting participation in orienteering. Ski orienteering is being considered for a slot in the 2002 Winter Olympics, which should cause an upsurge in interest. "Being in the Olympics never hurts," he says.

Participation in Orienteering

(percent of persons aged 16 or older who participated in orienteering at least once in the past year, by selected demographic characteristics, 1994-95)

Total	**2.4%**
Age	
Aged 16 to 24	4.1
Aged 25 to 29	3.3
Aged 30 to 39	2.7
Aged 40 to 49	2.4
Aged 50 to 59	1.5
Aged 60 or older	0.9
Income	
Under $15,000	1.2
$15,000 to $24,999	1.9
$25,000 to $49,999	2.6
$50,000 to $74,999	3.2
$75,000 to $99,999	2.7
$100,000 or more	3.1
Sex	
Men	3.6
Women	1.3
Race and Hispanic origin	
White	2.4
Black	1.7
Other, including Hispanic	3.3
Education	
Not a high school graduate	3.0
High school graduate	1.8
Some college	2.1
College graduate	3.0
Number of persons in household	
One	2.0
Two	1.9
Three	2.4
Four	3.0
Five or more	3.4

(continued)

(continued from previous page)

**Number of persons aged
16 or older in household**

One	2.1%
Two	2.1
Three or more	3.5

**Number of persons under
age 6 in household**

None	2.4
One or more	2.5

Source: USDA Forest Service, 1994-95 National Survey on Recreation and the Environment

Rock Climbing

Who rock climbs:
- *young adults*
- *men*
- *whites*

Rock climbing trends:
- *slower growth*

Over 7 million people aged 16 or older are rock climbers, which is defined by the National Survey of Recreation and the Environment as "technical climbing that involves the use of specialized equipment to move up a route on a rock wall or face." Because of the rigorous nature of this sport, it appeals to the young. Among 16-to-24-year-olds, 8 percent participated in rock climbing at least once in the past 12 months. Fewer than 1 percent of people aged 60 or older have been rock climbing in the past year.

Because rock climbing appeals to young adults—and young adults typically have low incomes—there is not much variation in climbing participation by household income.

Men are twice as likely to be rock climbers than women, 5 versus 2.5 percent. Whites are much more likely to participate than blacks, with only 0.4 percent of blacks aged 16 or older involved in the sport.

Rock climbing participation does not vary much by educational level. It is more

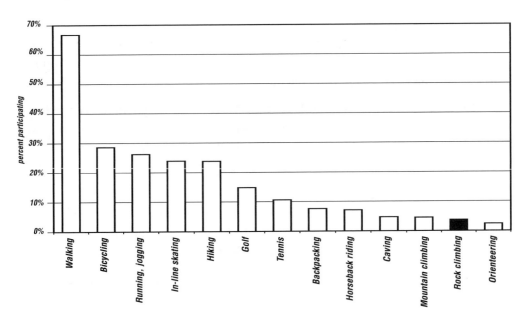

common in larger households, particularly in those with three or more adults. Some of these households may be college students sharing a house and a passion for rock climbing.

The Future of Rock Climbing

"The way we look at it, there are only about 500,000 real climbers in this country," says Sally Moser, executive director of the Access Fund, an international climbing advocacy and conservation group.

Although the National Survey for Recreation and the Environment counts over 7 million rock climbers in the United States, Moser and other dedicated climbers have more stringent qualifications for who counts as a rock climber. "Real climbers own gear, climb regularly, and have technical climbing skills," says Moser. The National Survey of Recreation and the Environment counts anyone who participated in the past 12 months.

It's important to be considered "real" in this sport, she says. Dabblers are not welcome when it's a matter of life and death—and in rock climbing it often is. "When there are more people, there are more accidents," says Moser. "Climbing is a sport where errors in judgment are costly and painful. It's a dangerous sport."

There has been growth in the sport in the past five years, fueled by increased participation in indoor climbing gyms, which often feel safer than a rock face. Although some people stay in the gyms, many people move out. That's how they get introduced to rock climbing.

This is not how it used to be, says Moser. Before climbing gyms, "climbing was a renegade sport. Your friends took you out, and you lived near rocks." But today, although climbing is "cool, chic and sexy, with a certain aura of danger to it," it is much more mainstream.

Rock climbing requires physical skill. But it also has a mental component to it, says Moser. This is more pronounced outdoors. "Climbing is like a chess game. You're always planning your next move," she notes.

"A lot of climbers are high-tech people," Moser says. They will use computers and the Internet to further their high-tech goals. Climbers work hard at staying in shape—lifting weights, for example. Some also participate in other outdoor activities like skiing or bicycling. But that's as far as the generalizations go. "Climbers are not a homogeneous group," she says.

Looking to the future, Moser sees the recent rock climbing boom leveling off, replaced by slow, steady growth unless it is included as an exhibition sport in the Olympics—a rumor which, she says, has been floating around for years.

"Climbing is more of a way of life than a sport," she says. "Some people will dabble in it, but most climbers are dedicated and tend to be in it for a very long time."

Participation in Rock Climbing

(percent of persons aged 16 or older who participated in rock climbing at least once in the past year, by selected demographic characteristics, 1994-95)

Total	**3.7%**
Age	
Aged 16 to 24	8.3
Aged 25 to 29	5.5
Aged 30 to 39	3.9
Aged 40 to 49	2.9
Aged 50 to 59	1.8
Aged 60 or older	0.7
Income	
Under $15,000	2.4
$15,000 to $24,999	3.3
$25,000 to $49,999	3.6
$50,000 to $74,999	5.7
$75,000 to $99,999	2.8
$100,000 or more	5.1
Sex	
Men	5.1
Women	2.5
Race and Hispanic origin	
White	4.2
Black	0.4
Other, including Hispanic	3.3
Education	
Not a high school graduate	3.8
High school graduate	3.3
Some college	3.8
College graduate	4.0
Number of persons in household	
One	3.1
Two	3.1
Three	4.3
Four	4.0
Five or more	4.9

(continued)

(continued from previous page)

**Number of persons aged
16 or older in household**

One	3.1%
Two	3.2
Three or more	5.4

**Number of persons under
age 6 in household**

None	3.7
One or more	3.6

Source: USDA Forest Service, 1994-95 National Survey on Recreation and the Environment

Running, Jogging

Who runs:
- *young adults*
- *men*
- *high-income households*

Running trends:
- *broadening demographics*
- *more marathons*

Running is a popular sport, involving 26 percent of Americans aged 16 or older. Participation is much higher in the 16-to-24 age group, however, than in older age groups. Fifty percent of 16-to-24-year-olds have been running or jogging in the past year—perhaps many of them through a high school sports program. Participation in running falls to 33 percent among 25-to-29-year-olds and declines steadily with rising age. For a high-impact sport, however, participation remains relatively strong in the older age groups. Even among those aged 60 or older, 8 percent take part in running or jogging.

Participation in running increases with income, to a peak of 38 percent among those with household incomes of $100,000 or more. Men are far more likely to run than women, 32 versus 21 percent.

Blacks and "others" (primarily Asians and Hispanics) are more likely to run than whites—32 percent of blacks and Hispanics have done so in the past year versus

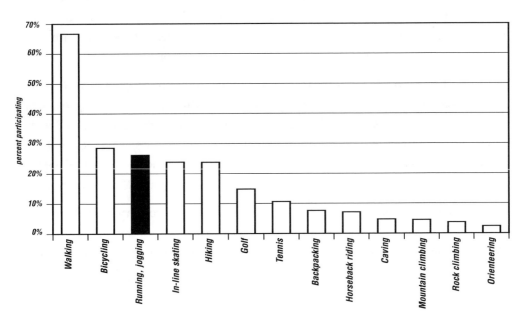

25 percent of whites. Behind this higher level of participation may be the fact that a larger proportion of blacks and Hispanics are young adults.

Participation in running does not vary much by whether young children are in the home. Thirty percent of people living in households with children under age 6 ran or jogged at least once in the past year versus 25 percent of those living without young children.

The Future of Running

In the sports world, running suffers from an image problem. It is often held up as a paragon of a high-impact, high-injury activity, and enthusiasts of other sports glee-fully count ex-runners with injured knees among their members. But the millions of runners and joggers in the United States might argue otherwise.

"Running does not have to be hard on the body, " says Linda Wack, list manager for the Dead Runners Society, a 2,000-member virtual community of runners who communicate through e-mail.

"As do people in any sport, a runner must listen to his or her body," says Wack. "A sensible training program is the key to avoiding injury." Advances in shoe tech-nology are also helping.

Although there are many different reasons why people begin to run, they must keep at it long enough to get hooked. The first few weeks of running are difficult, Wack says, "with all of the work and few of the benefits. Many people don't have the patience to continue until it becomes fun."

But many do tough it out, and the sport is benefiting. Wack says, "Races now attract more people who are not male, or young, or thin, or fast. They're less exclusive and draw more of a cross-section of the population. The median finish time in many marathons has gotten slower as people who never considered themselves athletes take up the sport and find a lot of encouragement from other runners."

Another trend Wack notices is the rise in the number of people who start run-ning with the immediate goal of running a marathon, rather than building up to mara-thon running gradually. Behind this trend is media coverage of the 100th Boston Mara-thon, she says. Other novices are drawn to marathons by charities using the events as fund raisers. Wack finds the marathon-or-bust trend disturbing because of its poten-tial for injury, since it takes time for runners to build strength for a marathon run.

But whether running a marathon or jogging on a quiet country road, there's no doubt the sport can be addictive. "Runners are social beings who like to run in groups," Wack concludes. "But runners also appreciate the time spent running alone when they can let their minds go free."

Participation in Running, Jogging

(percent of persons aged 16 or older who participated in running or jogging at least once in the past year, by selected demographic characteristics, 1994-95)

Total	**26.2%**
Age	
Aged 16 to 24	50.4
Aged 25 to 29	33.3
Aged 30 to 39	28.4
Aged 40 to 49	23.3
Aged 50 to 59	17.2
Aged 60 or older	8.0
Income	
Under $15,000	18.6
$15,000 to $24,999	20.8
$25,000 to $49,999	26.4
$50,000 to $74,999	29.6
$75,000 to $99,999	30.9
$100,000 or more	38.1
Sex	
Men	31.6
Women	21.1
Race and Hispanic origin	
White	24.9
Black	31.9
Other, including Hispanic	31.7
Education	
Not a high school graduate	31.6
High school graduate	20.5
Some college	25.3
College graduate	30.5
Number of persons in household	
One	20.2
Two	20.8
Three	29.5
Four	31.5
Five or more	35.2

(continued)

(continued from previous page)

Number of persons aged 16 or older in household	
One	22.4%
Two	23.7
Three or more	35.5
Number of persons under age 6 in household	
None	25.2
One or more	29.9

Source: USDA Forest Service, 1994-95 National Survey on Recreation and the Environment

Tennis

Who plays tennis:

- ***young and middle-aged adults***
- ***high-income households***
- ***college-educated people***

Tennis trends:

- ***campaigns aimed at children***
- ***attempts to broaden the demographics***

Millions of Americans play tennis regularly. Overall, 11 percent of the population aged 16 or older played tennis at least once in the past year. Among people aged 16 to 24, fully 21 percent have played tennis—the highest participation rate of any age group. Many are playing tennis in high school physical education programs.

The prevalence of tennis playing increases with income. Participation is above average in households with incomes of $50,000 or more and below average in households with lower incomes. Nearly one in five persons in households with incomes of $100,000 or more played tennis in the past year.

Men are only slightly more likely to play tennis than women, 12 versus 10 percent. People of "other" race (most of them Asians and Hispanics) are most likely to play tennis (13 percent), followed by whites (11 percent). Black participation in tennis is below average, at 8 percent.

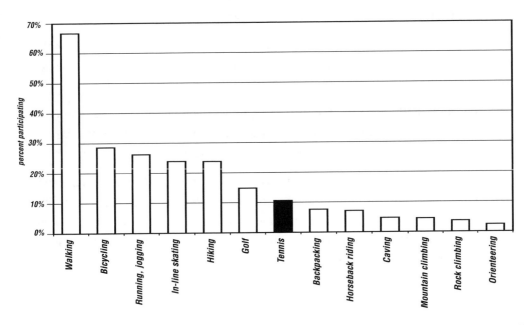

Tennis participation is highest for college graduates, at 15 percent. Next highest in particiation are people who do not have a high school diploma—many of them high school students who play in physical education programs. Tennis participation is highest in the largest households—most of them families with teenaged children.

The Future of Tennis

"On a one-to-ten coolness scale, tennis is about a five, which is up from a few years ago," says Brad Patterson, executive director of the Tennis Industry Association. After the sport experienced enormous growth in the 1970s, its popularity began to fade.

What made tennis uncool? According to Patterson, tennis is neither a good physical activity nor a whole lot of fun unless the skill is there to sustain a rally. "Most people spent time picking up balls at the net, so they went on to other things. We have a need in this society for instant gratification."

Today, with better instructors and better racquets, it's easier to develop the skills necessary to become a recreational player. But the sport must overcome the perception that it's time consuming, expensive, and passé.

So the coolness campaign has begun. "People don't tend to pick up tennis later in life," says Patterson. He hopes a relationship with the Cartoon Network will have kids clamoring for the courts. "We need to get to the kids before they're 10," he says. The message will be that tennis is cool and fun.

Adults are being targeted differently: "The message is, tennis fits into the 90s lifestyle. It's relatively affordable. It's relatively accessible, a great year-round activity. And it's more fun than running on a treadmill," Patterson says. The message will also emphasize tennis as a good workout in a short amount of time.

"We're trying to showcase that tennis can be as competitive or as recreational as you'd like it to be," he explains, although most players relish the competitive aspect of the game.

Off court, Patterson says, tennis players are homeowners, have computers, and enjoy gardening. They are active politically and environmentally. They also participate in sports such as jogging, basketball, and other racquet sports.

Looking toward the future, the industry is trying to counter its white, upper-crust image by promoting tennis programs in inner cities. People can enjoy tennis into old age, he says, and it's one sport where men and women are now on equal footing. With strong marketing, the Tennis Industry Association hopes, more people will get onto the courts—and stay there.

Participation in Tennis

(percent of persons aged 16 or older who participated in tennis at least once in the past year, by selected demographic characteristics, 1994-95)

Total	**10.6%**
Age	
Aged 16 to 24	21.4
Aged 25 to 29	12.2
Aged 30 to 39	11.7
Aged 40 to 49	9.7
Aged 50 to 59	6.1
Aged 60 or older	3.1
Income	
Under $15,000	6.3
$15,000 to $24,999	7.1
$25,000 to $49,999	10.0
$50,000 to $74,999	13.8
$75,000 to $99,999	15.3
$100,000 or more	19.2
Sex	
Men	11.7
Women	9.6
Race and Hispanic origin	
White	10.8
Black	7.8
Other, including Hispanic	12.9
Education	
Not a high school graduate	11.0
High school graduate	6.8
Some college	10.1
College graduate	14.8
Number of persons in household	
One	7.9
Two	8.5
Three	12.1
Four	12.9
Five or more	14.0

(continued)

(continued from previous page)

Number of persons aged 16 or older in household	
One	8.1%
Two	9.9
Three or more	14.8
Number of persons under age 6 in household	
None	10.5
One or more	10.7

Source: USDA Forest Service, 1994-95 National Survey on Recreation and the Environment

Walking

Who walks:	• *middle-aged and older adults*
	• *women*
	• *college-educated people*
Walking trends:	• *mall walking*
	• *walking for health*

Walking is the most-popular outdoor activity in the nation. Sixty-seven percent of Americans have walked for exercise or pleasure in the past year—or 134 million people. Unlike with most other recreational activities, young adults are not the ones most likely to walk. Instead, people aged 30 to 39 are most likely to do so, with 75 percent having walked for exercise or pleasure in the past 12 months. A majority of every age group walks for exercise or pleasure at least occasionally, including 52 percent of people aged 60 or older.

Participation walking does not vary much by income, although people in the poorest households are least likely to walk for exercise or pleasure. Still, half have done so in the past year. Men and women are about equally likely to walk for exercise or pleasure.

While whites are more likely to walk for exercise or pleasure than blacks or Hispanics, a majority of all racial and ethnic groups have done so in the past 12 months.

Walking increases with educational level, in part because the educated are more aware of walking's health benefits. Fully 76 percent of college graduates have walked

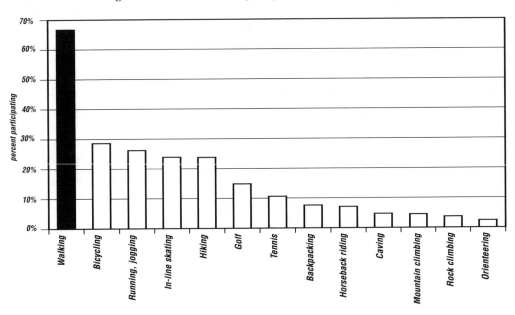

for exercise or pleasure in the past year, versus a smaller 51 percent of people who did not graduate from high school.

Participation in walking does not vary much by household size, although people living alone are slightly less likely to walk for exercise or pleasure than those in larger households. Behind this pattern is the older age of people who live alone.

The Future of Walking

Walking has become the most-popular sport in America, and that's no surprise to Mark Fenton, editor-at-large of *Walking* magazine. Fenton is a five-time member and former coach of the U.S. National Race Walking team and co-author of *The 90 Day Fitness Plan*.

"Walking is absolutely the easiest thing to do," Fenton explains. "It's inexpensive, there's no instruction necessary, and you need no expensive gear." Walking is so low-budget and ordinary that it's hard to market, he says.

Three types of people become walkers, Fenton says. For some, walking is their first experience with athletic participation. They are led to it by a doctor because of a health problem or because they're overweight. Mall walkers are this type, walking for health reasons and usually under doctor's orders. Most mall walkers are aged 55 or older, have medium incomes, and are women, says Tom Cabot, president of the National Organization of Mall Walkers. "At the mall, they're not going to get wet or cold, and they don't need to worry about vehicular traffic," Cabot explains.

An important aspect of mall walking is the companionship and camaraderie it provides. Walkers form clubs, and they walk in the morning before stores open. When a club is sponsored by a wellness or health center, Cabot says, there will be monthly meetings on diet, cardiovascular issues, and other health concerns. "As the population gets older, mall walking is going to become more popular. It's going to be around for a while unless they put in moving sidewalks," Cabot concludes.

The second type of walker is physically fit but "is looking for a more intelligent way" to exercise says *Walking* magazine's Fenton. "They have a softer attitude toward fitness. Maybe they were runners and now have trashed knees. Maybe they have kids and they put them in a stroller and walk with them," he says.

The third type of walker—younger women—is driving the trend, says Fenton. "They've found out that walking is a great workout. It's less expensive. You don't have to be anywhere at a certain time, and you don't have to belong to a club," Fenton explains.

But will the popularity of walking continue? Fenton sees what he calls "four points of light" that promise a strong future for walking.

- **The Surgeon General's Report on Physical Fitness**. This report called physical inactivity an epidemic and recommended at least 30 minutes of exercise most days of the week. Because walking is easy, it's a natural way for people to get in their quota.

- **The re-creation of communities.** Suburbanization and crime in the cities have made America a pedestrian-unfriendly country, but this is beginning to change. There are bicycle and pedestrian coordinators in every state, says Fenton, and planners are beginning to design new construction to enhance walkability.

- **Women walkers.** "Women are a strong influence on physical activity because of Title IX and their increased role in the Olympics." Fenton says. Women bring a more-balanced view to exercise, which also tends to favor walking.

- **The health care industry.** With insurers getting involved, "there's a financial incentive to keep people healthy," Fenton explains. Paying for a walking club is cheaper than paying for a heart attack. The people who move and shake America are the people who control the purse strings."

Participation in Walking

(percent of persons aged 16 or older who participated in walking at least once in the past year, by selected demographic characteristics, 1994-95)

Total	**66.7%**
Age	
Aged 16 to 24	68.2
Aged 25 to 29	72.5
Aged 30 to 39	74.7
Aged 40 to 49	72.0
Aged 50 to 59	65.5
Aged 60 or older	51.8
Income	
Under $15,000	49.9
$15,000 to $24,999	62.2
$25,000 to $49,999	71.9
$50,000 to $74,999	74.9
$75,000 to $99,999	77.1
$100,000 or more	74.8
Sex	
Men	65.1
Women	68.5
Race and Hispanic origin	
White	69.0
Black	55.8
Other, including Hispanic	58.6
Education	
Not a high school graduate	50.9
High school graduate	61.2
Some college	71.2
College graduate	75.8
Number of persons in household	
One	57.4
Two	66.6
Three	70.9
Four	71.0
Five or more	68.6

(continued)

(continued from previous page)

Number of persons aged
16 or older in household

One	60.0%
Two	69.6
Three or more	67.8

Number of persons under
age 6 in household

None	65.5
One or more	72.1

Source: USDA Forest Service, 1994-95 National Survey on Recreation and the Environment

Chapter 6

Nature Observation

Wildlife viewing, observing nature near water, and bird watching are some of the most popular outdoor recreational activities in the United States. With 31 percent of Americans participating at least once in a year's time, wildlife viewing ranks just behind swimming in popularity. Studying nature near water and bird watching are more popular than running and almost as popular as bicycling. Overall, 28 percent of people aged 16 or older observed nature near water (such as along seacoasts, lake shores, and so on) in 1994-95, and 27 percent took part in bird watching.

Fish viewing (e.g., going to a fish ladder or aquarium) is a much-less-popular activity, but it is more popular than many recreational activities that get much more attention—such as tennis, downhill skiing, and sailing. With 14 percent of people aged 16 or older participating in fish viewing, its popularity is about equal to that of volley-ball and golf.

Americans spent $31 billion in 1996 observing, photographing, or feeding wild-life, according to the 1996 National Survey of Fishing, Hunting, and Wildlife-Associated Recreations, sponsored by the U.S. Fish and Wildlife Service. Between 1991 and 1996, spending on wildlife watching increased 27 percent.

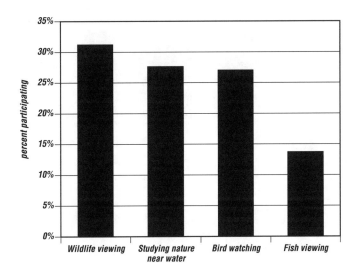

The aging of the population is certain to boost participation in and spending on these activities, since older people favor less physically demanding sports. Also driving the growth of these activities is the rising educational level of the population, which heightens interest in the natural world.

Bird Watching

Who watches birds:	• **older Americans** • **college-educated people**
Bird watching trends:	• **rapid growth** • **birding as tourist attraction**

Bird watching is one of America's most-popular recreational activities, with 27 percent of people aged 16 or older having watched birds in the past year. Unlike for many recreational activities, participation is lowest among young adults and rises with age. Participation peaks among 40-to-59-year-olds, with one-third of this age group watching birds. Even among people aged 60 or older, 29 percent participate in bird watching—a larger share than among adults aged 25 to 39.

Because of bird watching's low cost, participation does not vary much by income. More than 20 percent of people with household incomes under $25,000 have been bird watching in the past 12 months.

Women are slightly more likely than men to participate in bird watching, 29 versus 25 percent. While whites are more likely than other racial or ethnic groups to watch birds, bird watching is popular among blacks, Asians, and Hispanics. A substantial one in five minority group members participates in bird watching.

Birding rises with education, from just 16 percent of people without a high school diploma to one-third of those with a college degree. Participation is highest in households with two adults—many being empty-nest and retired couples who have time to observe birds.

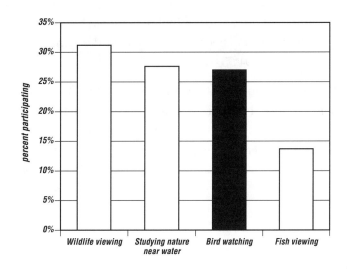

The Future of Bird Watching

"The first thing to understand about people who observe birds is that if they are serious about it, they will not want to be called 'bird watchers,'" says Paul Green, director of conservation and education for the American Birding Association. "Bird watchers will observe birds in their gardens. A 'birder' spends a lot of time and money to watch birds and may be offended" by the term, says Green.

Most people become involved in bird observation by spending time in their gardens, Green says. The next step is buying a pair of binoculars, then traveling to a local state park to see birds that would not show up in a garden, then subscribing to a birding magazine, and finally, for a few, traveling to far-flung places to see even more birds.

Why watch birds? Some people are motivated by the urge to collect. Green calls them "listers." While most birders keep lists of the species they have seen, for listers, growing the list is the goal. "They're only in it for themselves," Green says, adding that listers are a minority in the birding community.

Other birders are interested in the plumage, biology, and psychology of birds. "The main appeal is aesthetics. Birds are wonderful creatures. There's a feeling of doing good, of feeding birds, and also the element of bringing wilderness into the garden," he notes.

Technology is also coming into play in bird watching, although a good pair of binoculars is the only necessary piece of equipment. Two recent technical advances are giving bird watching a boost. One is the rare-bird beeper, which transmits the location of rare species when they are spotted. Another is software to help birders manage their lists. "People have a life list, a United States list, a county list, a year list, a month list. It's not a question of one list," Green says.

Bird observation is not limited to the old, although retirees are the ones with the time and money to make expensive excursions. In fact, bird watching is the fastest-growing activity among those analyzed by the National Survey for Recreation and the Environment. The number of people involved in bird watching increased 155 percent between 1982-83 and 1994-95.

Birding will continue to grow, Green says. As it does, "the business community will become more aware of the economic importance of birders." Areas that are natural habitats or migration stopovers will find people coming to see birds—and spending money while they are there. The more birders, the greater is the financial incentive to conserve habitat. Green says, business won't "want to kill the goose that laid the golden egg."

Participation in Bird Watching

(percent of persons aged 16 or older who participated in bird watching at least once in the past year, by selected demographic characteristics, 1994-95)

Total	**27.0%**
Age	
Aged 16 to 24	16.4
Aged 25 to 29	21.2
Aged 30 to 39	28.4
Aged 40 to 49	33.8
Aged 50 to 59	32.8
Aged 60 or older	28.9
Income	
Under $15,000	20.8
$15,000 to $24,999	26.6
$25,000 to $49,999	28.6
$50,000 to $74,999	29.9
$75,000 to $99,999	32.3
$100,000 or more	29.3
Sex	
Men	24.7
Women	29.2
Race and Hispanic origin	
White	28.4
Black	20.5
Other, including Hispanic	21.4
Education	
Not a high school graduate	15.9
High school graduate	25.1
Some college	28.9
College graduate	32.5
Number of persons in household	
One	24.0
Two	32.0
Three	33.2
Four	33.4
Five or more	32.1

(continued)

(continued from previous page)

Number of persons aged	
16 or older in household	
One	24.0%
Two	29.9
Three or more	23.9
Number of persons under	
age 6 in household	
None	27.7
One or more	24.5

Source: USDA Forest Service, 1994-95 National Survey on Recreation and the Environment

Wildlife Viewing, Observing Nature near Water, and Fish Viewing

Who views:
- *all age groups*
- *college graduates*

Viewing trends:
- *recognition as a legitimate sport*
- *technological advances*

Nearly one-third of Americans aged 16 or older participated in wildlife viewing in the past 12 months. Twenty-eight percent observed nature near water (such as on a seacoast), while 14 percent participated in fish viewing.

Unlike many recreational activities, these activities peak in middle-age. Thirty-eight percent of people aged 40 to 49 participated in wildlife viewing in the past year, 35 percent observed nature near water, and 17 percent took part in fish viewing. People in their 30s are slightly less likely to participate in wildlife viewing or observing nature near water, and slightly more likely to participate in fish viewing. Those least likely to participate in these activities are Americans aged 60 or older. Nevertheless, a substantial one-fifth of this age group participated in wildlife viewing in the past year, while 17 percent observed nature near water and 10 percent took part in fish viewing.

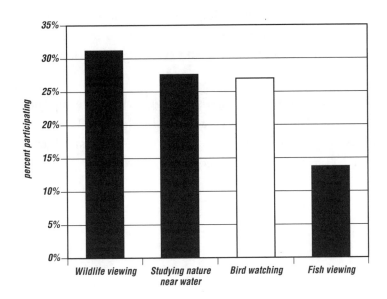

Participation in these activities does not vary much by income, although people with household incomes below $25,000 are less likely to take part. Men and women are about equally likely to view wildlife and fish and to observe nature near water.

Whites are more likely to view wildlife than are blacks or people of "other" race, which includes Asians and Hispanics. But people of "other" race are almost as likely as whites to observe nature near water and slightly more likely to view fish. Behind this high level of participation by "others" is the fact that many Asians and Hispanics live near coastal areas where water and fish are more accessible.

Participation in these activities does not vary much by household size, although people who live alone are less likely to take part than people living in larger households. All three activities are slightly more common among people living in households with preschoolers than among those without young children at home.

The Future of Nature Observation

Wildlife viewing is a simple activity. "You start out by driving down the road," explains Mark Damian Duda, executive director and president of Responsive Management, a Virginia-based natural resource research organization, and author of *Watching Wildlife*. Eventually, a dedicated wildlife viewer will travel to see animals such as bears and whales. Fish viewing is similar, but instead of watching deer, a fish viewer will go to see salmon jump, for example. "It's really a question of what resource is available," Duda says.

"Unlike hunting and fishing, wildlife viewing is a sport you pick up on your own. It's relatively easy and inexpensive, a wholesome family activity, a positive way to get back to the natural world," Duda says. Wildlife viewing also attracts a more diverse crowd than consumptive outdoor activities, he says.

Duda sees a strong future for wildlife viewing because of the "increased awareness of the environment and the natural world. You have to have the resource to enjoy it." Another trend is the recognition of wildlife viewing as a legitimate activity, not a side show.

Technological advances, like night-vision goggles, will "open up another world," Duda predicts. "The challenge is to view ethically," he says. When people get too close to animals, they can trample habitat, hurt themselves, and hurt the animals. "Guidelines haven't been established. People have to realize it's not a petting farm," he concludes.

Participation in Wildlife Viewing, Observing Nature near Water, and Fish Viewing

(percent of persons aged 16 or older who participated in wildlife viewing, nature observation near water, and fish viewing at least once in the past year, by selected demographic characteristics, 1994-95)

	wildlife viewing	studying nature near water	fish viewing
Total	**31.2%**	**27.6%**	**13.7%**
Age			
Aged 16 to 24	28.8	25.7	11.9
Aged 25 to 29	32.3	30.7	14.0
Aged 30 to 39	36.5	32.7	16.7
Aged 40 to 49	37.7	34.6	16.5
Aged 50 to 59	32.8	29.1	13.8
Aged 60 or older	21.9	16.6	9.9
Income			
Under $15,000	20.4	15.3	7.5
$15,000 to $24,999	27.2	23.6	10.9
$25,000 to $49,999	35.1	30.0	15.4
$50,000 to $74,999	37.2	35.8	16.6
$75,000 to $99,999	40.4	40.2	17.9
$100,000 or more	35.5	35.5	18.4
Sex			
Men	31.4	28.4	13.9
Women	31.2	27.0	13.5
Race and Hispanic origin			
White	33.6	29.5	14.3
Black	18.1	15.5	8.4
Other, including Hispanic	25.1	25.8	14.7
Education			
Not a high school graduate	20.3	1.7	9.2
High school graduate	28.5	2.3	12.1
Some college	34.1	2.9	15.4
College graduate	36.5	3.6	15.8
Number of persons in household			
One	23.6	20.9	11.1
Two	33.0	28.9	13.7
Three	33.2	29.5	15.0
Four	33.4	30.3	13.9
Five or more	32.1	27.6	15.0

(continued)

(continued from previous page)

	wildlife viewing	studying nature near water	fish viewing
Number of persons aged			
16 or older in household			
One	25.7%	22.7%	11.7%
Two	33.6	30.3	14.3
Three or more	32.0	27.1	14.5
Number of persons under			
age 6 in household			
None	30.8	27.3	13.6
One or more	33.2	29.0	13.9

Source: USDA Forest Service, 1994-95 National Survey on Recreation and the Environment

Chapter 7

Outdoor Team Sports

Outdoor team sports are a popular recreational activity in the United States, with almost one in four Americans having played on a team in the past 12 months.

Those most likely to participate in outdoor team sports are young adults aged 16 to 24. Nearly half (47 percent) did so in the past 12 months—many through organized high school sports programs. Although the percentage falls with age, at least 20 percent of people play team sports through their 40s. After that, outdoor team sports participation drops off dramatically.

Participation in outdoor team sports does not vary much by income, although those living in households with incomes below $15,000 are least likely to do so. Many people living in low-income households are elderly, which accounts for those households' lower level of participation.

Men are nearly twice as likely to participate in outdoor team sports as women, 31 versus 19 percent. Blacks are more likely to participate than both whites and "others" (primarily Asians and Hispanics), making it one of the few recreational activities in which black participation exceeds that of whites. Participation in outdoor team

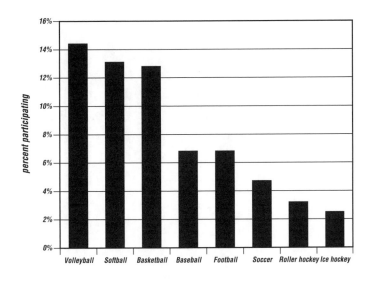

sports falls with education, primarily because teens—who have not yet completed their high school education—are the biggest participants. People living in households with three or more people are more likely to take part in outdoor team sports than those living in households with only one or two people. Behind this is the fact that larger households are more likely to contain people aged 16 to 24. Similarly, people living in households with children under age 6 are more likely than average to participate in outdoor team sports because many of these households include teens and young adults.

Participation in Any Outdoor Team Sport

(percent of persons aged 16 or older who participated in any outdoor team sport at least once in the past year, by selected demographic characteristics, 1994-95)

Total	**24.7%**
Age	
Aged 16 to 24	47.4
Aged 25 to 29	37.2
Aged 30 to 39	30.2
Aged 40 to 49	20.2
Aged 50 to 59	12.9
Aged 60 or older	4.0
Income	
Under $15,000	16.3
$15,000 to $24,999	22.0
$25,000 to $49,999	27.6
$50,000 to $74,999	27.6
$75,000 to $99,999	27.1
$100,000 or more	24.3
Sex	
Men	31.2
Women	18.6
Race and Hispanic origin	
White	23.6
Black	31.4
Other, including Hispanic	25.1
Education	
Not a high school graduate	30.0
High school graduate	24.1
Some college	25.7
College graduate	21.7
Number of persons in household	
One	16.0
Two	16.8
Three	29.6
Four	33.3
Five or more	36.2

(continued)

(continued from previous page)

Number of persons aged 16 or older in household	
One	18.9%
Two	23.0
Three or more	34.1
Number of persons under age 6 in household	
None	22.6
One or more	32.6

Source: USDA Forest Service, 1994-95 National Survey on Recreation and the Environment

Baseball

Who plays baseball:
- *young adults*
- *men*
- *blacks*

Trends in baseball:
- *more coverage of amateur baseball*
- *adults returning to the sport*
- *more women players*

Baseball likes to think of itself as America's favorite sport, but it is far from number one in participation. Only 7 percent of people aged 16 or older played baseball in the past year.

Younger Americans are most likely to play baseball. Fourteen percent of people aged 16 to 24 have played it in the past year. This figure falls to 8 percent among 25-to-39-year-olds and declines with age to just 1 percent of people aged 60 or older.

Participation in baseball does not vary much by income. Men are more than twice as likely as women to have played baseball in the past year, 10 versus 4 percent. Baseball is one of the few sports in which blacks are more likely to participate than whites. Ten percent of blacks have played baseball at least once in the past 12 months, versus 6 percent of whites. People of "other" race, including Asians and Hispanics, are also more likely to play baseball than whites, with a participation rate of 8 percent.

Unlike in many sports, participation in baseball declines with increasing education. While 11 percent of people who have not graduated from high school play base-

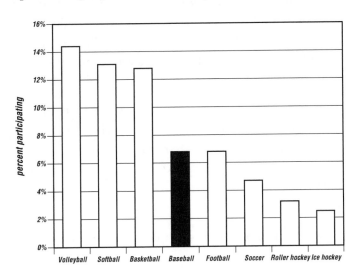

ball (many of them high school students), only 5 percent of college graduates have played it in the past year.

Baseball participation increases with household size because teenagers and young adults are most likely to play baseball, and larger households are more likely to include this age group. Baseball participation is also higher for households with preschoolers than for those without young children at home.

The Future of Baseball

Baseball is struggling—not only as a participatory sport, but also as a spectator sport. The game so closely associated with American culture has survived ups and downs in public opinion before, explains Wanda Rutledge, deputy director of USA Baseball, the governing body for amateur baseball. But it has endured because "kids thoroughly love the game." Most people are introduced to the game as children, and some return to it as adults because of their childhood experience.

Baseball is suffering as a participatory sport because it is competing against so many other sports for people's free time. It is suffering as a spectator sport because of Major League Baseball's labor and image problems. The Major League Baseball players' strike "had a trickle-down effect" on amateur baseball, Rutledge says.

Some contend that baseball is too slow for the video generation. Others claim it does not compete well with sports like basketball and soccer, which require less equipment. Children who play baseball today do so with uniforms and umpires, says Rutledge. "Kids don't go down and play baseball on their blocks anymore. Baseball has almost regulated itself out of existence at the sandlot," she says. And compared to other sports, baseball lacks heroes. There is no Michael Jordan or Tiger Woods out there to create enthusiasm at the grassroots level.

To drum up excitement at the grassroots level, Little League Baseball sold the rights to cover not only the 1997 world series but also the regional finals to ESPN2. The public is interested: When ESPN2 covered the 1996 Little League World Series, its ratings rose from 0.4 to 0.9, meaning that 440,000 households tuned in, according to *The Wall Street Journal*.

Participation in baseball has been limited by the scarcity of opportunities for women to play in high school and college, and as adults. USA Baseball is trying to change this, Rutledge says. Men account for the majority of amateur players, but given the opportunity, more women would play. "Major League Baseball research has found that 50 percent of baseball fans are women, and that women enjoy baseball more than any other sport," Rutledge says.

Yet another problem for baseball—and most outdoor team sports—is a shortage of playing fields.

Despite the problems, Rutledge says, baseball is "pretty healthy." Although it has obstacles to overcome, it will retain a special place in America's heart.

There are positive signs. One is the growing participation of girls, thanks in part to the expansion of T-ball for the 4-to-7-year-old set. Another sign of life is the return of adults to their childhood sport, which she describes as "a thriving growth market."

Participation in Baseball

(percent of persons aged 16 or older who participated in baseball at least once in the past year, by selected demographic characteristics, 1994-95)

Total	**6.8%**
Age	
Aged 16 to 24	14.1
Aged 25 to 29	8.1
Aged 30 to 39	8.0
Aged 40 to 49	6.1
Aged 50 to 59	3.8
Aged 60 or older	1.1
Income	
Under $15,000	4.0
$15,000 to $24,999	5.7
$25,000 to $49,999	7.3
$50,000 to $74,999	7.2
$75,000 to $99,999	7.4
$100,000 or more	6.4
Sex	
Men	9.7
Women	4.0
Race and Hispanic origin	
White	6.3
Black	9.5
Other, including Hispanic	7.8
Education	
Not a high school graduate	11.0
High school graduate	7.4
Some college	6.3
College graduate	4.6
Number of persons in household	
One	3.0
Two	3.9
Three	8.8
Four	9.6
Five or more	11.9

(continued)

(continued from previous page)

**Number of persons aged
16 or older in household**

One	4.2%
Two	6.2
Three or more	10.6

**Number of persons under
age 6 in household**

None	6.2
One or more	9.1

Source: USDA Forest Service, 1994-95 National Survey on Recreation and the Environment

Basketball

Who plays basketball:
- *young adults*
- *men*
- *blacks*

Trends in basketball:
- *more women*
- *women's professional basketball*

Basketball is one of the most-popular team sports, with 13 percent of people aged 16 or older having played basketball at least once in the past 12 months. It is a sport dominated by young adults. Among 16-to-24-year-olds, fully 31 percent played basketball in the past year. This proportion falls to a still-substantial 19 percent among 25-to-29-year-olds. Even among people in their 30s, a significant 14 percent play basketball. After age 40, however, participation drops into the single-digits.

Basketball participation does not vary much by income. Men are more than twice as likely to play basketball as women, 19 versus 7 percent.

Blacks are more likely to play basketball than whites. Nearly 22 percent of blacks have played basketball at least once in the past year, versus just 11 percent of whites and 13 percent of "others" (primarily Asians and Hispanics). Behind the high level of black participation is basketball's accessibility. It is a sport anyone can enjoy no matter where he or she lives, from inner city to countryside. It requires no travel and little equipment.

Basketball participation falls with education. Behind the lofty 20 percent participation rate of people without a high school diploma are high school kids playing in

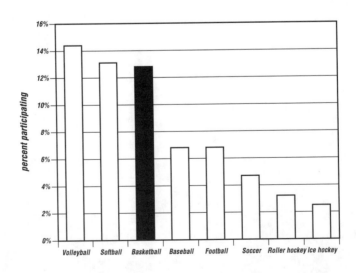

school programs or after school in their neighborhoods. Only 10 percent of college graduates have played basketball in the past year.

Basketball participation rises sharply with household size because larger households are more likely to include teens and young adults than small households. Basketball participation is much higher in households with preschoolers (again, because these households are likely to include teens) than in households without young children in the home.

The Future of Basketball

"Basketball is cheap, fun and exciting," explains Craig Miller, assistant executive director of media/public relations at USA Basketball, the national governing body for amateur basketball in the United States. "It's easy to set up a basketball court. You can use a garbage can lid, a hub cap, a crate as a basket. Equipment needs are minimal."

Extensive media coverage of professional basketball generates excitement among younger fans, who emulate the moves of their favorite players. Especially for minority children, basketball is often seen as "a major avenue to wealth and success. If you're good in basketball, the odds are high against you [playing in the NBA], but it can happen," says Miller.

The opportunity to become a professional player is one reason why basketball is an important sport for minorities, especially blacks. This chance, in turn, boosts participation in the sport and attendance at both amateur and professional games. But this perspective may not be healthy for minority youth. Basketball has been "portrayed by the media as a way out of poverty," says Richard Lapchik, director of Northeastern University's Center for the Study of Sport in Society. The chances of making it are so slim, however, that this belief can be dangerous to a child's future, preventing him or her from preparing for a more realistic career.

The growing popularity of professional basketball is due, in part, to the increasingly fast pace of the game, a characteristic that appeals to children and young adults. Men's basketball has become more action intensive, with a trend toward the dramatic shot. Consequently, there has been a decline in below-the-rim play and lower scores. Critics maintain that the skill of players has diminished while the grandstanding grows.

Some suggest that the emergence of women's leagues will temper this change in playing style. The growing popularity of women's sports "is the most refreshing aspect of sports today," says Lapchik "It's very grassroots."

Today, there are two professional women's basketball leagues—the American Basketball League (ABL) and the National Basketball League's women's team (WNBA). "We've seen phenomenal growth in the area of women's basketball. It will take years to really develop, but there is steady and positive interest," Miller notes. The hope is that women players will become role models for girls, just as today's male stars are role models for boys.

There is growing corporate interest in women's professional basketball as well, because the games' spectators are more family oriented. "Sponsors want to reach that active female and family niche," Miller says.

With women playing basketball professionally, the participation of girls in high school and neighborhood basketball is certain to rise. But not all signs are positive for basketball participation. Miller concedes that basketball is a physically demanding sport. The aging of the population could dampen participation, which drops with age. Miller believes, however, that many middle-aged and older people will continue to shoot baskets at local parks and in their backyard. "There's competition at every level and for every age," he says.

Participation in Basketball

(percent of persons aged 16 or older who participated in basketball at least once in the past year, by selected demographic characteristics, 1994-95)

Total	**12.8%**
Age	
Aged 16 to 24	31.0
Aged 25 to 29	18.7
Aged 30 to 39	14.1
Aged 40 to 49	8.7
Aged 50 to 59	4.7
Aged 60 or older	1.1
Income	
Under $15,000	9.5
$15,000 to $24,999	11.2
$25,000 to $49,999	13.2
$50,000 to $74,999	14.2
$75,000 to $99,999	15.0
$100,000 or more	11.8
Sex	
Men	18.5
Women	7.4
Race and Hispanic origin	
White	11.4
Black	21.9
Other, including Hispanic	13.4
Education	
Not a high school graduate	19.9
High school graduate	12.4
Some college	12.4
College graduate	10.2
Number of persons in household	
One	6.6
Two	7.8
Three	15.8
Four	18.5
Five or more	20.5

(continued)

(continued from previous page)

Number of persons aged 16 or older in household	
One	8.7%
Two	11.2
Three or more	20.2
Number of persons under age 6 in household	
None	11.6
One or more	17.1

Source: USDA Forest Service, 1994-95 National Survey on Recreation and the Environment

Football

Who plays football:
- *young adults*
- *men*
- *minorities*

Trends in football:
- *more women players*

Only 7 percent of the people aged 16 or older played football at least once in the past 12 months. Participation is much higher among young adults than among older people. More than one in five 16-to-24-year-olds played football in the past year—many of them in high school sports programs. Participation drops to a still-substantial 12 percent among 25-to-29-year-olds. Thereafter football participation declines steeply with age.

Participation in football does not vary much by income. Men are far more likely to play football than women; 12 percent of men have played in the past 12 months versus just 2 percent of women. Unlike in many other sport and recreational activities, blacks are more likely to participate in football than whites. Ten percent of blacks have played football in the past 12 months, versus just 6 percent of whites. People of "other" race (primarily Asians and Hispanics) also participate at a higher rate than whites.

Football participation drops with increasing education. Behind this pattern is the high level of participation among teens and young adults, many of whom have not yet graduated from high school. Football participation rises with household size because larger households are more likely to include teens and young adults.

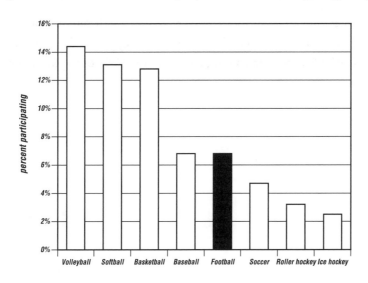

The Future of Football

Playing football gives people "a release they normally wouldn't be afforded in the normal workplace. Even the shyest or most diminutive person becomes larger than life on the field," says Stephen Russell, executive director of the National Touch Flag Football League. Plus, there's always "the chance to be the Joe Montana of your local league," he adds.

Most people get exposure to amateur football in college. "Intramural sports—that's where people cut their teeth," Russell notes. "The average player will come straight out of college and continue."

College football is one reason why the National Football League is sitting pretty today. Its fan base is assured by the popularity of college football, and the popularity of college football is assured by football scholarships, which become especially coveted as the cost of a college education increases. The rush for college scholarships starts in high school, when boys play hard to grab the attention of college scouts.

Today, girls do not formally participate in football in high school or college. Despite this absence, Russell says, the most important trend in amateur football is the growth of women players. "The last five to ten years have seen enormous growth," he says. "It's still a novelty to some, but women want to be taken seriously. There's conviction when they take the field. They're pioneers," he says. Women who play football are avid pro-football fans. They will never play on Sundays because they would miss the pros' play.

Football's dominance by men is its greatest weakness, especially as other sports open their doors to women. Another problem for football is the "free agency" of teams, allowing them to leave one geographic area for another. When teams leave, fans feel betrayed. This can reduce the public's interest not only in watching football, but also in playing the sport.

Americans play amateur football for reasons very different from those that motivate professional players. "The players aren't being paid," Russell says. "The only quest is victory." Players keep coming back for "the thrill of the hunt and chase."'

Participation in Football

(percent of persons aged 16 or older who participated in football at least once in the past year, by selected demographic characteristics, 1994-95)

Total	**6.8%**
Age	
Aged 16 to 24	20.6
Aged 25 to 29	11.6
Aged 30 to 39	6.2
Aged 40 to 49	2.3
Aged 50 to 59	1.1
Aged 60 or older	0.3
Income	
Under $15,000	4.3
$15,000 to $24,999	5.5
$25,000 to $49,999	6.8
$50,000 to $74,999	7.1
$75,000 to $99,999	6.1
$100,000 or more	6.6
Sex	
Men	11.9
Women	2.0
Race and Hispanic origin	
White	6.1
Black	10.1
Other, including Hispanic	9.5
Education	
Not a high school graduate	13.4
High school graduate	6.7
Some college	6.1
College graduate	4.5
Number of persons in household	
One	3.9
Two	3.8
Three	8.6
Four	9.8
Five or more	11.1

(continued)

(continued from previous page)

Number of persons aged	
16 or older in household	
One	4.6%
Two	5.0
Three or more	12.8
Number of persons under	
age 6 in household	
None	6.3
One or more	8.7

Source: USDA Forest Service, 1994-95 National Survey on Recreation and the Environment

Hockey

Who plays hockey:
- *children and young adults*
- *men*

Hockey trends:
- *rapid growth*
- *more women*

Nearly 6 million people aged 7 or older played hockey in 1995, according to the Sporting Goods Manufacturers Association of Mount Prospect, Illinois. The participation data for this sport, which were not collected by the National Survey on Recreation and the Environment, are not comparable with those for other sports in this book. Roller hockey (played on roller skates), with 3.2 million players, is more popular than ice hockey with its 2.5 million players.

Roller hockey players are much younger than people who play ice hockey. While 50 percent of ice hockey players are under age 18, 73 percent of roller hockey players are children. Among adults who play ice or roller hockey, most are under age 35. Women account for only about one in five hockey players.

The Future of Hockey

Hockey, an import from Canada, has become an important player in the sport scene. The sport is growing, with participation in ice hockey up 29 percent between 1994 and 1995, according to the Sporting Goods Manufacturers Association. Roller hockey participation rose 43 percent between 1994 and 1995.

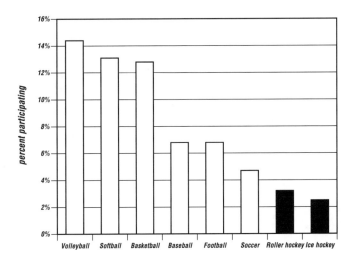

But hockey has a big problem—the lack of female players and fans. According to a 1994 ESPN/Chilton Sports Poll, hockey ranked last among major league sports in the percentage of women professing "some" or "a lot" of interest in the game.

This may be changing, however. Hockey is the sport that benefits most from the mixed-gender popularity of in-line skating, which has given rise to the hybrid sport of in-line hockey. The popularity of field hockey among teenaged girls and the inclusion of women's ice hockey in the 1998 Winter Olympics should help attract more female players and spectators.

Participation in Hockey

(number and percent distribution of persons participating in ice and roller hockey at least once in 1995, by sex and age)

	ice hockey	roller hockey
Total (millions)	**2.5**	**3.2**
Sex (percent)		
Male	82.0%	79.3%
Female	18.0	20.7
Age (percent)		
Aged 7 to 11	21.2	36.8
Aged 12 to 17	28.8	36.1
Aged 18 to 24	20.9	12.0
Aged 25 to 34	12.8	8.3
Aged 35 to 44	12.6	4.4
Aged 45 to 54	2.2	0.5
Aged 55 to 64	1.7	0.7
Aged 65 to 74	-	0.6
Aged 75 or older	-	0.7

Note: (-) means sample is too small to make a reliable estimate.
Source: Sporting Goods Manufacturers Association, Mt. Prospect, Illinois

Soccer

Who plays soccer: • *young people*

Trends in soccer: • *introduction of Major League Soccer*
                         • *multicultural appeal*

Only 5 percent of people aged 16 or older played soccer in the past 12 months. This figure does not include the many players who are under age 16.

Among adults, participation is highest in the 16-to-24-age group, at 13 percent. Participation falls sharply to just 6 percent of 25-to-29-year-olds. Only 5 percent of people in their 30s and 3 percent of those in their 40s have played soccer in the past 12 months.

Soccer participation increases with income, but not dramatically. Men are almost twice as likely to participate as women, 6 versus 3 percent. People of "other" race (primarily Asians and Hispanics) are more likely to play soccer than blacks and whites, in part because many Hispanics come from countries where soccer is enormously popular.

Soccer participation falls with education. Behind this pattern is the higher level of participation among young adults, many of whom have not yet completed high school. Participation is also higher for people living in larger households and for those in households with preschoolers. These types of households are more likely to include teens and young adults, who are most likely to play soccer.

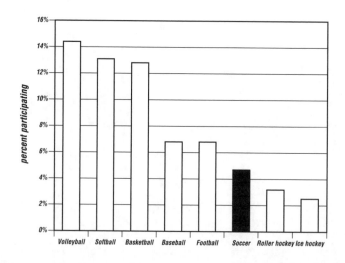

The Future of Soccer

"Soccer was viewed as an immigrant sport because it was not invented in the United States, as baseball or basketball were," says Sandy Briggs, executive director of the Soccer Industry Council of America (SICA). But soccer is becoming an American sport. Behind the change, Briggs says, is the growing participation of children.

SICA's 1996 National Soccer Participation Survey found 13.3 million players under age 18. "It's never been a huge sport for adults," Briggs acknowledges. According to the National Survey of Recreation and the Environment, soccer is about as popular as rowing and caving. But this could change as young soccer enthusiasts grow up and continue to play the game.

Soccer's popularity among American children hasn't escaped the attention of business. Bandai, the Japanese company best known for its Mighty Morphin' Power Rangers, is now marketing Major League Soccer action figures.

A big plus for soccer, according to Briggs, is its appeal to both boys and girls. Title IX brought millions of girls into the sport, and Briggs forecasts that this growth will continue. "The United States is considered the leading country in women's soccer," he notes. The licensing of Major League Soccer hair accessories, such as barrettes and scrunchies, is proof of its appeal to girls.

The United States has been one of the few countries in the world where soccer is not a major professional sport, but no longer. Major League Soccer (MLS) kicked off for the first time in 1996, and its reception was better than expected. With an average of about 17,000 fans attending each game, the sport is already making its mark. High-powered sponsors, such as Pepsi and Kellogg, will make the game even more visible. Look for an upsurge in interest in women's soccer when the women's professional soccer league takes to the field in 1998.

Another plus for soccer is its "appeal to all ethnic groups," says Rafael Morffi, manager of communications for Major League Soccer. Over one-third of soccer fans are Hispanic, giving the sport an edge with one of the country's fastest-growing demographic segments.

Participation in Soccer

(percent of persons aged 16 or older who participated in soccer at least once in the past year, by selected demographic characteristics, 1994-95)

Total	**4.7%**
Age	
Aged 16 to 24	13.2
Aged 25 to 29	6.0
Aged 30 to 39	5.0
Aged 40 to 49	3.0
Aged 50 to 59	1.5
Aged 60 or older	0.1
Income	
Under $15,000	3.3
$15,000 to $24,999	3.8
$25,000 to $49,999	4.4
$50,000 to $74,999	5.8
$75,000 to $99,999	5.5
$100,000 or more	6.6
Sex	
Men	6.2
Women	3.4
Race and Hispanic origin	
White	4.7
Black	3.6
Other, including Hispanic	7.1
Education	
Not a high school graduate	9.3
High school graduate	3.5
Some college	4.1
College graduate	4.6
Number of persons in household	
One	2.2
Two	2.3
Three	5.1
Four	7.7
Five or more	9.6

(continued)

(continued from previous page)

**Number of persons aged
16 or older in household**

One	2.8%
Two	3.9
Three or more	8.6

**Number of persons under
age 6 in household**

None	4.4
One or more	6.2

Source: USDA Forest Service, 1994-95 National Survey on Recreation and the Environment

Major League Soccer Spectators, 1996

(percent distribution of in-stadium Major League Soccer spectators aged 18 or older, by selected characteristics, 1996)

Total	**100%**
Age	
Aged 18 to 24	23
Aged 25 to 34	29
Aged 35 to 44	25
Aged 45 to 54	14
Aged 55 or older	5
Household income	
Under $25,000	23
$25,000 to $49,999	31
$50,000 to $74,999	19
$75,000 or more	27
Sex	
Men	72
Women	28
Race and Hispanic origin	
Anglo	54
Latino	36
Black	1
Asian	2
Other	7
Education	
Not a high school graduate	1
High school graduate only	22
Some college	26
College graduate	30
Graduate school	21

Source: Major League Soccer's 1996 Survey of In-Stadium Spectators, ©1996 Major League Soccer. Reprinted with permission.

Softball

Who plays softball:
- *young and middle-aged adults*
- *blacks*
- *households with young children*

Trends in softball:
- *more women*
- *teams for older people*

More than twice as many Americans play softball than baseball—13 percent of people aged 16 or older have played softball at least once in the past 12 months. Participation in softball is substantial for both young and middle-aged adults. It peaks at 23 percent among 25-to-29-year-olds. Even among people in their 40s, however, more than 12 percent play softball.

Softball participation is highest for people living in households with incomes between $25,000 and $74,999, at more than 15 percent. In contrast, a smaller 10 percent of people in the most-affluent households play softball.

Sixteen percent of men have played softball in the past year, a higher rate of participation than that of women. Nevertheless, a substantial 10 percent of women have played softball at least once in the past year.

Blacks are slightly more likely to play softball than whites and "others" (primarily Asians and Hispanics). Sixteen percent of blacks have played softball in the past year, versus 13 percent of whites and 10 percent of others.

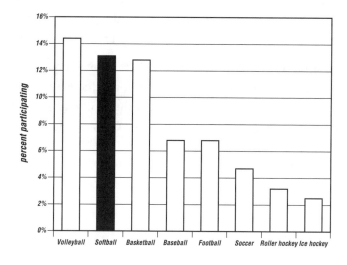

Softball participation does not vary much by education. It is much more popular in larger households and in households with preschoolers. Fully 19 percent of people living in households with children under age 6 have played softball in the past year versus only 12 percent of those living in households without young children.

The Future of Softball

Like the players of many team sports, softball players are introduced to the game in high school or college. Many then participate in amateur adult games after graduation. Children who play baseball often become adult softball enthusiasts.

Tom O'Hara, Northeast regional vice-president for the National Softball Association, says softball is becoming more competitive and attracting more people.

Many people think softball players are a bunch of guys playing for a keg of beer and then "going into the parking lot and getting drunk," says O'Hara. To the contrary, the competition is serious, there are opportunities to play in tournaments, and both women and men are more likely to play now than 20 years ago. Behind the increased participation, according to O'Hara, is the game's low cost compared to other adult leisure activities (he cites golf as an example) and the increased interest in physical fitness.

While softball enjoys high rates of participation today, it is in the midst of tough competition from other team sports. Children are not playing baseball or softball as much as they once did, and that will affect future participation in the sport. The direct competitors are soccer and lacrosse, which are played during the same season. "When kids who've played soccer all of their lives graduate, they're going to want to continue to play soccer as adults."

Softball also faces competition from these sports for field space. If more people play soccer, for example, fewer fields are available for softball. Because of this competition, O'Hara foresees softball groups becoming multisport organizations—including sports like baseball and volleyball—in order to get the competitive edge.

But "the future for softball is not bleak," O'Hara says. Look for more leagues and teams for "masters" players (people aged 35 or older), especially for women. Also on the way are improvements in equipment that will make the game easier to play, and year-round training. "Softball is resilient," O'Hara says.

Participation in Softball

(percent of persons aged 16 or older who participated in softball at least once in the past year, by selected demographic characteristics, 1994-95)

Total	**13.1%**
Age	
Aged 16 to 24	20.4
Aged 25 to 29	22.6
Aged 30 to 39	17.7
Aged 40 to 49	12.1
Aged 50 to 59	6.3
Aged 60 or older	1.9
Income	
Under $15,000	7.5
$15,000 to $24,999	11.7
$25,000 to $49,999	15.2
$50,000 to $74,999	16.6
$75,000 to $99,999	14.3
$100,000 or more	10.4
Sex	
Men	16.2
Women	10.1
Race and Hispanic origin	
White	12.9
Black	15.8
Other, including Hispanic	10.2
Education	
Not a high school graduate	12.4
High school graduate	12.8
Some college	14.4
College graduate	12.2
Number of persons in household	
One	8.5
Two	9.4
Three	14.5
Four	18.4
Five or more	18.4

(continued)

(continued from previous page)

**Number of persons aged
16 or older in household**

One	10.0%
Two	13.2
Three or more	15.8

**Number of persons under
age 6 in household**

None	11.5
One or more	18.8

Source: USDA Forest Service, 1994-95 National Survey on Recreation and the Environment

Volleyball

Who plays volleyball:
- *young and middle-aged adults*
- *women*

Trends in volleyball:
- *older players*
- *beach volleyball*

With 14 percent of Americans aged 16 or older having played volleyball at least once in the past 12 months, volleyball is the most popular team sport. Young adults are most likely to play volleyball, with 28 percent of people aged 16 to 24 participating. The share drops slightly to 23 percent among 25-to-29-year-olds and remains at a relatively high 18 percent among people in their 30s. Even among fortysomethings, more than 1 in 10 has played volleyball at least once in the past year.

Volleyball participation does not vary much by income. While men are more likely to participate than women, the difference is not great—17 percent of men and 12 percent of women. Of all the outdoor team sports, in fact, volleyball has the highest level of participation by women. Blacks are slightly more likely to play volleyball than whites, 16 versus 14 percent.

Volleyball participation does not vary much by education. It does rise with household size. This is because large households are more likely to include teens and young adults, the age group most likely to participate in volleyball.

The Future of Volleyball

"Everyone plays volleyball in school," says John Kessel, director of beach volleyball and grassroots programs for USA Volleyball, the national governing body for amateur volleyball in the U.S.

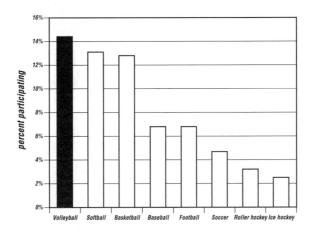

In both high school and college, girls have higher rates of participation in volleyball than boys, thanks to Title IX, which requires colleges to offer equal numbers of athletic scholarships to men and women. Because college football offers so many scholarships to men, an equal number must be made available to women. Volleyball is one of the team sports that has benefited from this legal requirement. For high school boys, it is football that offers the greatest opportunity to get a college scholarship; for girls, it is volleyball.

"In order for schools to achieve a sense of proportionality," Kessel says, they need to give out many more volleyball scholarships to women than to men. There are about 10,000 varsity volleyball scholarships for women, but fewer than 100 for men, according to Kessel. After college, however, men are more likely to play volleyball than women.

Besides its appeal to both men and women, volleyball has other things going for it as well. While other team sports require lots of land, volleyball is "the most concentrated sport for the space," Kessel says. "You can fit two volleyball courts onto one basketball court." Outdoors, volleyball does not require a permanent location. Perhaps the only space issue with volleyball is finding a place to play indoors during the winter in cold climates.

Volleyball is also unique in that it is not a contact team sport. "Because of that, there's a huge amount of coed volleyball," says Kessel. It is also an inexpensive game compared to other team sports, with little equipment required. But volleyball is not an easy sport to play, and there is little that can be done to make it easier. "We're dealing with gravity," Kessel explains. Volleyball organizations are trying to introduce lightweight beach balls to interest younger children in the sport.

Beach volleyball is growing especially rapidly right now, Kessel says, with sand courts being built around the country. The growth of volleyball should continue, says Kessel, since it is a lifetime sport.

Participation in Volleyball

(percent of persons aged 16 or older who participated in volleyball at least once in the past year, by selected demographic characteristics, 1994-95)

Total	**14.4%**
Age	
Aged 16 to 24	28.0
Aged 25 to 29	23.2
Aged 30 to 39	17.8
Aged 40 to 49	11.3
Aged 50 to 59	6.9
Aged 60 or older	1.6
Income	
Under $15,000	10.2
$15,000 to $24,999	12.6
$25,000 to $49,999	16.7
$50,000 to $74,999	16.0
$75,000 to $99,999	16.4
$100,000 or more	12.2
Sex	
Men	16.6
Women	12.2
Race and Hispanic origin	
White	14.1
Black	16.2
Other, including Hispanic	14.2
Education	
Not a high school graduate	15.9
High school graduate	13.5
Some college	15.4
College graduate	13.3
Number of persons in household	
One	10.0
Two	10.3
Three	16.6
Four	18.6
Five or more	20.8

(continued)

(continued from previous page)

Number of persons aged 16 or older in household	
One	11.8%
Two	13.0
Three or more	19.8

Number of persons under age 6 in household	
None	13.1
One or more	19.2

Source: USDA Forest Service, 1994-95 National Survey on Recreation and the Environment

Chapter 8

Watersports

Watersports are some of the most-popular outdoor recreational activities in the United States. Swimming ranks fifth among the outdoor sports and recreational activities examined by the National Survey on Recreation and the Environment, behind walking, sightseeing, picnicking, and attending an outdoor sports event. Fully 44 percent of Americans aged 16 or older swam in a pool during the past 12 months, while 39 percent swam in an ocean, lake, river, or pond.

Boating is enjoyed by 30 percent of people aged 16 or older each year, with 23 percent motorboating. Other types of boating are far less popular: Only 7 percent have been canoeing and 5 percent sailing.

Fewer people take part in more-strenuous watersports. Just 9 percent of people aged 16 or older have been water-skiing in the past year, 7 percent have been snorkeling, and only 1 percent have been surfing or windsurfing.

With the nation's Sunbelt population growing, the percentage of Americans participating in watersports should increase. In warmer climates, more people will have the opportunity to enjoy watersports year-round.

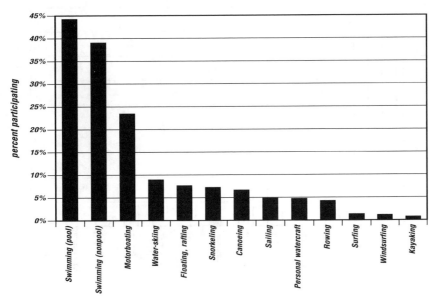

Canoeing

Who canoes:
- *people under age 50*
- *men*
- *high-income households*

Canoeing trends:
- *better equipment*
- *access concerns*
- *canoeing in different places*

Canoeing is the most-popular human-powered watercraft sport in the United States, with 7 percent of the population having canoed at least once in the past 12 months. Those most likely to canoe are adults under age 50, with the highest rate of participation among 16-to-24-year-olds, at 12 percent. Participation in canoeing is below average among older people, with only 2 percent of Americans aged 60 or older having canoed in the past year.

Because canoeing requires buying or renting equipment, participation in canoeing rises with income. Among those with household incomes of $50,000 or more, about 1 in 10 has canoed in the past 12 months. Men are more likely to canoe than women, 9 versus 5 percent.

Whites are more likely to canoe than blacks, in part because their incomes are higher. While 8 percent of whites have been canoeing in the past 12 months, only 2 percent of blacks have.

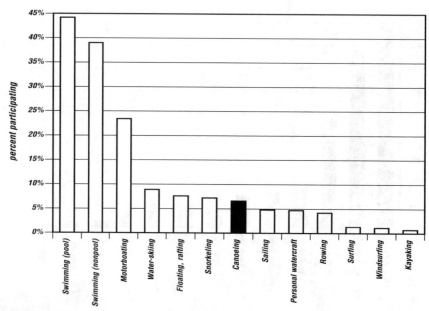

The college-educated are most likely to canoe, with 9 percent having done so in the past 12 months. In part, this is due to the higher incomes of people with college degrees.

The Future of Canoeing

"It's a great sport. A lot of people fall in love with it," says James Leasure, director of marketing and communications for the American Canoe Association.

The appeal of canoeing, he says, is how well the activity meshes with so many trends. It can be a social sport or an individual sport, providing the opportunity for family time or the chance to get away. Canoeing is "calisthenically rewarding," he says, and so is in step with the fitness movement. It is environmentally sound. And it can satisfy the urge to compete as well.

"Canoeing has been around for a long time," he says. Now, "it's being rediscovered."

An important trend in the sport of canoeing is traveling to unique places to enjoy the activity. Another trend is canoeing in unusual ways, such as in white water or standing up. Boat technology is improving, creating boats that are more durable and cheaper. This could open the sport up to people with lower incomes. If media coverage of canoe competitions improves, this too could open up the sport, says Leasure.

Canoeing is not immune from access considerations. "Conservation is the key," Leasure notes. Despite some access problems, "participation is booming, absolutely booming."

Participation in Canoeing

(percent of persons aged 16 or older who participated in canoeing at least once in the past year, by selected demographic characteristics, 1994-95)

Total	**6.6%**
Age	
Aged 16 to 24	11.7
Aged 25 to 29	9.3
Aged 30 to 39	8.2
Aged 40 to 49	7.4
Aged 50 to 59	4.9
Aged 60 or older	1.9
Income	
Under $15,000	2.8
$15,000 to $24,999	4.7
$25,000 to $49,999	7.3
$50,000 to $74,999	10.8
$75,000 to $99,999	10.1
$100,000 or more	9.9
Sex	
Men	9.1
Women	5.1
Race and Hispanic origin	
White	7.9
Black	1.6
Other, including Hispanic	5.2
Education	
Not a high school graduate	6.8
High school graduate	5.3
Some college	7.1
College graduate	8.9
Number of persons in household	
One	4.4
Two	6.2
Three	7.9
Four	8.6
Five or more	9.2

(continued)

(continued from previous page)

**Number of persons aged
16 or older in household**

One	5.0%
Two	7.1
Three or more	9.1

**Number of persons under
age 6 in household**

None	7.0
One or more	7.4

Source: USDA Forest Service, 1994-95 National Survey on Recreation and the Environment

Floating and Rafting

Who floats and rafts:

- *young adults*
- *whites*
- *large households*

Floating and rafting trends:

- *better equipment*
- *raft exploration*

Floating and rafting are popular water sport activities, just behind water-skiing in the number of participants. Nearly 8 percent of Americans have been floating or rafting in the past 12 months. As with most sports, participation is highest among young adults. Sixteen percent of 16-to-24-year-olds have been floating or rafting in the past 12 months, as have 12 percent of those aged 25 to 29. Floating and rafting participation remains above average in the 30-to-39 age group, then falls below average after age 40.

Participation in floating and rafting is above average for people with household incomes of $50,000 or more, with about 1 in 10 participating in the past year. Only 4 percent of those in households with incomes below $15,000 have participated, in part because many low-income householders are retirees.

There is no difference in floating and rafting participation by education. But whites are much more likely to participate than blacks and "others" (primarily Asians and Hispanics).

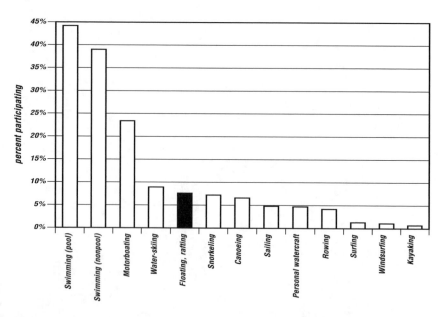

Participation in floating and rafting is highest for those living in households with three or more people aged 16 or older. Behind this pattern are families with teens who participate in the sport.

The Future of Floating and Rafting

Floating and rafting are not the same thing. Floating is "throwing a six-pack into the raft, flowing the current, and socializing," says Ron Hilbert, paddle sport expert and partner in Adventure Sports On-Line. Hilbert was executive officer of the American Canoe Association, a certified A.C.A. paddling instructor, and on the board of the Eppies Great Race (the oldest Triathalon in the world).

Rafting, on the other hand, is a sport. It involves a guide and rafters who "work as a crew to get down the river," Hilbert says. Rafting appeals to people who like group water experiences, unlike kayaking or canoeing. Also, Hilbert notes that rafting "allows people to share a river experience without having to learn all of the skills."

Rafting allows people to "use the river as a water trail," Hilbert says. "The raft is your truck or your four-wheel-drive vehicle." It can give people access to places they would never be able to get to via land.

Rafting is dominated by commercial outfitters, says Hilbert, because rafts are more expensive than other nonmotorized boats.

The trends are positive for rafting and floating. "There's much better gear than we used to have. We're very close to the perfect raft," Hilbert remarks. This allows participants to get more enjoyment from their rafting experience in safety. Another trend is the growth in traveling. "People use their rafts to explore," Hilbert says, and people are willing to go far from home—even internationally—to do that.

Participation in Floating and Rafting

(percent of persons aged 16 or older who participated in floating and rafting at least once in the past year, by selected demographic characteristics, 1994-95)

Total	**7.6%**
Age	
Aged 16 to 24	15.8
Aged 25 to 29	11.9
Aged 30 to 39	8.4
Aged 40 to 49	6.3
Aged 50 to 59	3.3
Aged 60 or older	1.4
Income	
Under $15,000	4.0
$15,000 to $24,999	5.3
$25,000 to $49,999	7.9
$50,000 to $74,999	10.6
$75,000 to $99,999	9.5
$100,000 or more	11.7
Sex	
Men	8.7
Women	6.6
Race and Hispanic origin	
White	8.6
Black	1.7
Other, including Hispanic	4.9
Education	
Not a high school graduate	8.8
High school graduate	6.8
Some college	8.0
College graduate	7.6
Number of persons in household	
One	5.3
Two	6.1
Three	9.3
Four	9.6
Five or more	9.2

(continued)

(continued from previous page)

Number of persons aged 16 or older in household	
One	5.9%
Two	7.0
Three or more	10.6
Number of persons under age 6 in household	
None	7.5
One or more	8.2

Source: USDA Forest Service, 1994-95 National Survey on Recreation and the Environment

Kayaking

Who kayaks:
- *young and middle-aged adults*
- *high-income households*

Kayaking trends:
- *more women*
- *more older people*

Few Americans have been kayaking in the past 12 months. Less than 1 percent of people aged 16 or older participated, making it the least-popular watersport surveyed here. Participation is highest in the 16-to-24 age group, at 2.7 percent. While participation falls with age, it remains at twice the national average among people in their 30s and 40s, at 1.3 and 1.4 percent, respectively.

Kayaking is a sport most popular among those with high incomes. The percentage of Americans who have been kayaking reaches a high of 3.1 percent among those with household incomes of $100,000 or more. But participation is above average for those with middle incomes as well. Men are twice as likely to kayak as women. Whites and "others" (primarily Asians and Hispanics) are much more likely to kayak than blacks. Kayaking participation does not vary much by education or by household type.

The Future of Kayaking

"The key to a sport like kayaking is that it's a total involvement recreation," says Ron Hilbert of Adventure Sports On-Line and a former officer of the American Canoe

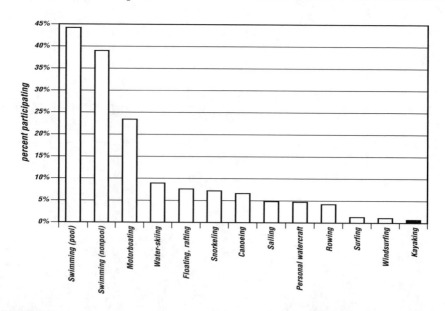

Association. "You're busy mentally and physically, and you don't have time to worry about balancing your checkbook. You're able to recharge your batteries because you're so involved in what you're doing." Because of this effect, he says, the sport attracts stressed-out professionals.

The sport also is "designed for women," he says. It will fare well with the aging population because it demands skill, not strength. Kayakers tend to be mountain bikers, Hilbert says. It is very common to see a car with both bike and kayak mounted on top.

Kayaking attracts the "been there, done that" type as much as it attracts the hardcore paddler. "The vast majority of people just like to be in the outdoors, soaking up the sunshine," he says.

Kayaking is benefiting from better technology. Although the initial outlay for equipment can be sizable, people are more likely to "outgrow a kayak than wear it out—there aren't any moving parts." And once you have your equipment, the large expenses are over—unlike with skiing.

Kayaking will benefit from the generally rising interest in outdoor sports. One factor that may limit its growth, however, is access. Many people do not live close enough to a body of water to become kayakers.

Participation in Kayaking

(percent of persons aged 16 or older who participated in kayaking at least once in the past year, by selected demographic characteristics, 1994-95)

Total	**0.7%**
Age	
Aged 16 to 24	2.7
Aged 25 to 29	1.8
Aged 30 to 39	1.3
Aged 40 to 49	1.4
Aged 50 to 59	0.9
Aged 60 or older	0.2
Income	
Under $15,000	0.7
$15,000 to $24,999	0.7
$25,000 to $49,999	1.3
$50,000 to $74,999	1.8
$75,000 to $99,999	1.8
$100,000 or more	3.1
Sex	
Men	1.8
Women	0.9
Race and Hispanic origin	
White	1.4
Black	0.2
Other, including Hispanic	1.8
Education	
Not a high school graduate	1.3
High school graduate	1.0
Some college	1.1
College graduate	1.9
Number of persons in household	
One	1.0
Two	1.2
Three	1.6
Four	1.4
Five or more	1.5

(continued)

(continued from previous page)

Number of persons aged
16 or older in household

One	1.2%
Two	1.2
Three or more	1.8

Number of persons under
age 6 in household

None	1.4
One or more	1.2

Source: USDA Forest Service, 1994-95 National Survey on Recreation and the Environment

Motorboating

Motorboating is one of the most-popular watersport activities, with 23 percent of Americans having been on a motorboat in the past 12 months. While young adults are more likely to have been boating than older Americans, a large proportion of people of all ages takes part in the activity. Motorboating participation peaks at 30 percent among people aged 25 to 29. But more than 20 percent of people up to age 60 have been motorboating in the past year. Even among the oldest Americans, more than 1 in 10 has been motorboating in the past 12 months.

Because of the expense of buying and maintaining a motorboat, motorboating is most popular among people with high incomes. One-third of people with household incomes of $75,000 or more have been motorboating in the past year. But even among those with the lowest household incomes, under $15,000, a substantial 12 percent have been motorboating recently.

Men are more likely than women to have been motorboating in the past 12 months, 27 versus 20 percent. Whites are far more likely to have been motorboating

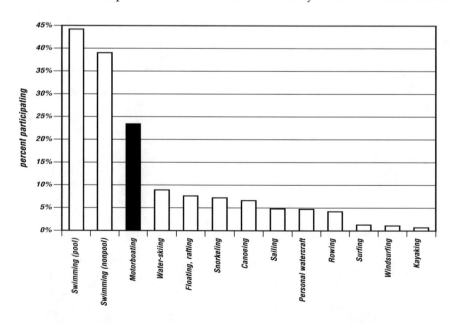

than blacks—27 versus just 7 percent. The popularity of motorboating does not vary much by education or household size—testimony to its broad demographic appeal.

The Future of Motorboating

"Boating carries a mystique for a lot of people," explains Daniel Bartell, executive officer of Somerset Power Squadrons, a division of U.S. Power Squadrons, a non-profit boating organization dedicated to the promotion of boating and boat safety.

The lifestyle of motorboating also has "tremendous appeal," Bartell says. "It's a way to go camping on the water."

Today, there is more interest in motorboats, and there is more power available, Bartell says. Personal watercrafts "have opened up the water to anyone," he says. "It's no longer just a rich man's toy."

Boats are now easier to use and easier to maintain. "In a lot of cases you can just get in and turn a key," says Bartell. "With navigation technology, like GPS, you can go just about anywhere and feel confident about getting back," he notes.

As more people motorboat, overcrowding, safety, and environmental concerns mount. "Licensing and required education for motorboaters are positive trends," Bartell concludes.

Participation in Motorboating

(percent of persons aged 16 or older who participated in motorboating at least once in the past year, by selected demographic characteristics, 1994-95)

Total	**23.4%**
Age	
Aged 16 to 24	27.8
Aged 25 to 29	30.2
Aged 30 to 39	27.7
Aged 40 to 49	24.2
Aged 50 to 59	21.1
Aged 60 or older	13.3
Income	
Under $15,000	11.7
$15,000 to $24,999	18.3
$25,000 to $49,999	25.8
$50,000 to $74,999	30.7
$75,000 to $99,999	34.1
$100,000 or more	33.8
Sex	
Men	27.4
Women	19.9
Race and Hispanic origin	
White	26.5
Black	7.0
Other, including Hispanic	13.9
Education	
Not a high school graduate	17.0
High school graduate	21.9
Some college	25.9
College graduate	25.9
Number of persons in household	
One	17.7
Two	22.9
Three	26.1
Four	27.7
Five or more	23.4

(continued)

(continued from previous page)

Number of persons aged	
16 or older in household	
One	18.8%
Two	25.3
Three or more	24.5
Number of persons under	
age 6 in household	
None	23.0
One or more	25.5

Source: USDA Forest Service, 1994-95 National Survey on Recreation and the Environment

Personal Watercraft Riding

Who rides personal watercraft:
- *young adults*
- *high-income households*
- *families with children*

Personal watercraft trends:
- *improved equipment*
- *expanding demographics*

Nearly 5 percent of Americans rode a personal watercraft (or PWC) at least once in the past 12 months. Those most likely to have done so are young adults. More than 1 in 10 people aged 16 to 24 has participated in the past year, as have 8 percent of those aged 25 to 29. Many of the 16-to-24-year-olds who rode a PWC may be teens who convinced their parents to buy or rent the equipment. Participation remains above average in the 30-to-39 age group, at 5.5 percent. It then falls below average to a low of just 0.4 percent among people aged 60 or older.

Riding personal watercraft rises sharply with income. People in households with incomes of $50,000 or more are more likely than the average person to have participated in the past year. Fully 10 percent of those in households with incomes of $100,000 or more have done so. Men are more likely than women to ride PWCs, 6 versus 4 percent. Whites are more likely to participate than blacks and "others" (primarily Asians and Hispanics).

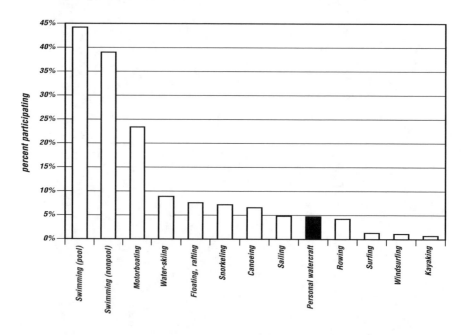

The popularity of riding personal watercraft does not vary much by educational level. But the larger the household, the higher is participation. Larger households are more likely to include teenagers, the age group with the greatest likelihood of taking part in the sport.

The Future of Personal Watercraft

Personal watercraft have changed waterfronts in the United States. Among larger powerboats and staid sailboats, PWCs are the new kids in town. According to Paul Carruthers, senior editor of *Personal Watercraft Illustrated*, most people started because they were curious. They see someone else doing it and they want to give it a try. Because PWCs can be rented, many people have their first experience on a rented craft. Carruthers says the appeal is simple: "It's outside, it's active, and it involves speed."

Technological changes have opened the personal watercraft experience to more participants. "The crafts started off as one-operator-only stand-up crafts. It was pretty physical, much like water-skiing. Today, the crafts are bigger, more stable," Carruthers explains. This has opened the door for older people and families. The crafts are easier to use and larger. More than one person can ride at a time, and riders don't have to be super athletes. Riding a PWC is now no more difficult than riding a boat.

"The sport is growing fast," Carruthers says. "I don't see any reason for it to slow down."

Riding Personal Watercraft

(percent of persons aged 16 or older who rode a personal watercraft at least once in the past year, by selected demographic characteristics, 1994-95)

Total	**4.7%**
Age	
Aged 16 to 24	10.4
Aged 25 to 29	8.1
Aged 30 to 39	5.5
Aged 40 to 49	3.3
Aged 50 to 59	1.8
Aged 60 or older	0.4
Income	
Under $15,000	1.9
$15,000 to $24,999	3.1
$25,000 to $49,999	4.7
$50,000 to $74,999	6.3
$75,000 to $99,999	8.5
$100,000 or more	10.0
Sex	
Men	6.0
Women	3.6
Race and Hispanic origin	
White	5.3
Black	1.3
Other, including Hispanic	3.6
Education	
Not a high school graduate	5.3
High school graduate	4.0
Some college	5.6
College graduate	4.5
Number of persons in household	
One	3.8
Two	3.5
Three	5.4
Four	5.9
Five or more	6.4

(continued)

(continued from previous page)

**Number of persons aged
16 or older in household**

One	3.9%
Two	4.2
Three or more	6.7

**Number of persons under
age 6 in household**

None	4.6
One or more	5.2

Source: USDA Forest Service, 1994-95 National Survey on Recreation and the Environment

Rowing

Who rows:
- *all age groups*
- *college-educated people*
- *high-income households*

Rowing trends:
- *more women*
- *local rowing clubs*

Rowing is a sport that appeals to all age groups. Unlike other human-powered boating sports, rowing does not show a sharp decline in participation with age. Overall, 4 percent of Americans have been rowing in the past 12 months. Participation peaks at 6 percent in the 16-to-24 age group and falls only gradually with age. Participation is at least 4 percent up to age 60. Even among people aged 60 or older, nearly 3 percent participate in rowing—a substantial share considering the physical demands of the sport.

While the likelihood of rowing rises with income, participation in the sport is above average for people with incomes of $25,000 or more. Men are slightly more likely than women to row, 5 versus 3.5 percent. Whites are twice as likely to participate in rowing as blacks.

Participation in rowing is highest among people with college degrees, in part because many people take up rowing as a college sport. This also explains why rowing participation is highest among 16-to-24-year-olds. Five percent of college gradu-

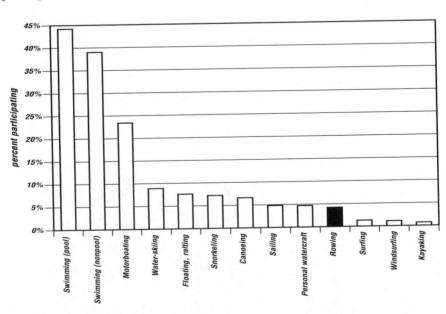

ates have been rowing in the past 12 months. Rowing participation does not vary by the presence of young children in the home, but it is more popular in larger households, probably because these households are most likely to contain people aged 16 to 24.

The Future of Rowing

Rowing is a sport people typically take up in college, says Mo Merhoff, director of member and communication services for USRowing, the national governing body for the sport. This is changing, with rowing becoming Europeanized as an increasing share of participants rows outside of the ivory tower in local clubs.

"Grassroots participation is on the upswing," Merhoff says. According to a USRowing membership survey, 22 percent of its rowers aged 24 or older started rowing in a community program. This compares with just 3 percent of rowers under age 24. More adults looking for fitness alternatives "outside the fluorescent confines of the gym" will drive this trend, she says.

Merhoff describes women's participation in rowing as "exploding," and predicts that women's rowing will get an added boost from the first-ever NCAA women's rowing championship in 1997. Other changes in rowing include an outreach effort to bring more minorities into the sport. "We have too many white people in boats today," she says. "We're trying to whittle away at the image of rowing as a wealthy person's sport."

Participation in Rowing

(percent of persons aged 16 or older who participated in rowing at least once in the past year, by selected demographic characteristics, 1994-95)

Total	**4.2%**
Age	
Aged 16 to 24	5.9
Aged 25 to 29	4.5
Aged 30 to 39	4.3
Aged 40 to 49	4.5
Aged 50 to 59	4.0
Aged 60 or older	2.7
Income	
Under $15,000	2.3
$15,000 to $24,999	3.8
$25,000 to $49,999	4.3
$50,000 to $74,999	5.7
$75,000 to $99,999	4.7
$100,000 or more	7.2
Sex	
Men	5.0
Women	3.5
Race and Hispanic origin	
White	4.6
Black	2.3
Other, including Hispanic	3.2
Education	
Not a high school graduate	4.4
High school graduate	3.7
Some college	3.5
College graduate	5.3
Number of persons in household	
One	2.6
Two	4.0
Three	4.5
Four	5.0
Five or more	5.4

(continued)

(continued from previous page)

**Number of persons aged
16 or older in household**

One	2.9%
Two	4.6
Three or more	4.7

**Number of persons under
age 6 in household**

None	4.2
One or more	4.3

Source: USDA Forest Service, 1994-95 National Survey on Recreation and the Environment

Sailing

Who sails:
- *all age groups*
- *high-income households*
- *college-educated people*

Sailing trends:
- *more young people*
- *community sailing programs*
- *smaller, simpler sailboats*

Slightly fewer than 5 percent of Americans have been sailing in the past 12 months. By comparison, a much larger 23 percent have been motorboating. Although the number of sailers is much smaller than the number of motorboaters, both activities appeal to a broad range of people.

While those most likely to sail are young adults aged 16 to 24, sailing participation remains above average until age 50. And the proportion of older Americans who sail is not much below average, with nearly 3 percent of people aged 60 or older having sailed in the past year.

Sailing is much more popular among the affluent than among those with lower incomes. Nearly 10 percent of people living in households with incomes of $100,000 or more have been sailing in the past 12 months versus fewer than 5 percent of those living in households with incomes below $50,000. Men are slightly more likely to

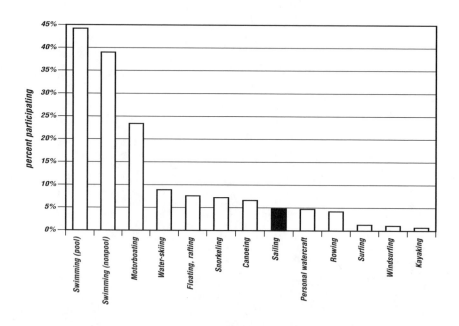

have been sailing in the past year than women, and whites are more likely to be sailers than blacks and "others" (primarily Asians and Hispanics).

Sailing participation peaks among those with a college education. Eight percent of college graduates have been sailing in the past 12 months. Sailing does not vary much by household size, but it is more popular in households without young children.

The Future of Sailing

"Sailing is radically different from how it was 20 years ago," says Terry Harper, executive director of US Sailing, the national governing body for sailing. There have been changes in the way people are introduced to the sport, the cost of participating, the time spent sailing, and what sailers do while on a sailboat.

Community sailing programs have exploded, Harper says. These programs increase public access to this once-exclusive sport, helping novices prepare boats for outings. The time-saving function may be the greatest appeal of community programs, since setting up a sailboat can consume much of a person's scarce recreational time. Between 1,500 and 1,700 community sailing programs exist across the country, Harper says; and he expects the number to grow.

Traditional private yacht clubs are another entry point to sailing. Still others get involved through commercial schools and boat shows. But no matter how people are pulled in, "they get the bug and stay with it," Harper says. "Most sailers are fairly loyal to sailing. They don't tend to go sport fishing. They don't have personal watercraft. A person who is relaxed enough to go sailing isn't going to go 40 miles an hour on a PWC with a rooster tail trailing behind." Sailers and powerboaters, Harper notes, are "two pretty divergent groups."

Sailing is experiencing an "influx of young people," he says. As a result, the average age of sailers is falling. Other trends include smaller and simpler boats and a relative decline in the price of boats. There has also been an increase in recreational chartering, which enables people to sail without an enormous investment of time and money. There is less sailboat racing today, however, because people don't have the time.

Like other watersports, sailing is grappling with access and regulation issues. Also like in other watersports, education is becoming a more important part of the experience. "People want to feel comfortable on the water. Learn it right the first time," Harper says.

Participation in Sailing

(percent of persons aged 16 or older who went sailing at least once in the past year, by selected demographic characteristics, 1994-95)

Total	**4.8%**
Age	
Aged 16 to 24	6.3
Aged 25 to 29	6.2
Aged 30 to 39	5.1
Aged 40 to 49	5.3
Aged 50 to 59	3.7
Aged 60 or older	2.8
Income	
Under $15,000	2.1
$15,000 to $24,999	2.3
$25,000 to $49,999	4.2
$50,000 to $74,999	7.5
$75,000 to $99,999	8.7
$100,000 or more	9.9
Sex	
Men	5.2
Women	4.3
Race and Hispanic origin	
White	5.2
Black	2.0
Other, including Hispanic	3.7
Education	
Not a high school graduate	3.7
High school graduate	2.3
Some college	4.3
College graduate	8.3
Number of persons in household	
One	5.1
Two	4.7
Three	4.4
Four	5.0
Five or more	4.6

(continued)

(continued from previous page)

Number of persons aged 16 or older in household	
One	4.9%
Two	4.5
Three or more	5.2
Number of persons under age 6 in household	
None	5.0
One or more	3.8

Source: USDA Forest Service, 1994-95 National Survey on Recreation and the Environment

Snorkeling

Who snorkels:
- *young and middle-aged adults*
- *high-income households*
- *college-educated people*

Snorkeling trends:
- *more older snorkelers*
- *travel to snorkeling sites*

Snorkeling is surprisingly popular, with participation rates higher than those for canoeing or sailing. Overall, 7 percent of Americans have snorkeled in the past 12 months.
Those most likely to participate are under age 30, with more than 10 percent involved
in the sport. But snorkeling is also popular among people in their 30s and 40s. Nearly
10 percent of people aged 30 to 39 have been snorkeling in the past year, as have 8
percent of those in their 40s.

Because snorkeling requires access to appropriate underwater sites, it appeals
most to those who can afford to travel. Nearly 18 percent of people living in households with incomes of $100,000 or more have been snorkeling in the past 12 months.
Snorkeling participation is below average for those with household incomes under
$50,000.

Men are more likely to snorkel than women, 9 versus 5.5 percent. Whites and
people of "other" race (primarily Asians and Hispanics) are more likely to snorkel
than blacks. Behind this pattern is the often lower income of blacks.

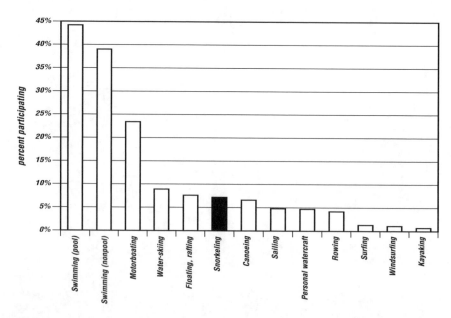

By education, snorkeling participation is above average only for college graduates, at 11 percent. It is more popular in larger households because they are more likely to include young adults. There is no difference in snorkeling participation by the presence of young children in the home.

The Future of Snorkeling

"Most snorkeling is done for the pleasure of looking around underwater, relaxing," says Mike Gower, president of the Underwater Society of America, a national federation involved in all types of water and underwater sports. "You don't expend a lot of energy, it's cheap, and you can spend the day swimming around," he explains. Snorkeling is also appealing because it does not require heavy scuba equipment, which is why it is called "free diving."

Snorkeling equipment has improved, allowing more people to enjoy the sport. Ultra-low-volume face masks, for example, allow snorkelers to stay underwater longer, says Gower.

Snorkeling is a sport that can be enjoyed even at older ages, with certain modifications. "You tailor your effort to the condition you're in," Gower says. He doesn't see much of an increase in participants aged 65 or older, but more "40- and 50-year-olds are getting involved," he says. The industry is trying to attract more younger people.

Snorkelers are involved in a variety of other outdoor sports, Gower says. Especially popular are rock climbing, skiing, and scuba diving. Scuba divers typically use two tanks of oxygen in a day, and a tank lasts one hour. "They'll snorkel the rest of the time they're in the water," he notes.

An important trend in snorkeling is travel to interesting underwater viewing sites. An important issue for snorkelers is protecting the marine environment.

As interest increases in scuba diving, there will be a heightened awareness of snorkeling, Gower predicts. But he "can't imagine there being any big change in snorkeling. It's such a simple recreational activity."

Participation in Snorkeling

(percent of persons aged 16 or older who went snorkeling at least once in the past year, by selected demographic characteristics, 1994-95)

Total	**7.2%**
Age	
Aged 16 to 24	10.4
Aged 25 to 29	10.7
Aged 30 to 39	9.5
Aged 40 to 49	8.1
Aged 50 to 59	4.7
Aged 60 or older	1.4
Income	
Under $15,000	2.5
$15,000 to $24,999	3.7
$25,000 to $49,999	6.1
$50,000 to $74,999	11.0
$75,000 to $99,999	14.0
$100,000 or more	17.6
Sex	
Men	9.1
Women	5.5
Race and Hispanic origin	
White	7.8
Black	3.0
Other, including Hispanic	7.5
Education	
Not a high school graduate	5.7
High school graduate	4.5
Some college	7.2
College graduate	10.9
Number of persons in household	
One	5.5
Two	7.0
Three	8.7
Four	7.4
Five or more	8.0

(continued)

(continued from previous page)

Number of persons aged 16 or older in household	
One	5.8%
Two	7.4
Three or more	8.5
Number of persons under age 6 in household	
None	7.2
One or more	7.5

Source: USDA Forest Service, 1994-95 National Survey on Recreation and the Environment

Surfing

Who surfs:
- *young adults*
- *men*
- *Asians, Hispanics*

Surfing trends:
- *travel to surfing spots*
- *boomer children becoming involved*

Despite its glamourous reputation, surfing is one of the least-popular watersports. Only 1 percent of Americans have been surfing in the past 12 months, in part because surfing is limited to coastal areas.

Young adults are most likely to surf. Nearly 4 percent of people aged 16 to 24 have been surfing in the past year, as have just under 2 percent of those aged 25 to 29. From age 30 on, participation in surfing is below average. Surfing participation does not vary much by income.

Men are four times as likely to surf as women. More than 2 percent of men have been surfing in the past 12 months, versus only 0.5 percent of women. People of "other" race (mostly Asians and Hispanics) are more likely to surf than whites and blacks, partly because many of the nation's Asians and Hispanics live in coastal states.

Surfing participation does not vary much by education. It is more common in households with three or more people aged 16 or older, in part because these house-

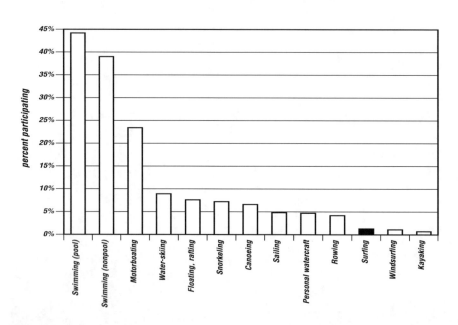

holds are most likely to include young adults. Surfing is also more popular among people without young children at home than among those with preschoolers.

The Future of Surfing

The appeal of surfing, according to Michael Angiulo, executive director and general counsel for the U.S. Surfing Federation, is the exhilaration that comes from "riding on a continually changing surface."

The thrill of riding a wave is something all surfers can agree on. Apart from that excitement, surfers as a whole have different philosophies about the sport.

"It's schizophrenic," Anguilo admits. One area of conflict surrounds the question of whether surfing should be competitive. Another surrounds the growing use of wave pools to bring surfing inland. "Purists don't like it," Anguilo explains.

Surfing is "an unrecognized leader in fashion and lifestyle, " Anguilo says—a trend that started with the Beach Boys. Surfing influences clothing styles and determines what is cool far from the ocean. This is helped along by the youthful demographics of the sport. Most people start surfing in their teens. "It's not something you pick up at 35," says Anguilo.

In the future, surfing will experience pressure because of the rising value of waterfront property. Pollution and erosion also compete with the surfer's resource. Compounding the problem is that "surfers aren't joiners," Anguilo says. That makes lobbying and organizational efforts difficult, although not impossible.

On the brighter side, as baby-boom surfers introduce the sport to their families, more money is coming in and the sport is becoming more mainstream. Travel is becoming a part of the sport, as surfers travel to prime surfing locations to ride the waves.

Technologically, lighter boards allow maneuvers that were once impossible. And by using personal watercraft, surfers can now be towed out to 40-foot waves they could not reach before.

"Performance is at an all-time high," Anguilo says.

Participation in Surfing

(percent of persons aged 16 or older who went surfing at least once in the past year, by selected demographic characteristics, 1994-95)

Total	**1.3%**
Age	
Aged 16 to 24	3.7
Aged 25 to 29	1.9
Aged 30 to 39	1.2
Aged 40 to 49	0.5
Aged 50 to 59	0.5
Aged 60 or older	0.3
Income	
Under $15,000	0.9
$15,000 to $24,999	0.8
$25,000 to $49,999	1.0
$50,000 to $74,999	1.8
$75,000 to $99,999	1.8
$100,000 or more	0.9
Sex	
Men	2.2
Women	0.5
Race and Hispanic origin	
White	1.4
Black	0.5
Other, including Hispanic	2.0
Education	
Not a high school graduate	1.5
High school graduate	1.0
Some college	1.3
College graduate	1.6
Number of persons in household	
One	1.2
Two	1.0
Three	1.8
Four	1.3
Five or more	1.6

(continued)

(continued from previous page)

**Number of persons aged
16 or older in household**

One	1.3%
Two	0.9
Three or more	2.3

**Number of persons under
age 6 in household**

None	1.4
One or more	0.9

Source: USDA Forest Service, 1994-95 National Survey on Recreation and the Environment

Swimming

Who swims:
- *all age groups*
- *whites*
- *households with children*

Swimming trends:
- *broadening access*
- *zero-depth pools*
- *family aquatic centers*

Swimming is America's second-most-popular recreational activity, with 44 percent of people aged 16 or older having swum in a pool in the past 12 months and 39 percent having swum in a lake, river, pond, or ocean.

Swimming is popular with adults of all ages, although participation is highest among young adults and declines with age. Over 60 percent of people aged 16 to 24 have been swimming in a pool in the past year, and more than 50 percent have been swimming in something other than a pool. A majority of 25-to-39-year-olds have also been swimming in a pool in the past 12 months, and nearly half have been swimming elsewhere. Even among people aged 60 or older, one in five has been swimming in a pool.

Sixty percent of people in households with incomes of $75,000 or more have been swimming in the past year, and over half have been swimming in a nonpool.

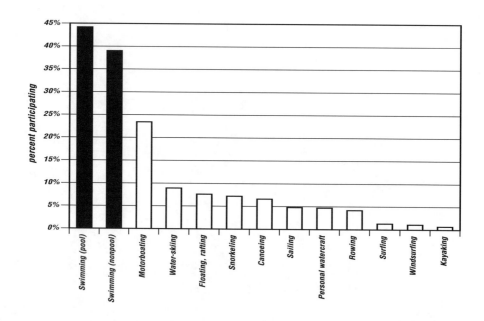

Swimming participation is below average for people with household incomes below $25,000, partly because many low-income households are in central cities with less access to swimming areas. This also explains why blacks and "others" (primarily Asians and Hispanics) are less likely to swim than whites.

Swimming is much more popular among people living in larger households. This is because larger households are more likely to include children. A 54 percent majority of people with children under age 6 at home have been swimming in a pool in the past 12 months, versus only 42 percent of those without young children at home.

The Future of Swimming

Swimming, which is already an extremely popular activity, is on the rise, says Walter C. Johnson, Great Lakes regional director of the National Recreation and Parks Association. The growing popularity of activities such as water aerobics, scuba diving, and aquatic therapy are getting more people into the water.

The idea of a swimming pool as a "square hole with water in it" is changing, Johnson notes. In the past, "the emphasis was on competitive swimming. Now, people are converting the traditional pool into a family aquatic center." Lap lanes must make room for water slides and wave pools. The concrete that once surrounded pools is being turned into grassy areas for lawn chairs. "There is a decrease in competitive swimming as a result," he says.

In order to accommodate everyone, another trend Johnson sees is "zero-depth pools." The water in these pools starts out only about an inch deep, with the depth increasing gradually. This allows the disabled and elderly access to the water, and it provides a shallow play area for children. In colder climates, family aquatic centers are moving indoors, with waterfalls, hot tubs, and spas.

Given today's emphasis on wellness and physical fitness, Johnson says participation in swimming will remain high. "Swimming has been deemed an outstanding physical activity," he says. Knowing how to swim can save your life. "There's a survival aspect to swimming," he says, noting that the fourth leading cause of death for children under age 7 is drowning. Because residents of inner cities often lack access to swimming pools, Johnson says, blacks and Hispanics are more likely to drown than whites. Efforts are being made to improve swimming opportunities in urban areas.

Johnson sees some factors that could limit swimming participation. These include less leisure time, competition from other sports, and liability issues. For non-pool swimming, water pollution can reduce participation. "Although I hate to think about it, we may have to create artificial environments," Johnson says. One recourse could be treating lake and other nonpool water with chemicals similar to those used in pools.

The rise of skin cancer will also have a negative effect on outdoor swimming in the future. As people become more aware of the dangers of extended sun exposure, they may limit their time outdoors.

The future of swimming depends on how we treat our environment, Johnson concludes.

Participation in Swimming: Pool and Nonpool

(percent of persons aged 16 or older who participated in pool and nonpool swimming at least once in the past year, by selected demographic characteristics, 1994-95)

	swimming (pool)	swimming (nonpool)
Total	**44.2%**	**39.0%**
Age		
Aged 16 to 24	60.6	51.3
Aged 25 to 29	54.7	49.5
Aged 30 to 39	53.0	48.2
Aged 40 to 49	44.8	42.4
Aged 50 to 59	34.8	30.5
Aged 60 or older	21.8	16.7
Income		
Under $15,000	25.2	23.7
$15,000 to $24,999	34.7	31.4
$25,000 to $49,999	48.1	42.3
$50,000 to $74,999	55.6	48.6
$75,000 to $99,999	60.1	52.8
$100,000 or more	59.6	54.7
Sex		
Men	45.6	42.8
Women	43.1	35.6
Race and Hispanic origin		
White	47.0	42.6
Black	29.1	16.8
Other, including Hispanic	36.1	32.2
Education		
Not a high school graduate	36.0	31.0
High school graduate	38.2	33.8
Some college	48.1	41.7
College graduate	50.9	45.7
Number of persons in household		
One	29.7	28.3
Two	38.3	34.9
Three	50.9	44.4
Four	55.5	46.7
Five or more	53.8	45.4

(continued)

(continued from previous page)

	swimming (pool)	swimming (nonpool)
Number of persons aged 16 or older in household		
One	33.7%	31.1%
Two	46.0	40.5
Three or more	51.4	44.0
Number of persons under age 6 in household		
None	41.8	37.5
One or more	53.8	45.1

Source: USDA Forest Service, 1994-95 National Survey on Recreation and the Environment

Water-Skiing

Who water-skis:
- *young and middle-aged adults*
- *whites*
- *households with children*

Water-skiing trends:
- *water-skiing behind personal watercraft*
- *more women*

Water-skiing is the third-most-popular watersport activity, after swimming and motorboating. Nevertheless, only 9 percent of Americans participated in water-skiing in the past 12 months. Participation is highest among adults under age 40. Eighteen percent of people aged 16 to 24 have been water-skiing at least once in the past year, as have 16 percent of those aged 25 to 29 and 11 percent of 30-to-39-year-olds.

Because water-skiing requires a boat, it is most popular among high-income households. At least 12 percent of people in households with incomes of $50,000 or more have been water-skiing in the past 12 months. Men are nearly twice as likely as women to water-ski, 12 versus 7 percent.

Whites are far more likely to water-ski than blacks and "others" (primarily Asians and Hispanics). In part, this is because of the higher income of whites and their greater access to water recreation sites. While 10 percent of whites participated in water-ski-

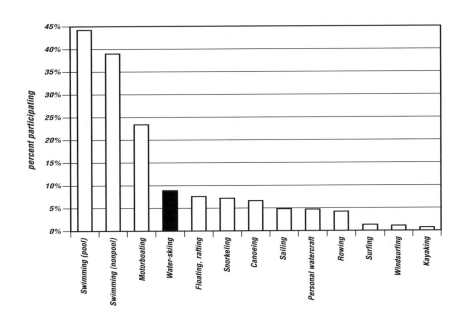

ing in the past 12 months, only 1 percent of blacks and 5 percent of "others" (primarily Asians and Hispanics) did.

Water-skiing participation does not vary much by education. It is more popular in households with three or more people because these households are more likely to include teenaged children. Water-skiing is slightly more popular in households that include at least one preschooler.

The Future of Water-Skiing

"Water-skiing is a family-oriented sport," says Don Cullimore, director of communication and public affairs for USA Water Ski, the national governing body for the sport, and publisher and editor-in-chief of *Waterskier*. People usually get involved through their families, but another entry point for the sport is recreational boating.

There are two types of water-skiers, Cullimore explains: those who do it competitively, and those who are in it for fun. One of the most-important trends in the sport is an effort by the industry to attract people who want to water-ski behind personal watercraft rather than large and expensive boats. Water-skiing equipment is also becoming more widely available and specialized.

There are many types of water-skiing. The hottest variation right now is wakeboarding, which uses a hybrid water ski that is a cross between a surfboard and a trick ski. "You can do tricks on it, and it's easier to learn," Cullimore says. It is comparable to snowboarding and "has strong appeal to young people." In the future, other forms of water-skiing are likely to evolve, according to Cullimore.

Women comprise a growing share of water-skiers. Cullimore attributes this growth to the fact that water-skiing is a family sport. Another factor behind women's growing presence is that "rules treat men and women equally" in competition, he says.

The downside to increased interest in water-skiing is the growing pressure on recreational water sites. Other water sports are competing for the same space. Unfortunately, this could result in "increased regulation of the water," notes Cullimore. "A governmental body needs to step in and make a plan."

Participation in Water-Skiing

(percent of persons aged 16 or older who participated in water-skiing at least once in the past year, by selected demographic characteristics, 1994-95)

Total	**8.9%**
Age	
Aged 16 to 24	17.7
Aged 25 to 29	15.8
Aged 30 to 39	10.7
Aged 40 to 49	7.1
Aged 50 to 59	3.6
Aged 60 or older	0.8
Income	
Under $15,000	3.9
$15,000 to $24,999	6.6
$25,000 to $49,999	9.4
$50,000 to $74,999	12.3
$75,000 to $99,999	13.5
$100,000 or more	14.8
Sex	
Men	11.5
Women	6.6
Race and Hispanic origin	
White	10.3
Black	1.1
Other, including Hispanic	5.3
Education	
Not a high school graduate	8.9
High school graduate	7.3
Some college	10.0
College graduate	9.7
Number of persons in household	
One	6.3
Two	7.1
Three	11.2
Four	11.2
Five or more	10.7

(continued)

(continued from previous page)

**Number of persons aged
16 or older in household**

One	7.2%
Two	8.5
Three or more	11.7

**Number of persons under
age 6 in household**

None	8.5
One or more	10.6

Source: USDA Forest Service, 1994-95 National Survey on Recreation and the Environment

Windsurfing

Who windsurfs:
- *young adults*
- *high-income households*
- *college-educated people*

Windsurfing trends:
- *windsurfing schools*
- *better equipment*

Only 1 percent of Americans have been windsurfing in the past 12 months. Because windsurfing participation is so low, rates of participation do not vary much by demographic characteristics. Young adults are most likely to have been windsurfing in the past year, with 1.7 percent of those under age 30 having done so. Because of the cost of equipment, windsurfing participation is highest for those with incomes of $100,000 or more, at 3 percent.

Men are somewhat more likely to windsurf than women, 1.3 versus 0.9 percent. Whites and blacks are equally likely to have been windsurfing in the past year, while "others" (primarily Asians and Hispanics) are somewhat less likely to have done so.

Windsurfing participation is highest for those with a college degree, at 1.8 percent. Participation is somewhat higher for larger households, but there is no variation by presence or absence of children under age six in the home.

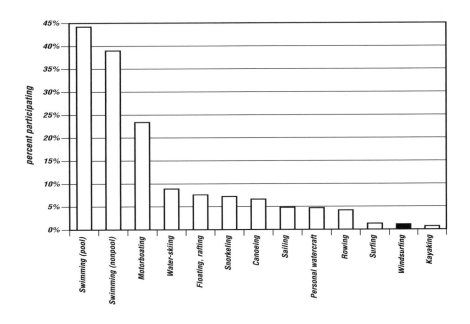

The Future of Windsurfing

"Windsurfing is like holding the wind in your hands," says Scott See, executive director of the American Windsurfing Industry Association. Windsurfers enjoy their sport on rivers, lakes, bays, and sometimes the ocean.

As a sport, See says it is quick and easy. "There aren't many sports as car-topable as windsurfing—it doesn't get any more convenient." Today, the equipment is more user friendly. "It's not a major project to put the thing together," See notes. And windsurfing is fast. In fact, the windsurfer is the fastest human-powered sailer on the water.

"Participation boomed in the 1980s and it's declined since then," says See. "If people knew what windsurfing was, it would go through the roof." The problem is the misconceptions people have about it, he says. The first misconception is that it is difficult to learn. Another is that windsurfing is "extreme." The windsurfing media take some of the blame for that, according to See, because of their quest for sensational photos. "Ninety-nine-point-nine percent of the windsurfing in America isn't extreme. It's a good family activity."

Despite the misconceptions, See thinks that if the sport "goes back to the basics" it should recover. More older people are getting involved. "It's a sport of finesse, not brute strength," he explains. A lot of older people who are getting into windsurfing have sailing backgrounds. The two activities share the same principles.

Other positive indicators for the future include increased affordability of equipment and better equipment. Small windsurfing schools are emerging, See says. The grassroots growth could feed on itself. "People tend to be evangelical about the sport," he explains.

Participation in Windsurfing

(percent of persons aged 16 or older who participated in windsurfing at least once in the past year, by selected demographic characteristics, 1994-95)

Total	**1.1%**
Age	
Aged 16 to 24	1.7
Aged 25 to 29	1.7
Aged 30 to 39	1.4
Aged 40 to 49	0.9
Aged 50 to 59	0.6
Aged 60 or older	0.4
Income	
Under $15,000	0.7
$15,000 to $24,999	0.4
$25,000 to $49,999	0.9
$50,000 to $74,999	1.8
$75,000 to $99,999	1.4
$100,000 or more	3.0
Sex	
Men	1.3
Women	0.9
Race and Hispanic origin	
White	1.1
Black	1.1
Other, including Hispanic	0.8
Education	
Not a high school graduate	1.2
High school graduate	0.6
Some college	0.9
College graduate	1.8
Number of persons in household	
One	1.0
Two	0.9
Three	1.4
Four	1.0
Five or more	1.4

(continued)

(continued from previous page)

**Number of persons aged
16 or older in household**

One	1.0%
Two	0.9
Three or more	1.5

**Number of persons under
age 6 in household**

None	1.1
One or more	1.1

Source: USDA Forest Service, 1994-95 National Survey on Recreation and the Environment

Spending on Boats

A motor makes a difference when it comes to spending on a boat. Because boats without motors tend to be less expensive than motorboats, the demographics of the households buying boats without motors are distinctly different from those of motorboat buyers.

Spending on boats without motors (such as canoes, rowboats, kayaks, and so on) is above average only for the youngest and oldest adults. Households headed by people under age 25 spend more than twice as much as the average household on boats without motors, while those headed by people aged 65 or older spend 27 percent more than average. The 26 percent market share held by older householders is much larger than the 17 percent share controlled by householders under age 25, however, because older householders are much more numerous.

The biggest spenders on motorboats are the most-affluent householders—those in the 45-to-54 age group, those with incomes of $70,000 or more, and college graduates. Households with incomes of $70,000 or more spend five times more than the average household, controlling 69 percent of all spending on motorboats.

Married couples without children at home (many of them empty nesters) outspend all other household types on boats, with or without motors. These couples spend more than twice as much as the average household on boats. Parents whose oldest child is under age 6 are also big buyers of motorboats. Households in the Northeast and West spend the most on motorboats, while those in the South and West spend the most on boats without motors.

Spending on Motorboats, 1995

(average annual, indexed, and market share of spending by consumer units on motorboats, by selected demographic characteristics, 1995; index definition: 100 is the average; an index of 132 means that spending by consumer units in the segment is 32 percent above average; an index of 68 means spending by consumer units in the segment is 32 percent below average)

	average	index	market share
Average consumer unit	**$44.34**	**100**	**100.0%**
Age			
Under age 25	27.72	63	4.3
Aged 25 to 34	64.82	146	27.7
Aged 35 to 44	28.22	64	14.5
Aged 45 to 54	78.79	178	32.1
Aged 55 to 64	61.10	138	16.9
Aged 65 or older	9.52	21	4.5
Income			
Under $20,000	2.72	7	2.4
$20,000 to $29,999	23.08	56	8.5
$30,000 to $39,999	11.47	28	3.6
$40,000 to $49,999	69.09	168	16.5
$50,000 to $69,999	1.35	3	0.4
$70,000 or more	222.12	540	68.6
Race			
White and "other"	45.25	102	90.5
Black	37.17	84	9.5
Hispanic origin			
Non-Hispanic	43.41	98	90.3
Hispanic	55.38	125	9.7
Education			
Not a high school graduate	0.15	0	0.1
High school graduate only	61.16	138	44.2
Some college	17.62	40	9.1
College graduate	85.33	192	46.7

(continued)

(continued from previous page)

	average	index	market share
Household type			
Married couples, total	$70.29	159	83.1%
Married couple only	100.10	226	48.3
Married couple with children	53.20	120	32.5
Oldest child under age 6	99.57	225	12.1
Oldest child aged 6 to 17	48.72	110	15.6
Oldest child aged 18 or older	28.37	64	4.8
Single parent with children under 18	10.13	23	1.5
Single person	-	-	-
Region			
Northeast	84.01	189	37.9
Midwest	9.56	22	5.4
South	39.82	90	30.6
West	55.52	125	26.1

Note: The average spending figures are extremely low because both purchasers and non-purchasers are included in the calculation. While the average spending figures do not show how much boat buyers spend, the patterns revealed by the index and market share figures do show who is most likely to spend on boats and how much spending is controlled by each demographic segment. (-) means sample is too small to make a reliable estimate.
Source: Bureau of Labor Statistics, 1995 Consumer Expenditure Survey; calculations by New Strategist

Spending on Boats without Motors and Boat Trailers, 1995

(average annual, indexed, and market share of spending by consumer units on boats without motors and boat trailers, by selected demographic characteristics, 1995; index definition: 100 is the average; an index of 132 means that spending by consumer units in the segment is 32 percent above average; an index of 68 means spending by consumer units in the segment is 32 percent below average)

	average	index	market share
Total	**$3.69**	**100**	**100.0%**
Age			
Under age 25	8.97	243	16.7
Aged 25 to 34	3.35	91	17.2
Aged 35 to 44	2.85	77	17.6
Aged 45 to 54	3.04	82	14.9
Aged 55 to 64	2.05	56	6.8
Aged 65 or older	4.69	127	26.4
Income			
Under $20,000	0.44	12	4.5
$20,000 to $29,999	11.59	319	48.4
$30,000 to $39,999	6.05	167	21.3
$40,000 to $49,999	-	-	-
$50,000 to $69,999	4.96	137	17.0
$70,000 or more	2.48	68	8.7
Race			
White and "other"	4.16	113	100.0
Black	-	-	-
Hispanic origin			
Non-Hispanic	3.79	103	94.7
Hispanic	2.52	68	5.3
Education			
Not a high school graduate	0.83	22	4.7
High school graduate only	8.28	224	71.9
Some college	1.60	43	9.9
College graduate	2.06	56	13.5

(continued)

(continued from previous page)

	average	index	market share
Household type			
Married couples, total	$5.11	138	72.6%
Married couple only	7.80	211	45.2
Married couple with children	3.73	101	27.4
Oldest child under age 6	1.99	54	2.9
Oldest child aged 6 to 17	4.29	116	16.6
Oldest child aged 18 or older	3.90	106	7.9
Single parent with children under 18	0.94	25	1.7
Single person	2.55	69	19.5
Region			
Northeast	1.57	43	8.5
Midwest	2.98	81	20.3
South	4.04	109	37.3
West	6.00	163	33.9

Note: The average spending figures are extremely low because both purchasers and non-purchasers are included in the calculation. While the average spending figures do not show how much boat buyers spend, the patterns revealed by the index and market share figures do show who is most likely to spend on boats and how much spending is controlled by each demographic segment. (-) means sample is too small to make a reliable estimate.
Source: Bureau of Labor Statistics, 1995 Consumer Expenditure Survey; calculations by New Strategist

Spending on Watersports Equipment

Spending on watersports equipment reveals two types of consumers—parents and hobbyists. Households headed by people aged 25 to 34 (parents) and 55 to 64 (hobbyists) spend more than average on watersports equipment. Together, these two age groups control over two-thirds of all spending in this market.

In the younger age group, parents are buying equipment for their children. Husbands and wives with children aged 6 to 17 spend 22 percent more than the average household on watersports equipment. In the older age group, hobbyists are buying snorkeling, scuba diving, and other gear. Married couples without children at home (many of them empty nesters) spend 86 percent more than the average household on watersports equipment.

Spending on watersports equipment is well above average for the most-affluent households and for those with incomes of $30,000 to $39,999 (many householders aged 25 to 34 are in this income group). It is also above average for college graduates, who account for nearly half the spending on watersports equipment.

Households in the West spend far more on watersports equipment than households in any other region. Western households spend more than twice as much as the average household, while those in the other three regions spend less than average. Western households control over half the spending on watersports equipment.

Spending on Watersports Equipment, 1995

(average annual, indexed, and market share of spending by consumer units on water sports equipment, by selected demographic characteristics, 1995; index definition: 100 is the average; an index of 132 means that spending by consumer units in the segment is 32 percent above average; an index of 68 means spending by consumer units in the segment is 32 percent below average)

	average	index	market share
Total	**$9.47**	**100**	**100.0%**
Age			
Under age 25	3.90	41	2.8
Aged 25 to 34	22.93	242	45.8
Aged 35 to 44	5.01	53	12.0
Aged 45 to 54	6.27	66	12.0
Aged 55 to 64	17.91	189	23.2
Aged 65 or older	1.85	20	4.2
Income			
Under $20,000	0.38	4	1.3
$20,000 to $29,999	2.04	19	2.9
$30,000 to $39,999	26.80	249	31.8
$40,000 to $49,999	7.69	71	7.0
$50,000 to $69,999	11.68	108	13.5
$70,000 or more	36.96	343	43.5
Race			
White and "other"	10.66	113	99.8
Black	0.16	2	0.2
Hispanic origin			
Non-Hispanic	9.96	105	97.0
Hispanic	3.55	37	2.9
Education			
Not a high school graduate	1.74	18	3.8
High school graduate only	8.78	93	29.7
Some college	7.74	82	18.7
College graduate	18.64	197	47.7

(continued)

(continued from previous page)

Household type	average	index	market share
Married couples, total	$12.10	128	67.0%
Married couple only	17.58	186	39.7
Married couple with children	8.82	93	25.2
Oldest child under age 6	6.60	70	3.8
Oldest child aged 6 to 17	11.60	122	17.4
Oldest child aged 18 or older	5.12	54	4.0
Single parent with children under 18	0.26	3	0.2
Single person	8.91	94	26.6
Region			
Northeast	3.92	41	8.3
Midwest	7.49	79	19.8
South	5.15	54	18.5
West	24.22	256	53.3

Note: The average spending figures are extremely low because both purchasers and non-purchasers are included in the calculation. While the average spending figures do not show how much buyers of watersports equipment spend, the patterns revealed by the index and market share figures do show who is most likely to spend on watersports equipment and how much spending is controlled by each demographic segment.
Source: Bureau of Labor Statistics, 1995 Consumer Expenditure Survey; *calculations by New Strategist*

Chapter 9

Winter Sports

Nineteen percent of Americans aged 16 or older participate in winter sports during a year's time. This surprisingly small proportion reflects the seasonality of these sports, the regionality of participation, and in some cases the high cost of participation.

The number-one winter sport is sledding. Downhill skiing ranks second, followed by ice skating, snowmobiling, and cross-country skiing. In last place is snowboarding, with fewer than 1 percent of people aged 16 or older participating. The small number of snowboard enthusiasts seems contrary to the extensive media coverage of the sport. Behind this discrepancy is the fact that most snowboarders are under age 18.

Participation in winter sports is above average among both young and middle-aged adults, falling below average only after age 50. Income is strongly linked to participation in winter sports. Nearly one-third of people in households with incomes of $100,000 or more have participated in the past year, compared with just 1 in 10 people in households with incomes below $15,000.

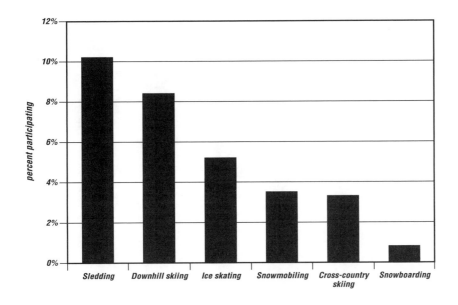

Men are slightly more likely to take part in winter sports than women, 22 versus 17 percent. Whites are far more likely to do so than blacks, 21 versus 8 percent. Behind this difference is the fact that a majority of blacks live in the South, where access to snow and ice is limited.

Participation in winter sports is greater for college graduates than for people with less education. Participation increases with household size and is significantly greater for people living in households with preschoolers than for those without young children at home.

Participation in Winter Sports

(percent of persons aged 16 or older who participated in winter sports at least once in the past year, by selected demographic characteristics, 1994-95)

	any winter sport
Total	**19.4%**
Age	
Aged 16 to 24	28.4
Aged 25 to 29	26.1
Aged 30 to 39	26.0
Aged 40 to 49	20.4
Aged 50 to 59	13.2
Aged 60 or older	4.9
Income	
Under $15,000	10.4
$15,000 to $24,999	13.5
$25,000 to $49,999	21.0
$50,000 to $74,999	25.9
$75,000 to $99,999	28.8
$100,000 or more	31.4
Sex	
Men	22.0
Women	17.1
Race and Hispanic origin	
White	21.3
Black	7.9
Other, including Hispanic	14.6
Education	
Not a high school graduate	16.1
High school graduate	14.8
Some college	20.5
College graduate	24.9
Number of persons in household	
One	12.9
Two	15.0
Three	21.8
Four	26.4
Five or more	26.0

(continued)

(continued from previous page)

	any winter sport
Number of persons aged 16 or older in household	
One	14.3%
Two	20.0
Three or more	23.4
Number of persons under age 6 in household	
None	18.1
One or more	24.5

Source: USDA Forest Service, 1994-95 National Survey on Recreation and the Environment

Cross-Country Skiing

Who cross-country skis:	• *middle-aged adults* • *whites* • *college graduates*
Trends in cross-country skiing:	• *groomed trails* • *simpler equipment* • *more older skiers*

Only 3 percent of Americans aged 16 or older have been cross-country skiing in the past 12 months. This is less than half the percentage of people who have been downhill skiing. Unlike in downhill skiing, however, participation in cross-country skiing increases with age, peaking at over 4 percent in the 40-to-59 age group. Only 1 percent of Americans aged 60 or older have been cross-country skiing in the past year.

The popularity of cross-country skiing rises with income. More than 6 percent of people living in households with incomes of $100,000 or more have been cross-country skiing in the past 12 months. Participation is below average for those with household incomes under $50,000.

Men are slightly more likely to cross-country ski than women, 3.5 versus 3 percent. Whites are much more likely to participate than blacks—4 versus 0.4 percent. Behind this difference is the fact that most blacks live in the South, where fewer op-

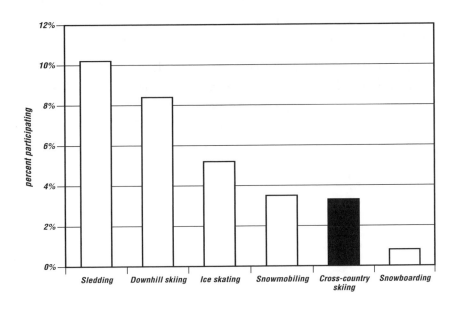

portunities to cross-country ski exist. People of "other" race (primarily Asians and Hispanics) are also less likely than whites to cross-country ski, with just 2 percent having participated in the past 12 months.

Cross-country skiing participation rises sharply with education. College graduates are the only ones to have an above-average rate of participation, at 6 percent.

Participation in cross-country skiing does not vary much by household size. It is more popular, however, among adults without preschoolers at home.

The Future of Cross-Country Skiing

Although cross-country skiing is appealing for many reasons, Paul Peterson, owner and manager of the Bear Valley Cross Country Ski Area in California, says the sport "is like a big secret. As a ski sport, it's really easy to learn. You can plop your skis down and go. You don't have to make it a vacation. And you have to earn your thrill."

One reason why few people participate in the sport is the perception that it is "a horrendous amount of physical exercise, which it doesn't have to be," Peterson says. Another reason is the competition Nordic skiing faces from other sports—in particular, mountain biking and in-line skating.

But the secret sport may not be so secret anymore. Some snow sports experts forecast a boom in cross-country skiing. The most encouraging development for the sport is the reduction in what Peterson calls "the misery factor." Groomed and marked trails make it a more civilized, predictable experience. "Twenty years ago, cross-country skiing was more of a mountaineering sport. You had to be good with a map, a compass, and first aid," Peterson says.

Waxless skis are another advance making the sport easier for the amateur. "You would have needed a degree in chemistry to figure out what wax you needed," says Peterson. "Now anyone can do it, anytime."

The growing media attention to the sport, as well as the fact that it can be enjoyed by families and older people, could lead to a surge in interest. "We're ready for them," Peterson says.

Participation in Cross-Country Skiing

(percent of persons aged 16 or older who participated in cross-country skiing at least once in the past year, by selected demographic characteristics, 1994-95)

Total	**3.3%**
Age	
Aged 16 to 24	3.5
Aged 25 to 29	3.5
Aged 30 to 39	3.7
Aged 40 to 49	4.4
Aged 50 to 59	4.0
Aged 60 or older	1.2
Income	
Under $15,000	1.4
$15,000 to $24,999	2.1
$25,000 to $49,999	3.2
$50,000 to $74,999	5.3
$75,000 to $99,999	5.9
$100,000 or more	6.2
Sex	
Men	3.5
Women	3.0
Race and Hispanic origin	
White	3.8
Black	0.4
Other, including Hispanic	1.7
Education	
Not a high school graduate	1.7
High school graduate	1.5
Some college	2.9
College graduate	6.2
Number of persons in household	
One	2.6
Two	3.4
Three	3.4
Four	3.7
Five or more	3.2

(continued)

(continued from previous page)

Number of persons aged	
16 or older in household	
One	2.7%
Two	3.4
Three or more	3.4
Number of persons under	
age 6 in household	
None	3.4
One or more	2.6

Source: USDA Forest Service, 1994-95 National Survey on Recreation and the Environment

Downhill Skiing

Who downhill skis:

- *young adults*
- *high-income households*
- *college graduates*

Trends in downhill skiing:

- *customized lift tickets*
- *family-oriented resorts*

Eight percent of Americans aged 16 or older have been downhill skiing at least once in the past 12 months, making it the second-most-popular winter sport after sledding. Participation in downhill skiing is greatest among young adults, with 16 percent of people aged 16 to 24 having participated in the past year. Participation is almost as high, at 14 percent, among 25-to-29-year-olds. It remains above average for people in their 30s, then falls to 8 percent for those in their 40s. Few people aged 50 or older downhill ski.

Downhill skiing is linked to income more than to any other demographic variable. Behind this relationship is the relatively high cost of ski equipment, lift tickets, and travel to ski resorts. Twenty-one percent of people in households with incomes of $100,000 or more have been downhill skiing at least once in the past 12 months. Participation is also above average in households with incomes of $50,000 to $99,999, but it is well below average in households with incomes under $50,000.

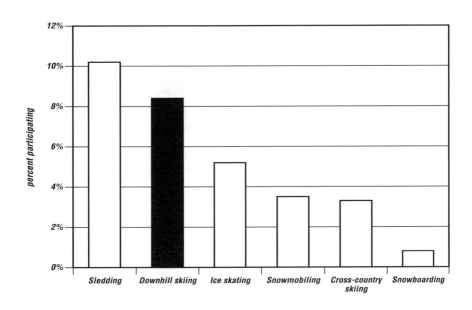

Men are more likely to downhill ski than women, 11 versus 7 percent. Whites are more likely to do so than blacks and people of "other" race (primarily Asians and Hispanics). Skiing participation rises with education—probably because well-educated people tend to have higher incomes. Thirteen percent of college graduates have been downhill skiing at least once in the past 12 months.

Downhill skiing is somewhat more popular in larger households—probably because large households are more likely to include young adults. But unlike with cross-country skiing, participation in downhill skiing does not vary by the presence of preschoolers in the home.

The Future of Downhill Skiing

"Skiing is the opportunity to dance with nature—to swoop and float down a slope with no other accouterments but your skis and gravity," says Charlie Leocha, author of the guidebooks *Ski America* and *Ski Europe*.

As if that isn't enough, downhill skiing provides a complete escape from "the hustle and bustle of the everyday world. I don't know anyone who skis down a mountain worries about the thirty-year bond," he says.

The sport isn't cheap. Not only is the equipment costly, but lift tickets are also expensive. To top it off, most people must travel some distance to get to a ski area. According to Snowsports Industries of America, alpine skiers travel an average of 3.3 hours to get to a ski resort.

"The cost is keeping people away," says Leocha. To control costs, he thinks "megaresorts will begin to break into smaller pieces." Instead of selling lift tickets allowing unlimited access to all ski lifts in a resort, they will offer customized lift tickets allowing skiers to choose the lifts they want to use and the number of times they want to use them. This could be accomplished through a computer chip in the lift ticket itself. Behind this trend are the budgetary constraints of families.

Skiing competes not so much with other sports as it does with other vacation options, like going to Europe or Disney World, Leocha notes. Because of this, he thinks ski resorts will begin to cater more to family vacationers.

On the slopes, downhill skiing is losing ground to snowboarding. In 20 years, Leocha predicts, resorts will be 30 percent downhill skiing, and 70 percent snowboarding. But downhill skiing won't disappear. New and more specialized equipment, like parabolic skis, will continue to attract people.

Participation in Downhill Skiing

(percent of persons aged 16 or older who participated in downhill skiing at least once in the past year, by selected demographic characteristics, 1994-95)

Total	**8.4%**
Age	
Aged 16 to 24	15.5
Aged 25 to 29	14.3
Aged 30 to 39	9.9
Aged 40 to 49	8.0
Aged 50 to 59	3.9
Aged 60 or older	1.0
Income	
Under $15,000	3.7
$15,000 to $24,999	4.6
$25,000 to $49,999	7.8
$50,000 to $74,999	11.9
$75,000 to $99,999	14.8
$100,000 or more	20.7
Sex	
Men	10.5
Women	6.5
Race and Hispanic origin	
White	9.3
Black	2.7
Other, including Hispanic	7.1
Education	
Not a high school graduate	7.5
High school graduate	4.5
Some college	8.7
College graduate	12.6
Number of persons in household	
One	6.6
Two	7.4
Three	9.7
Four	9.5
Five or more	10.0

(continued)

(continued from previous page)

**Number of persons aged
16 or older in household**

One	6.5%
Two	7.9
Three or more	11.3

**Number of persons under
age 6 in household**

None	8.5
One or more	8.2

Source: USDA Forest Service, 1994-95 National Survey on Recreation and the Environment

Ice Skating

Who ice skates:

- *young adults*

Trends in ice skating:

- *more older people*
- *oversaturation by the media*

Only 5 percent of Americans aged 16 or older have been ice skating at least once in the past 12 months. Those most likely to ice skate are young adults aged 16 to 24, with a participation rate of 10 percent. While ice skating participation falls with age, it remains above average to age 50.

Participation in ice skating is above average for people in households with incomes of $50,000 or more, peaking at 9 percent for those with household incomes of $75,000 to $99,999. Ice skating is one of the few sports in which women are as likely to participate as men.

Ice skating is much more popular among whites than among blacks and people of "other" race (primarily Asians and Hispanics). Participation in ice skating increases sharply with household size because larger households are more likely to include young adults—the age group most likely to ice skate.

The Future of Ice Skating

Ice skating interests people of all ages, says Cindy Lang, in charge of public relations for Ice-Castle, an international training center and ice rink in California.

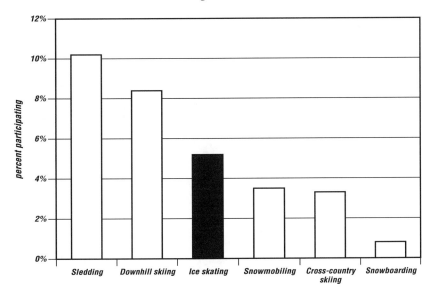

Although the sport is dominated by young people, especially at the competitive level, the United States Figure Skating Association's adult competitors series is encouraging more adults to participate. "People are competing at the age of 40 or 50 years old," Lang says.

Ice skating is experiencing a boom thanks to the media attention on figure skating's many stars. The infamous Nancy Kerrigan/Tonya Harding conflict also brought a lot of attention to the sport.

"The last years have been the craziest years," Lang says. "Ice skating has become huge—more than anyone could have imagined." Although she says more rinks are being built, she doesn't think the boom can last. "It's cyclical," she explains.

But today, at the peak, things are looking good. Almost every weekend, an ice-skating competition is televised. Lang thinks the point of oversaturation is fast approaching. "All the competition is counterproductive to the sport," she says.

Behind the appeal of the sport are ice skating's unique qualities, Lang says. "It's a combination of athletics and aesthetics."

The best hope for ice skating's future is to keep producing ice-skating stars—especially Olympic winners. Lang thinks this will happen. "In the United States, we're producing some of the best figure skaters in the world," she says.

Participation in Ice Skating

(percent of persons aged 16 or older who participated in ice skating at least once in the past year, by selected demographic characteristics, 1994-95)

Total	**5.2%**
Age	
Aged 16 to 24	9.9
Aged 25 to 29	6.2
Aged 30 to 39	6.7
Aged 40 to 49	5.6
Aged 50 to 59	2.5
Aged 60 or older	0.8
Income	
Under $15,000	2.7
$15,000 to $24,999	3.0
$25,000 to $49,999	5.4
$50,000 to $74,999	7.4
$75,000 to $99,999	8.6
$100,000 or more	7.7
Sex	
Men	5.2
Women	5.3
Race and Hispanic origin	
White	5.9
Black	1.7
Other, including Hispanic	2.6
Education	
Not a high school graduate	5.6
High school graduate	3.7
Some college	5.3
College graduate	6.6
Number of persons in household	
One	2.7
Two	3.3
Three	6.1
Four	7.5
Five or more	8.9

(continued)

(continued from previous page)

Number of persons aged
16 or older in household

One	3.4%
Two	5.2
Three or more	7.2

Number of persons under
age 6 in household

None	4.9
One or more	6.7

Source: USDA Forest Service, 1994-95 National Survey on Recreation and the Environment

Sledding

Who sleds:	• *young and middle-aged adults*
	• *whites*
	• *families with children*
Trends in sledding:	• *more sledding at resorts*
	• *more older people*

Ten percent of Americans aged 16 or older have been sledding in the past 12 months, making sledding the most popular winter sport—ahead of downhill skiing and ice skating.

Sledding participation peaks in two age groups. Nearly 16 percent of 16-to-24-year-olds have been sledding in the past year. The proportion dips slightly among 25-to-29-year-olds, then rises again to nearly 16 percent among people in their 30s. Behind this pattern is children's enthusiasm for sledding. Not only do teens enjoy the activity, but people in their 30s are big participants because so many have children who sled. Sledding participation falls to 11 percent among people in their 40s, then drops to 4 percent among those in their 50s. Fewer than 2 percent of people in their 60s have been sledding in the past 12 months.

Sledding participation is above-average at most income levels. It is below average only among those with household incomes under $25,000. Behind the lower par-

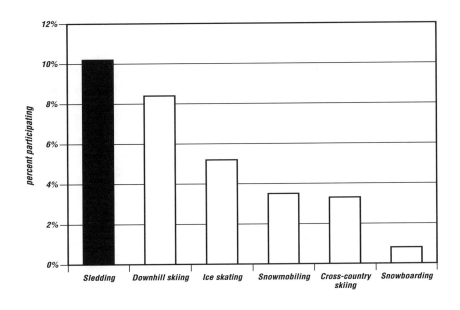

ticipation rate of this income group is the fact that many low-income householders are retirees—the age group least likely to participate in sledding.

Men are only slightly more likely to sled than women. Whites are much more likely to sled than blacks—12 versus 3 percent. Behind this difference is the fact that most blacks live in the South, where the warm climate limits participation in winter sports. Sledding is slightly more popular among the college educated than among those with less education.

The biggest factor driving participation in sledding is the presence of children in the home. This is why people living in larger households (which are more likely to include children) are much more likely to sled (18 percent) than those living in small households. It also explains why adults living with preschoolers are much more likely to sled than those without young children at home—17 versus 9 percent.

The Future of Sledding

"Ski area managers are finding that people are interested in snow play. Vacationers want a diversity of snow sports," says Diane Scholfield, freelance snow sports journalist. Snowboarding paved the way, and now the door is open for sledding, snowshoeing, tubing, ice skating, and anything else that gets someone active in a winter environment, she says.

What's behind all this snow play? One group of enthusiasts is made up of dedicated skiers and snowboarders who like winter sports for their own sake. Others simply enjoy being outdoors in the winter. It is this second group to whom snow play is most appealing. This group includes families with children who are too young to downhill or cross-country ski. It also includes older people who do not want the risk associated with more physically challenging winter sports. And it includes people who participate in traditional winter sports but want a break from their regular activities.

"The diversity of equipment on the mountain lets you pick whatever is going to give you the most fun. People want a different experience," she concludes.

Participation in Sledding

(percent of persons aged 16 or older who participated in sledding at least once in the past year, by selected demographic characteristics, 1994-95)

Total	**10.2 %**
Age	
Aged 16 to 24	15.7
Aged 25 to 29	13.0
Aged 30 to 39	15.7
Aged 40 to 49	10.5
Aged 50 to 59	4.4
Aged 60 or older	1.8
Income	
Under $15,000	4.9
$15,000 to $24,999	7.2
$25,000 to $49,999	11.4
$50,000 to $74,999	14.4
$75,000 to $99,999	13.9
$100,000 or more	12.2
Sex	
Men	10.8
Women	9.7
Race and Hispanic origin	
White	11.5
Black	3.2
Other, including Hispanic	5.9
Education	
Not a high school graduate	9.8
High school graduate	8.3
Some college	11.2
College graduate	11.6
Number of persons in household	
One	4.6
Two	5.8
Three	11.4
Four	17.0
Five or more	17.6

(continued)

(continued from previous page)

Number of persons aged
16 or older in household

One	6.4%
Two	11.0
Three or more	12.5

Number of persons under
age 6 in household

None	8.6
One or more	16.6

Source: USDA Forest Service, 1994-95 National Survey on Recreation and the Environment

Snowboarding

Who snowboards:

- **young adults**

Trends in snowboarding:

- **more older people**
- **better equipment**

Among Americans aged 16 or older, fewer than 1 percent have been snowboarding in the past 12 months. Although snowboarding supposedly is one of the "hot" sports among young adults, only 1.5 percent of 16-to-24-year-olds have been snowboarding in the past year. This compares with 16 percent who have been downhill skiing and 4 percent who have been cross-country skiing. In the 25-to-29 age group, 1 percent participated in snowboarding in the past 12 months. The share drops below 1 percent among people aged 30 or older.

Participation in snowboarding does not vary much by income. Men are slightly more likely to snowboard than women, 1 versus 0.7 percent. People of "other" race (primarily Asians and Hispanics) are slightly more likely to snowboard than both whites and blacks.

Reflecting the fact that many snowboarders are young adults, people who have not graduated from high school are most likely to snowboard—many of them still high school students. Snowboarding is more popular in large households because large households are most likely to include young adults.

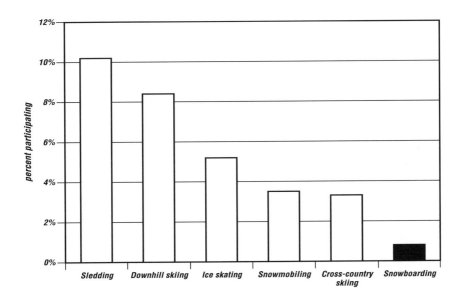

The Future of Snowboarding

Snowboarding has received more media coverage than its few adult participants would seem to warrant. But the adult participation figures may be misleading, since most snowboarders are under age 18. According to estimates by the National Sporting Goods Association, the number of snowboarders has increased by 800,000 since 1990, reaching 2.3 million in 1995.

As happens with many sports, people are introduced to snowboarding by a friend who shows them how to do it, says Jack Turner, former member of the U.S. ski team and snow sports industry expert. Snowboarding is a sport that carries the image of rebellious youth. This makes it a "whole social thing," says Turner. Teenagers see their heroes doing it and want to become involved.

For a sport that did not exist a few years ago, it has gained acceptance quickly and is now welcomed at almost every ski resort in the country. "The industry is maturing," says Turner. Although its growth rate will eventually flatten, he doesn't think snowboarding is a passing fad. It is here to stay.

What's so great about this hybrid sport? "Most people have no danger in their lives," Turner explains. Danger is snowboarding's appeal. "Hypothetically, you can get hurt," he says. "These are real mountains, real trees. Snowboarding functions as an oasis of excitement."

Despite the perception that snowboarding is for "young radicals" while skiing is for "old Republicans," Turner says, older people are getting involved in the sport. This trend is likely to pick up momentum as snowboarding equipment becomes easier and more comfortable to use.

Participation in Snowboarding

(percent of persons aged 16 or older who participated in snowboarding at least once in the past year, by selected demographic characteristics, 1994-95)

Total	**0.8%**
Age	
Aged 16 to 24	1.5
Aged 25 to 29	1.1
Aged 30 to 39	0.9
Aged 40 to 49	0.9
Aged 50 to 59	0.6
Aged 60 or older	0.1
Income	
Under $15,000	0.8
$15,000 to $24,999	0.6
$25,000 to $49,999	1.0
$50,000 to $74,999	1.0
$75,000 to $99,999	0.6
$100,000 or more	0.9
Sex	
Men	1.0
Women	0.7
Race and Hispanic origin	
White	0.8
Black	0.5
Other, including Hispanic	1.0
Education	
Not a high school graduate	1.3
High school graduate	0.8
Some college	0.8
College graduate	0.7
Number of persons in household	
One	0.5
Two	0.5
Three	0.9
Four	1.1
Five or more	1.5

(continued)

(continued from previous page)

Number of persons aged 16 or older in household	
One	0.7%
Two	0.6
Three or more	1.4
Number of persons under age 6 in household	
None	0.8
One or more	1.0

Source: USDA Forest Service, 1994-95 National Survey on Recreation and the Environment

Snowmobiling

Who snowmobiles:	• *young and middle-aged adults*
	• *men*
	• *families*
Trends in snowmobiling:	• *expanded trail systems*

Snowmobiling is slightly more popular than cross-country skiing among Americans aged 16 or older, with 3.5 percent having participated in the past 12 months. Participation is highest among 16-to-24-year-olds, at nearly 6 percent. Participation remains above average for people aged 25 to 39, then falls with age to a tiny 0.8 percent of people aged 60 or older.

Snowmobiling participation is above average for people in households with incomes of $25,000 or more. It peaks among those with household incomes between $75,000 and $99,999, at over 5 percent. Men are more likely to snowmobile than women, 4.7 versus 2.5 percent.

Whites are four times more likely to snowmobile than blacks. Behind the lower participation of blacks is the fact that most live in the South, where the warm climate limits participation in winter sports.

College graduates are less likely to snowmobile than people with less education. Because snowmobiling is often a family activity, people living in larger house-

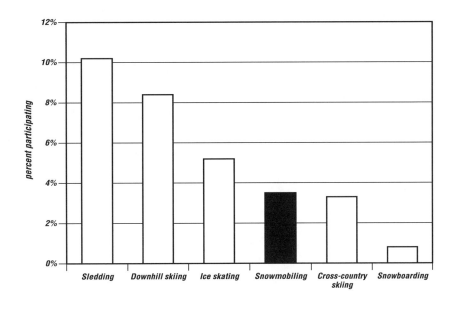

holds (which often include teens and young adults) are more likely to snowmobile than those living in smaller households. In addition, households with preschoolers are more likely to snowmobile than those without preschoolers at home.

The Future of Snowmobiling

Most snowmobilers become involved in the activity through friends and family, says Chris Jourdain, executive director of the American Council of Snowmobile Associations. "It's fun, you get to see a lot of the country, and it's exciting," she says.

Snowmobiling is different from what it was 20 years ago. Vehicles are quieter and more sophisticated. "Snowmobiles have dramatically improved," says Jourdain, providing features like hand warmers and better suspension. In the future, features "that used to be considered a luxury will become standard—like reverse, and mirrors."

Another development in snowmobiling is a more-extensive trail system, built because of the dedication of snowmobilers themselves. "Snowmobilers take care of their own trails. They rebuild bridges, brush them out, and groom them all winter," she says. The trail system will continue to grow, eventually approaching an organized interstate system.

"If you're in shape, you can snowmobile," Jourdain says. The growing awareness of physical fitness will help boost the sport's numbers. The more snowmobilers there are, the better it is for the economy, she says. "Snowmobiles allow businesses that used to shut down for the winter to become year-round. It's created a big boom in business in a lot of northern states."

Participation in Snowmobiling

(percent of persons aged 16 or older who participated in snowmobiling at least once in the past year, by selected demographic characteristics, 1994-95)

Total	**3.5%**
Age	
Aged 16 to 24	5.9
Aged 25 to 29	5.4
Aged 30 to 39	4.7
Aged 40 to 49	3.0
Aged 50 to 59	2.1
Aged 60 or older	0.8
Income	
Under $15,000	1.3
$15,000 to $24,999	2.6
$25,000 to $49,999	4.5
$50,000 to $74,999	4.6
$75,000 to $99,999	5.4
$100,000 or more	4.3
Sex	
Men	4.7
Women	2.5
Race and Hispanic origin	
White	4.0
Black	1.0
Other, including Hispanic	2.1
Education	
Not a high school graduate	3.7
High school graduate	3.8
Some college	3.9
College graduate	2.9
Number of persons in household	
One	2.4
Two	2.7
Three	4.5
Four	4.4
Five or more	4.6

(continued)

(continued from previous page)

Number of persons aged
16 or older in household

One	2.6%
Two	3.6
Three or more	4.4

Number of persons under
age 6 in household

None	3.3
One or more	4.7

Source: USDA Forest Service, 1994-95 National Survey on Recreation and the Environment

Spending on Winter Sports Equipment

Spending on winter sports equipment is dominated by young adults. Spending peaks among householders aged 35 to 44, who spend 78 percent more than the average household on sleds, ice skates, skis, and other winter sports equipment. Two-thirds of all spending on these items is controlled by householders aged 25 to 44. Most of these big spenders are parents, buying equipment for themselves and their children.

Spending on winter sports equipment rises sharply with income. Households with incomes of $100,000 or more spend three times more than the average household on these items, controlling 42 percent of all household spending in this market. Many affluent households are purchasing downhill skis, while lower-income households are buying sleds, ice skates, and other less-expensive equipment.

College graduates spend twice as much as the average household on winter sports equipment. Whites far outspend both blacks and "others" (primarily Asians and Hispanics) on these items.

Married couples with children aged 6 to 17 spend more than twice as much as the average household on winter sports equipment. Married couples without children at home, many of them empty nesters, also spend more than average on these items. Many couples with children are probably buying sleds and ice skates, while older couples are buying cross-country and downhill ski equipment.

Not surprisingly, households in the Northeast spend the most on winter sports equipment—92 percent more than the average household. Those in the Midwest also spend more than average, while households in the South spend 70 percent less than the average household on winter sports equipment.

Spending on Winter Sports Equipment, 1995

(average annual, indexed, and market share of spending by consumer units on winter sports equipment, by selected demographic characteristics, 1995; index definition: 100 is the average; an index of 132 means that spending by consumer units in the segment is 32 percent above average; an index of 68 means spending by consumer units in the segment is 32 percent below average)

	average	index	market share
Total	**$3.78**	**100**	**100.0%**
Age			
Under age 25	4.84	128	8.8
Aged 25 to 34	5.48	145	27.4
Aged 35 to 44	6.72	178	40.4
Aged 45 to 54	3.26	86	15.6
Aged 55 to 64	1.45	38	4.7
Aged 65 or older	0.53	14	3.0
Income			
Under $20,000	1.09	29	10.9
$20,000 to $29,999	2.40	64	9.8
$30,000 to $39,999	3.78	101	12.9
$40,000 to $49,999	2.18	58	5.7
$50,000 to $69,999	5.62	151	18.8
$70,000 or more	12.30	330	41.9
Race			
White and "other"	4.22	112	99.0
Black	0.30	8	0.9
Hispanic origin			
Non-Hispanic	4.09	108	99.8
Hispanic	-	-	-
Education			
Not a high school graduate	0.50	13	2.8
High school graduate only	3.16	84	26.8
Some college	3.08	81	18.6
College graduate	8.06	213	51.7

(continued)

(continued from previous page)

	average	index	market share
Household type			
Married couples, total	$5.67	150	78.6%
Married couple only	4.72	125	26.7
Married couple with children	6.65	176	47.7
Oldest child under age 6	6.42	170	9.1
Oldest child aged 6 to 17	7.90	209	29.8
Oldest child aged 18 or older	4.42	117	8.8
Single parent with children under 18	2.30	61	4.0
Single-person	2.15	57	16.1
Region			
Northeast	7.27	192	38.5
Midwest	4.98	132	33.1
South	1.15	30	10.4
West	3.26	86	18.0

Note: The average spending figures are extremely low because both purchasers and non-purchasers are included in the calculation. While the average spending figures do not show how much buyers of winter sports equipment spend, the patterns revealed by the index and market share figures do show who is most likely to spend on winter sports equipment and how much spending is controlled by each demographic segment. (-) means sample is too small to make a reliable estimate.
Source: Bureau of Labor Statistics, 1995 Consumer Expenditure Survey; calculations by New Strategist

Chapter 10

High School Sports Participation

Many of the sports enjoyed by teenagers today will become popular sport and fitness activities among adults tomorrow. An examination of teen sports participation reveals several important trends.

Perhaps most important is the dramatic increase in the number of girls participating in sports. Title IX allowed girls equal access to high school athletics, and with that change came a surge in the number of girls taking part in sports. Today, girls constitute about 40 percent of participants in high school sports. When they grow up, their interest in sports is likely to continue. Expect them to organize more women's team sports in communities across the country and to boost women's participation in individual sports as well.

Budget tightening is another trend in teen sports. Sports programs are often targeted for cutbacks when schools must trim expenses. To make ends meet, many schools are asking parents to fund their children's sports programs. Others are taking a cue from professional sports and turning toward sponsorships. Companies such as Nike and Adidas are providing some schools with free footwear, apparel, and even stipends for coaches.

A third trend in teen athletics is the growing popularity of individual sports. In part, this is due to the recognition by physical education programs that adult fitness starts young. Consequently, these programs now stress lifetime sports. Also contributing to the trend is that teens today spend more time alone than did previous generations because so many have working parents. Some of them spend that time engaged in individual sports. Summer camps have also contributed to the growth of individual sports among teens. "Camps continue to be a place to participate in non-traditional sports activities," explains Bob Schultz, public relations director for the American Camping Association, an educational organization that accredits summer camps. While old stand-bys such as baseball and swimming are still alive and well, camp directors are continually adding new activities to the mix.

"In the last ten years, camps have gone from team sports to a renewed emphasis on individual challenge, mental strength, and problem solving," Schultz explains. Teenagers, he says, are "rugged individuals" and the segment of the population most interested in adventure sports. Camps are responding to the demand by adding activities like rock climbing, caving, rappelling, and white-water rafting.

Participation in High School Athletics

The number of girls participating in high school athletics has grown sharply over the past 25 years, thanks to Title IX. This law, passed in 1972, gave girls equal access to high school athletic programs. The number of girls participating in high school athletics soared from 294,000 in 1971-72 to more than 2 million just six years later. By 1995-96, the 2.4 million girls taking part in high school athletics accounted for 40 percent of the 6 million total participants, up from a tiny 7 percent of participants in 1971-72.

The number of participants in high school athletics is also affected by the size of each generation. The number of boys and girls in high school athletics fell in the late 1970s and early 1980s because the small Generation X was in its teens. By the early 1990s, the number of participants was on the rise again as the high school population expanded. The growth of high school athletics should continue as the baby boomlet (the children of the baby-boom generation) enters its teens. The number of births peaked in 1990. This group won't reach high school age until after the turn of the century.

More Girls Play Sports

(girls as a percent of total participants in high school athletics, 1971-72 to 1995-96)

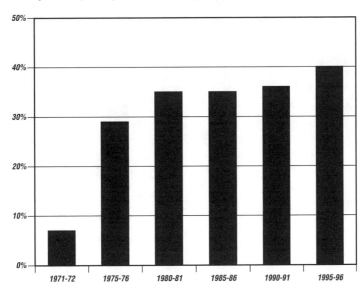

Participation in High School Athletics by Sex, 1971-72 to 1995-96

(number and percent distribution of persons participating in high school athletics by sex, 1971-72 to 1995-96)

	number			percent	
	total	boys	girls	boys	girls
1995-96	6,001,988	3,634,052	2,367,936	60.5%	39.5%
1994-95	5,776,820	3,536,359	2,240,461	61.2	38.8
1993-94	5,603,282	3,472,967	2,130,315	62.0	38.0
1992-93	5,413,878	3,416,389	1,997,489	63.1	36.9
1991-92	5,370,654	3,429,853	1,940,801	63.9	36.1
1990-91	5,298,671	3,406,355	1,892,316	64.3	35.7
1989-90	5,256,851	3,398,192	1,858,659	64.6	35.4
1988-89	5,256,196	3,416,844	1,839,352	65.0	35.0
1987-88	5,275,461	3,425,777	1,849,684	64.9	35.1
1986-87	5,200,438	3,364,082	1,836,356	64.7	35.3
1985-86	5,151,396	3,344,275	1,807,121	64.9	35.1
1984-85	5,112,168	3,354,284	1,757,884	65.6	34.4
1983-84	5,050,905	3,303,559	1,747,346	65.4	34.6
1982-83	5,135,530	3,355,558	1,779,972	65.3	34.7
1981-82	5,219,752	3,409,081	1,810,671	65.3	34.7
1980-81	5,356,913	3,503,124	1,853,789	65.4	34.6
1979-80	5,268,093	3,517,829	1,750,264	66.8	33.2
1978-79	5,563,912	3,709,512	1,854,400	66.7	33.3
1977-78	6,450,482	4,367,442	2,083,040	67.7	32.3
1975-76	5,754,060	4,109,021	1,645,039	71.4	28.6
1973-74	5,370,294	4,070,125	1,300,169	75.8	24.2
1972-73	4,587,694	3,770,621	817,073	82.2	17.8
1971-72	3,960,932	3,666,917	294,015	92.6	7.4

Source: National Federation of State High School Associations, 1996 High School Athletics Participation Survey

Participation in High School Athletics by Sport

In high school athletics, many sports are still dominated by boys. These include some of the most-popular programs, such as baseball, football, and wrestling. Other sports in which boys account for over 90 percent of participants are archery, decathlon, and ice hockey.

Girls account for over 90 percent of participants in competitive spirit squads, both fast-pitch and slow-pitch softball, volleyball, heptathalon, and field hockey.

A variety of sports are evenly split between male and female participants. These include basketball, bowling, crew, cross-country running, fencing, both alpine and Nordic skiing, soccer, tennis, and indoor and outdoor track and field.

Participation in High School Athletics by Sport and Sex, 1995-96

(number of persons participating in high school athletics by sport, and percent distribution of participants by sex, 1995-96)

	total number	percent	
		boys	girls
Archery	117	91.5%	8.5%
Badminton	11,371	29.1	70.9
Baseball	445,816	99.7	0.3
Basketball	991,465	55.0	45.0
Bowling	15,422	52.5	47.5
Canoeing	462	41.3	58.7
Competitive spirit squads	33,279	1.6	98.4
Crew	2,003	51.8	48.2
Cross-country running	308,390	54.5	45.5
Decathalon	140	91.4	8.6
Equestrian	422	18.5	81.5
Fencing	1,219	56.8	43.2
Field hockey	56,142	0.0	100.0
Football (11 players)	958,364	99.9	0.1
Football (9 players)	6,179	100.0	0.0
Football (8 players)	13,384	99.9	0.1
Football (6 players)	4,372	99.7	0.3
Golf	179,645	77.9	22.1
Gymnastics	22,033	12.0	88.0
Heptathlon	63	0.0	100.0
Ice hockey	25,752	94.3	5.7
Judo	165	86.1	13.9
Lacrosse	38,818	62.1	37.9
Pentathalon	19	78.9	21.1
Riflery	2,504	75.2	24.8
Skiing (cross-country)	8,189	50.7	49.3
Skiing (downhill)	10,318	56.3	43.7
Soccer	493,015	57.5	42.5
Softball (fast pitch)	307,149	0.6	99.4
Softball (slow pitch)	34,356	0.5	99.5
Swimming and diving	192,360	42.1	57.9
Tennis	283,107	48.2	51.8
Track and field (indoor)	79,335	52.9	47.1
Track and field (outdoor)	833,705	54.5	45.5
Volleyball	389,129	8.1	91.9
Water polo	14,802	69.2	30.8
Weight lifting	15,784	86.3	13.7
Wrestling	222,326	99.5	0.5

Source: National Federation of State High School Associations, 1996 High School Athletics Participation Survey

Most-Popular High School Sports

Basketball is the most widely available high school sport for both boys and girls, offered by more than 16,000 schools nationwide. In second place is track and field, offered to boys and girls in more than 14,000 high schools across the country.

Football is the fourth-most-offered boy's sport program, available in 13,000 schools, but it ranks number one in participants. Nearly 1 million high school boys played football in 1995-96. Far behind in second place is basketball, with 546,000 boys participating.

Among girls, basketball is number one in participants, with 446,000 high school girls on the courts in 1995-96. It is followed by track and field and volleyball, each with more than 300,000 participants.

Some high school sports rank among the top ten in participants among both boys and girls. They are: basketball, track and field, soccer, tennis, cross-country running, golf, and swimming. Several sports are in the top 10 for one sex, but don't make the cut with the opposite sex. For boys, they are football, baseball, and wrestling. For girls, they are volleyball, fast-pitch softball, and field hockey.

Top Ten High School Sports Programs and Sports by Sex, 1995-96

(number of schools with sports program for the 10 most widely offered sports and number of partici-pants for the 10 most-popular high school sports by sex, 1995-96)

Most Widely Offered

BOYS
Number of schools

Basketball	16,574
Track and field (outdoor)	14,505
Baseball	14,174
Football	13,004
Golf	11,394
Cross-country running	11,360
Tennis	9,214
Wrestling	8,677
Soccer	8,182
Swiming and diving	4,852

Most Popular

Number of participants

Football	957,573
Basketball	545,596
Track and field (outdoors)	454,645
Baseball	444,476
Soccer	283,728
Wrestling	221,162
Cross-country running	168,203
Golf	140,011
Tennis	136,534
Swimming and diving	81,000

GIRLS
Number of schools

Basketball	16,198
Track and field (outdoors)	14,410
Volleyball	12,669
Softball (fast pitch)	11,452
Cross-country running	10,774
Tennis	9,165
Soccer	6,526
Golf	5,469
Swimming and diving	4,948
Competitive spirit squads	1,913

Number of participants

Basketball	445,869
Track and field (outdoor)	379,060
Volleyball	357,576
Softball (fast pitch)	305,217
Soccer	209,287
Tennis	146,573
Cross-country running	140,187
Swimming and diving	111,360
Field hockey	56,142
Golf	39,634

Source: National Federation of State High School Associations, 1996 High School Athletics Participation Survey

Participation in High School Athletics by State

Although participation in high school athletics is influenced by the number of high schoolers living in a state, it is also affected by the degree to which different states emphasize sports in high school and encourage children to participate. Thus, although California is the nation's number one state in population, it ranks number two in the number of high school students participating in sports. Texas is number one by far in participation, with a margin of almost 200,000 participants.

Some differences in athletic participation by state can be accounted for by the age structure of a state's population. Florida, for example, ranks only 11th in high school athletic participation although it is fourth in overall population. Behind Florida's relatively low ranking is the fact that many of the state's residents are elderly.

Participation in High School Athletics by State, 1995-96

(number of participants in high school athletics by state, 1995-96)

Texas	706,847
California	514,139
New York	301,702
Illinois	296,840
Ohio	277,993
Michigan	270,420
Pennsylvania	226,361
New Jersey	198,065
Wisconsin	164,090
Massachusetts	162,909
Florida	160,585
Indiana	152,776
Missouri	148,128
Iowa	145,428
Washington	138,902
Minnesota	131,673
North Carolina	122,940
Georgia	122,087
Virginia	115,529
Oregon	99,597
Kansas	96,696
Colorado	92,156
Maryland	82,334
Louisiana	80,578
Tennessee	80,253
Nebraska	78,960
Alabama	78,609
Connecticut	77,256
Arizona	76,536
Kentucky	74,148
Oklahoma	71,070
South Carolina	67,353
Mississippi	65,033
Arkansas	60,634
Maine	49,485
Utah	47,169
Idaho	39,959
New Mexico	37,571

(continued)

(continued from previous page)

West Virgina	36,832
Montana	34,880
New Hampshire	33,072
South Dakota	29,713
Nevada	28,924
North Dakota	27,547
Hawaii	21,428
Delaware	20,256
Rhode Island	19,666
Wyoming	18,314
Vermont	17,468
Alaska	15,835
District of Columbia	3,143

Note: Participants are counted in each sport in which they participate. If they participate in two sports, they are counted twice. If they participate in three sports, they are counted three times.
Source: National Federation of State High School Associations, 1996 High School Athletics Participation Survey

Chapter 11

College Sports Participation

The number of men and women participating in National Collegiate Athletic Association (NCAA) sports increased 17 percent between 1982-83 and 1995-96, to more than 300,000. Behind this increase is the expansion in the number of women taking part in college athletic programs. Women's participation grew 45 percent between 1982-83 and 1995-96 as more colleges offered sports for women and as more women participated in sports. In contrast, the number of men participating in NCAA sports rose just 4.5 percent during those years.

Women represent a growing share of NCAA athletes. They accounted for 38 percent of total participants in 1995-96, up from 31 percent in the early 1980s. With teenaged girls accounting for 40 percent of participants in high school athletic programs, women's share of NCAA athletes may stabilize at about 40 percent.

Women Surge into College Sports

(percent increase in number of men and women participating in NCAA sports, 1982-83 to 1995-96)

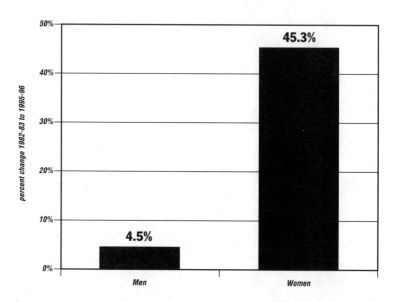

Participation in National Collegiate Athletic Association Sports by Sex, 1982-83 to 1995-96

(number and percent distribution of persons participating in National Collegiate Athletic Association sports by sex, 1982-83 to 1995-96)

	number			percent	
	total	*men*	*women*	*men*	*women*
1995-96	304,671	188,399	116,272	61.8%	38.2%
1994-95	299,608	189,084	110,524	63.1	36.9
1993-94	295,174	189,642	105,532	64.2	35.8
1992-93	286,900	187,038	99,859	65.2	34.8
1991-92	282,512	186,045	96,467	65.9	34.1
1990-91	277,371	184,593	92,778	66.6	33.4
1989-90	266,368	177,165	89,212	66.5	33.5
1988-89	271,550	180,145	91,409	66.3	33.7
1987-88	268,766	178,941	89,825	66.6	33.4
1986-87	281,118	190,017	91,101	67.6	32.4
1985-86	295,382	200,031	95,351	67.7	32.3
1984-85	292,732	201,063	91,669	68.7	31.3
1983-84	273,359	188,594	84,813	69.0	31.0
1982-83	260,875	180,235	80,040	69.1	30.7
Percent change					
1982-83 to 1995-96	16.8%	4.5%	45.3%	-	-

Source: National Collegiate Athletic Association's 1997 Participation Statistics Report, 1982-96. Reproduced with permission of the National Collegiate Athletic Association, 1997; this information is subject to annual review and change.

Men's Participation by Sport

Football has long been the most popular college sport, with big budgets, much-sought-after scholarships, and a national audience numbering in the millions. In 1995-96, nearly 54,000 men played National Collegiate Athletic Association (NCAA) football, making it number one in participation by far. Ranking second in popularity is track and field, with about 35,000 men participating. Baseball, soccer, basketball, and cross-country running also counted more than 10,000 male participants in 1995-96.

Growth in men's participation in NCAA athletics varies by sport. The number of men playing NCAA basketball fell 0.6 percent between 1966-67 and 1995-96. Other sports have had much steeper declines. The number of men participating in wrestling fell 19 percent during those years. Also down were men's swimming, crew, fencing, skiing, riflery, gymnastics, and squash.

One reason for men's declining participation is Title IX. This law, passed in 1972, requires colleges receiving federal funds to offer women equal access to sports programs. Schools have been scrambling to expand their sports programs for women, and some have done so by offering fewer sports to men. The percentage of NCAA-member schools offering men's wrestling, for example, fell from 46 to 27 percent between 1982-83 and 1995-96, which explains why fewer men are wrestling in college today than several decades ago.

Top Sports for College Men

(number of men participating in NCAA sports, for top ten sports)

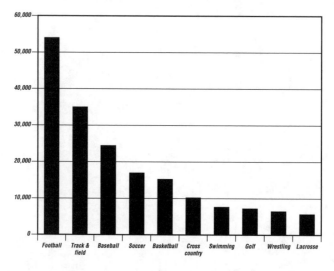

Men's Participation in the National Collegiate Athletic Association by Sport, 1966-67 and 1995-96

(number of men participating in the National Collegiate Athletic Association by sport, and percent change in participation, 1966-67 and 1995-96; ranked by number participating in 1995-96)

	1995-96	*1966-67*	*percent change, 1966-67 to 1995-96*
Football	53,900	36,799	46.5%
Track and field	34,926	18,697	86.8
Baseball	24,332	17,101	42.3
Soccer	16,885	10,370	62.8
Basketball	15,160	15,247	-0.6
Cross-country running	10,113	6,281	61.0
Tennis	7,961	7,155	11.3
Swimming	7,580	8,269	-8.3
Golf	7,163	6,160	16.3
Wrestling	6,385	7,889	-19.1
Lacrosse	5,592	4,620	21.0
Ice hockey	3,554	2,360	50.6
Rowing, crew	1,693	2,871	-41.0
Volleyball	1,053	405	160.0
Water polo	877	755	16.2
Fencing	731	1,337	-45.3
Skiing	504	928	-45.7
Riflery	481	1,776	-72.9
Gymnastics	457	1,938	-76.4
Squash	302	690	-56.2

Source: National Collegiate Athletic Association's 1997 Participation Statistics Report, 1982-96. Reproduced with permission of the National Collegiate Athletic Association, 1997; this information is subject to annual review and change.

Women's Participation by Sport

Women have surged into college athletic programs over the past few decades thanks to Title IX. This law, passed in 1972, requires schools receiving federal funds to provide women with equal access to sports programs. Not only has the variety of sports available to women expanded over the years, but the number of women participating in those sports has also grown rapidly.

The number of women participating in National Collegiate Athletic Association (NCAA) track and field grew the fastest. In 1966-67, a miniscule 309 women participated in track and field. By 1995-96, the figure stood at more than 28,000. Other NCAA sports with more than 10,000 women participating include soccer, basketball, softball, and volleyball.

All NCAA sports available to women have seen participation grow sharply. Field hockey—long a traditional women's sport—has experienced the slowest growth, up 54 percent since 1966-67. The number of women participating in fencing grew 77 percent. All other NCAA sports available to women have at least doubled in participation since the mid-1960s. Soccer, cross-country running, lacrosse, rowing, ice hockey, water polo, and squash were not available to college women in the 1960s. Today, more than 13,000 women play college soccer and nearly 10,000 take part in cross-country running.

Top Sports for College Women

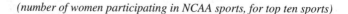

(number of women participating in NCAA sports, for top ten sports)

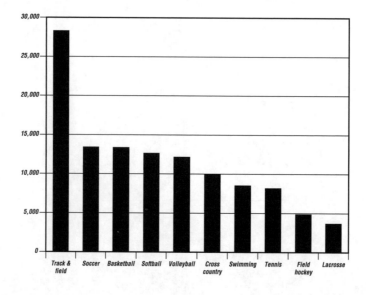

Women's Participation in the National Collegiate Athletic Association by Sport, 1966-67 and 1995-96

(number of women participating in the National Collegiate Athletic Association by sport, and percent change in participation, 1966-67 and 1995-96; ranked by number participating in 1995-96)

	1995-96	1966-67	percent change, 1966-67 to 1995-96
Track and field	28,254	309	9,043.7%
Soccer	13,394	-	-
Basketball	13,343	4,253	213.7
Softball	12,606	1,366	822.8
Volleyball	12,122	2,178	456.6
Cross-country running	9,949	-	-
Swimming	8,499	1,184	617.8
Tennis	8,156	1,361	499.3
Field hockey	4,828	3,126	54.4
Lacrosse	3,635	-	-
Rowing, crew	3,569	-	-
Golf	2,083	384	442.4
Gymnastics	1,323	579	128.5
Fencing	575	325	76.9
Skiing	455	117	288.9
Ice hockey	416	-	-
Water polo	365	-	-
Squash	364	-	-

Source: National Collegiate Athletic Association's 1997 Participation Statistics Report, 1982-96. Reproduced with permission of the National Collegiate Athletic Association, 1997; this information is subject to annual review and change.

College Sports Programs for Men

Participation in college sports depends largely on the number of colleges offering sports programs. Nearly every school belonging to the National Collegiate Athletic Association (NCAA) offers men's basketball, while more than 80 percent have men's baseball and cross-country running. Other men's sports offered by at least half the NCAA-member schools are football, golf, soccer, tennis, and indoor and outdoor track. Fewer than 10 percent of NCAA-member schools offer sports such as volleyball, rowing, skiing, or gymnastics for men.

For a variety of sports, the percentage of schools offering men's programs has been declining because of Title IX. This law, passed in 1972, requires colleges receiving federal funds to offer women equal access to sports programs. After passage of the law, most colleges had to revamp their sports programs to include more women. Consequently, many men's sports programs were reduced or eliminated.

Among the 22 men's sports shown in the accompanying table, 17 were less widely available in 1996 than in 1982. The only sports that have not experienced a decline in availability are baseball, basketball, lacrosse, soccer, and indoor track. Men's wrestling was available in 46 percent of NCAA-member schools in 1982, but in only 27 percent in 1996. Sailing has been eliminated as an NCAA sport. Other sports with significant declines are men's gymnastics, swimming, tennis, and outdoor track.

Fewer Sports for Men

(percentage point change in percent of NCAA-member institutions offering selected men's sports, 1982 to 1996)

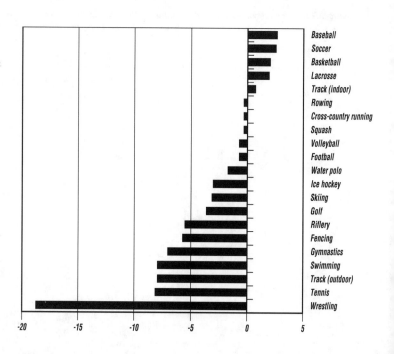

National Collegiate Athletic Association Member Institutions
Offering Selected Men's Sports, 1982 and 1996

(percentage of all divisions of National Collegiate Athletic Association member institutions offering selected men's sports, 1982 and 1996; percentage point change, 1982-96; ranked by percent offering sport in 1996)

	1996	1982	percentage point change 1982-96
Basketball	96.0%	94.0%	2.0
Baseball	84.1	81.5	2.6
Cross-country running	82.2	82.5	-0.3
Tennis	79.5	87.6	-8.1
Golf	71.3	74.9	-3.6
Soccer	68.6	66.1	2.5
Track (outdoor)	65.3	73.2	-7.9
Football	62.4	63.1	-0.7
Track (indoor)	54.3	53.6	0.7
Swimming	39.9	47.8	-7.9
Wrestling	27.4	46.1	-18.7
Lacrosse	19.4	17.5	1.9
Ice hockey	13.5	16.5	-3.0
Volleyball	7.3	8.0	-0.7
Rowing	5.8	6.1	-0.3
Riflery*	5.0	10.5	-5.5
Water polo	4.5	6.2	-1.7
Fencing	4.3	10.0	-5.7
Skiing	3.9	7.0	-3.1
Gymnastics	3.0	10.0	-7.0
Squash	2.4	2.7	-0.3
Sailing	-	1.9	-

* Includes some women in coeducational rifle programs.
Source: National Collegiate Athletic Association's 1997 Participation Statistics Report, 1982-96. *Reproduced with permission of the National Collegiate Athletic Association, 1997; this information is subject to annual review and change.*

College Sports Programs for Women

Women's college sports programs have been expanding, thanks to Title IX. This law, passed in 1972, requires colleges receiving federal funds to offer women equal access to sports programs. In response, most colleges had to revamp their programs by offering more sports to women.

In 1996, over 90 percent of schools belonging to the National Collegiate Athletic Association (NCAA) offered women's basketball and volleyball, and more than 80 percent had women's tennis and cross-country running. Other women's sports offered by at least half the NCAA-member schools are softball, track, and soccer. Fewer than 10 percent of schools have sports such as women's rowing, fencing, or skiing.

Most women's sports are offered by a larger share of NCAA-member schools today than in 1982. The only exceptions are field hockey, gymnastics, fencing, and skiing. Women's soccer saw the biggest increase in availability. It was offered by just 10 percent of NCAA-member schools in 1982 but by fully 64 percent of schools in 1996. Women's cross-country running (rising from 53 to 85 percent of schools), indoor track (from 30 to 56 percent), and softball (from 53 to 75 percent) also experienced big gains.

As generations of women athletes graduate from college and get jobs, expect to see growing demand for women's team sport opportunities in communities across the country.

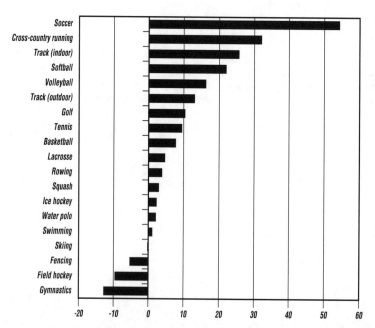

More Sports for Women

(*percentage point change in percent of NCAA-member institutions offering selected women's sports, 1982 to 1996*)

National Collegiate Athletic Association Member Institutions
Offering Selected Women's Sports, 1982 and 1996

(percentage of all divisions of National Collegiate Athletic Association member institutions offering selected women's sports, 1982 and 1996; percentage point change, 1982-96; ranked by percent offering sport in 1996)

	1996	1982	percentage point change 1982-96
Basketball	97.1%	89.5%	7.6
Volleyball	92.6	76.5	16.1
Tennis	86.8	77.4	9.4
Cross-country running	84.9	52.9	32.0
Softball	74.7	52.8	21.9
Track (outdoor)	67.2	54.2	13.0
Soccer	64.4	10.2	54.2
Track (indoor)	55.9	30.3	25.6
Swimming	45.2	44.2	1.0
Golf	26.2	15.9	10.3
Field hockey	24.5	34.0	-9.5
Lacrosse	17.8	13.3	4.5
Gymnastics	10.1	22.7	-12.6
Rowing	9.2	5.5	3.7
Fencing	4.4	9.6	-5.2
Skiing	4.1	4.2	-0.1
Squash	2.8	0.0	2.8
Ice hockey	2.2	0.0	2.2
Water polo	2.0	0.0	2.0

Source: National Collegiate Athletic Association's 1997 Participation Statistics Report, 1982-96. Reproduced with permission of the National Collegiate Athletic Association, 1997; this information is subject to annual review and change.

Recreational Travel

Millions of Americans travel in pursuit of their sport and recreational interests. Travel by Americans increased by an enormous 45 percent between 1985 and 1995, according to the Travel Industry Association of America, based in Washington, D.C. During those years, the population grew by just 10 percent.

Pleasure travel far surpasses business travel in the U.S.—and the margin is growing. Of the 1.2 billion person-trips taken by Americans in 1995 (a person trip is a trip by one person traveling 100 or more miles one-way from home), 78 percent were for pleasure, according to the Travel Industry Association. Ten years earlier, 67 percent of trips were for pleasure.

Most pleasure travelers go by car. Eighty percent of all person-trips were taken by automobile in 1995, and 73 percent of automobile trips were for pleasure. Only 17 percent of person-trips are by air, with bus and train trailing at just 1 percent each,

Traveling for Pleasure on the Rise

(percent of person-trips in the U.S. for pleasure or business, 1985 and 1995)

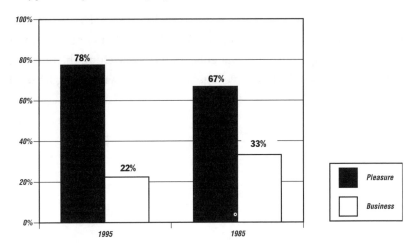

according to Tourism Works for America, a Washington, D.C.-based coalition of travel trade associations and businesses.

Travel has been increasing for two reasons—the aging of the population and the rising educational level of Americans. Educated people travel more than those with less education. As the educational level of the population rises, pleasure travel is becoming a popular hobby. The biggest travelers are older Americans, aged 55 to 64. In second place are those aged 45 to 54. With the baby-boom generation now entering the prime travel years, the number of travelers and trips is growing.

"Travel means different things to different people," explains Cathy Keefe, manager of public relations for Tourism Works for America. "For some people, there's an educational aspect—traveling in pursuit of a hobby, or visiting another culture. For others, it's a way to get away," she says. Many families want the educational benefit of an authentic cultural experience when they travel. Others want to escape the stress of their jobs and daily routines.

The most important trend in domestic travel is shorter trips, says Keefe. "People aren't taking two weeks off at a time," she says. Instead, they are taking more long weekends and one- or two-day trips. Shorter trips may explain why the number of person-trips has increased so sharply, rising from 808 million in 1985 to 1.2 billion in 1995. If a couple takes a one-week vacation, it counts as two person-trips in travel statistics. But if a couple takes three weekend getaways, it counts as six person-trips.

Another important trend is the specialization of the travel industry. According to Keefe, one area to watch is the gay and lesbian market. "They spend more, stay longer, and take more trips," she says. Another growth area is travel by people with disabilities. As baby boomers age and face more disability, accessibility is likely to become an increasingly important issue. Travel agents are already helping the disabled plan accessible trips, Keefe says.

Technology is also affecting the travel industry. The Internet, electronic ticketing, and other advances are changing the role of both traveler and travel agent. "People are always going to use travel agents," Keefe says, citing the human touch as important to a lot of people. But travel agents are "still trying to figure out their new role."

Travel in the United States, 1985 to 1995

(total number of person-trips in the U.S. and percent for pleasure or business, 1985-95; numbers in millions)

	total	percent	
		pleasure	*business*
1995	1,173	77.6%	22.4%
1994	1,139	68.6	31.4
1993	1,058	69.9	30.1
1992	1,063	69.2	30.8
1991	980	68.1	31.9
1990	956	67.9	32.1
1989	945	67.0	33.0
1988	925	67.1	32.9
1987	894	67.4	32.6
1986	841	68.5	31.5
1985	808	66.8	33.2

Note: A person-trip is one person traveling 100 or more miles one-way away from home.
Source: Travel Industry Association of America, Washington, D.C.

Characteristics of Pleasure Trips, 1985 to 1995

(total number of pleasure trips taken by Americans and selected characteristics of trips and travelers, 1985, 1990, and 1995)

	1995	1990	1985
Total pleasure trips (millions)	**413**	**361**	**301**
Also a vacation trip (percent)	74%	82%	80%
Average number of nights per trip*	3.8	4.4	5.6
Average number of miles per trip**	818	867	1,010
Characteristics of pleasure trips (in percent)			
Travel primarily by car, truck, RV, or rental car	75%	77%	73%
Travel primarily by air	16	18	21
Rental car used on trip	8	7	6
Hotel stay while on trip	38	37	39
Travel agent used	6	12	13
Characteristics of pleasure travelers (in percent)			
Male travelers	53%	49%	48%
Female travelers	47	51	52
Household income under $40,000	47	63	73
Household income $40,000 or more	53	38	27
Average number of household members on trip	1.9	1.8	1.8

Includes trips with no overnight stays.
**United States only.*
Source: U.S. Travel Data Center, Washington, D.C. National Travel Survey, annual. Reprinted with permission.

Spending on Air Fares

Air travel is the second-most-popular mode of transportation on pleasure trips. In 1995, Americans took 232 million person-trips by air. But air travel accounts for a shrinking share of all pleasure trips, falling from 21 percent in 1985 to just 16 percent in 1995.

Two factors limit the use of air travel on pleasure trips: perceived cost and safety. Air travel is much more expensive than travel by automobile. Adding to the expense is the need to rent a car at the destination. While no-frills airlines offer cheaper fares, they can be plagued by safety problems. As government regulators try to make planes safer, the cost of flying increases.

Spending on air fares peaks among the most-affluent householders—those aged 45 to 54. This age group spends 27 percent more than average on air transportation. Householders aged 55 to 64 spend 14 percent more than the average household on plane fares. The largest share of spending on air fares, however, is controlled by house-holders aged 35 to 44. Although the age group spends only 9 percent more than aver-age on air travel, it controls the largest share of the market simply because it includes so many households. As boomers fill the 45-to-54 age group, the market share held by older householders will soon surpass that of 35-to-44-year-olds.

Households with incomes of $70,000 or more spend more than three times as much as the average household on air fares, accounting for 40 percent of all consumer spending in this market. Households with incomes between $50,000 and $69,999 also spend more than average on air fares.

Whites are much more likely to spend on air travel than blacks. Whites spend 8 percent more than average, while blacks spend 59 percent less than average. Simi-larly, non-Hispanics spend 2 percent more than the average household on air fares, while Hispanics spend 25 percent less.

Householders with college degrees spend more than twice as much as the aver-age household on air fares. Those with some college experience spend an average amount, while householders with less education spend well below average on air transportation.

Married couples without children at home spend more than other household types on air fares—46 percent more than average. Couples with children also spend above average on air fares, while single parents and people who live alone spend less than average on air transportation.

People in the West spend 33 percent more than the average household on air fares, while those in the Northeast spend 7 percent more than average. Households in the Midwest and South spend less than average on air transportation.

Spending on Air Fares, 1995

(average annual, indexed, and market share of spending by consumer units on airline fares, by selected demographic characteristics, 1995; index definition: 100 is the average; an index of 132 means that spending by consumer units in the segment is 32 percent above average; an index of 68 means spending by consumer units in the segment is 32 percent below average)

	average	index	market share
Total	**$225.58**	**100**	**100.0%**
Age			
Under age 25	98.77	44	3.0
Aged 25 to 34	195.73	87	16.4
Aged 35 to 44	245.75	109	24.8
Aged 45 to 54	285.52	127	22.9
Aged 55 to 64	257.84	114	14.0
Aged 65 or older	201.77	89	18.9
Income			
Under $20,000	89.71	38	14.2
$20,000 to $29,999	141.49	60	9.1
$30,000 to $39,999	207.46	88	11.3
$40,000 to $49,999	208.67	89	8.7
$50,000 to $69,999	323.16	138	17.1
$70,000 or more	731.34	311	39.5
Race			
White and "other"	242.65	108	95.4
Black	91.95	41	4.6
Hispanic origin			
Non-Hispanic	230.31	102	94.2
Hispanic	169.50	75	5.8
Education			
Not a high school graduate	64.63	29	6.0
High school graduate only	136.81	61	19.4
Some college	226.81	101	23.0
College graduate	480.20	213	51.6

(continued)

(continued from previous page)

	average	index	market share
Household type			
Married couples, total	$303.57	135	70.5%
Married couple only	329.59	146	31.2
Married couple with children	282.96	125	34.0
Oldest child under age 6	226.37	100	5.4
Oldest child aged 6 to 17	296.00	131	18.7
Oldest child aged 18 or older	298.84	132	9.9
Single parent with children under 18	103.08	46	3.0
Single person	149.97	66	18.8
Region			
Northeast	240.70	107	21.3
Midwest	199.46	88	22.2
South	189.76	84	28.6
West	301.05	133	27.8

Note: The average spending figures are extremely low because both purchasers and non-purchasers are included in the calculation. While the average spending figures do not show how much buyers of airline fares spent, the patterns revealed by the index and market share figures do show who is most likely to spend on plane tickets and how much spending is controlled by each demographic segment.
Source: Bureau of Labor Statistics, 1995 Consumer Expenditure Survey; calculations by New Strategist

Spending on Automobile Rentals While on Out-of-Town Trips

Renting a car is not the most-enjoyable part of a pleasure trip. Even the highest-rated rental car company failed to get top marks from consumers, according to a J.D. Powers survey published in *Travel Weekly* (May 16, 1997). The survey found speed, cleanliness, and value to be the three characteristics desired most by customers of rental car companies.

Although cost is important to most travelers, image matters to some. A growing trend in the rental car industry is luxury rentals. For the right price, consumers can rent Jaguars or BMWs. For the adventurous, Harley Davidson motorcycles are available from some rental companies. By renting a luxury car or motorcycle, pleasure travelers can maximize the fun of their shorter trips. "Smart cars" are another option in rental cars, with some vehicles equipped with satellite navigation units.

Householders aged 55 to 64 spend the most on auto rentals, 73 percent more than average. Householders in this age group control 21 percent of all consumer spending on auto rentals. As boomers enter this peak-spending age group, the market share controlled by 55-to-64-year-olds will easily surpass that of younger householders.

Households with incomes of $70,000 or more spend more than three times as much as the average household on rental cars, accounting for 39 percent of household spending in this market. College graduates spend twice as much on rental cars as the average household. This is the only educational segment with above-average spending.

By household type, married couples without children at home spend the most on rental cars—52 percent more than the average household. This household type controls about one-third of all consumer spending on rental cars.

Spending on rental cars is well above average only in the West, where households spend 39 percent more than average on this item. Spending is about average in the Northeast and Midwest, and below average in the South.

Spending on Rented Automobiles While on Out-of-Town Trips, 1995

(average annual, indexed, and market share of spending by consumer units on rented automobiles while on out-of-town trips, by selected demographic characteristics, 1995; index definition: 100 is the average; an index of 132 means that spending by consumer units in the segment is 32 percent above average; an index of 68 means spending by consumer units in the segment is 32 percent below average)

	average	index	market share
Total	**$25.95**	**100**	**100.0%**
Age			
Under age 25	7.37	28	1.9
Aged 25 to 34	21.29	82	15.5
Aged 35 to 44	28.41	109	24.9
Aged 45 to 54	33.19	128	23.1
Aged 55 to 64	44.80	173	21.2
Aged 65 or older	16.37	63	13.3
Income			
Under $20,000	9.91	37	13.7
$20,000 to $29,999	19.32	72	10.9
$30,000 to $39,999	19.15	71	9.1
$40,000 to $49,999	28.07	104	10.3
$50,000 to $69,999	37.00	138	17.1
$70,000 or more	82.52	307	38.9
Race			
White and "other"	28.08	108	96.0
Black	9.29	36	4.1
Hispanic origin			
Non-Hispanic	26.96	104	95.8
Hispanic	13.94	54	4.2
Education			
Not a high school graduate	5.36	21	4.3
High school graduate only	11.87	46	14.6
Some college	26.06	100	22.9
College graduate	62.16	240	58.1

(continued)

(continued from previous page)

	average	index	market share
Household type			
Married couples, total	$34.23	132	69.1%
Married couple only	39.37	152	32.4
Married couple with children	31.22	120	32.6
Oldest child under age 6	22.10	85	4.6
Oldest child aged 6 to 17	32.94	127	18.1
Oldest child aged 18 or older	34.52	133	10.0
Single parent with children under 18	6.15	24	1.5
Single person	21.02	81	22.9
Region			
Northeast	26.61	103	20.5
Midwest	24.78	95	24.0
South	20.27	78	26.6
West	36.00	139	28.9

Note: The average spending figures are extremely low because both purchasers and non-purchasers are included in the calculation. While the average spending figures do not show how much renters of automobiles on out-of-town trips spend, the patterns revealed by the index and market share figures do show who is most likely to rent cars while on trips and how much spending is controlled by each demographic segment.
Source: Bureau of Labor Statistics, 1995 Consumer Expenditure Survey; calculations by New Strategist

Spending on Gasoline on Out-of-Town Trips

Automobiles are the most-popular mode of transportation for travelers. Three in four pleasure trips were taken by car, truck, recreational vehicle, or rental car in 1995. The proportion of trips taken by car has been stable for the past decade. In contrast, the proportion of pleasure trips taken by air has fallen from 21 to 16 percent.

The biggest spenders on gasoline for trips are also the biggest travelers: householders aged 45 to 64. Spending on gasoline peaks among householders aged 55 to 64, at 37 percent above average. Those controlling the largest share of spending on gasoline for trips, however, are householders aged 35 to 44. This age group includes the most households and accounts for 23 percent of all spending on gasoline for trips. As boomers enter the 55-to-64 age group, however, the market share controlled by older householders will surpass that of younger Americans.

Affluent households spend nearly twice as much as the average household on gasoline for trips. Whites and non-Hispanics spend about an average amount, while blacks and Hispanics spend less than average on this item. By education, householders with at least some college experience spend more than average on gasoline for trips, while those with less education spend less.

Married couples without children at home account for 31 percent of spending on gasoline for trips—a larger share than any other household type. These couples spend 43 percent more than the average household on gasoline for trips. Couples with children aged 18 or older at home spend 51 percent more than average on this item.

Households in the West spend more than those in other regions on gasoline for trips—31 percent more than the average household. But the South controls the largest market share (32 percent) because it is home to the most households.

Spending on Gasoline on Out-of-Town Trips, 1995

(average annual, indexed, and market share of spending by consumer units on gasoline while on out-of-town trips, by selected demographic characteristics, 1995; index definition: 100 is the average; an index of 132 means that spending by consumer units in the segment is 32 percent above average; an index of 68 means spending by consumer units in the segment is 32 percent below average)

	average	index	market share
Total	**$81.98**	**100**	**100.0%**
Age			
Under age 25	53.09	65	4.4
Aged 25 to 34	77.21	94	17.8
Aged 35 to 44	83.57	102	23.2
Aged 45 to 54	102.61	125	22.6
Aged 55 to 64	112.15	137	16.8
Aged 65 or older	58.75	72	15.1
Income			
Under $20,000	42.50	49	18.3
$20,000 to $29,999	63.67	74	11.2
$30,000 to $39,999	97.43	113	14.5
$40,000 to $49,999	109.81	119	12.5
$50,000 to $69,999	128.56	149	18.6
$70,000 or more	168.93	196	24.9
Race			
White and "other"	88.61	108	95.8
Black	30.08	37	4.2
Hispanic origin			
Non-Hispanic	84.83	103	95.4
Hispanic	48.19	59	4.6
Education			
Not a high school graduate	43.02	52	11.0
High school graduate only	63.39	77	24.8
Some college	98.08	120	27.3
College graduate	124.89	152	36.9

(continued)

(continued from previous page)

	average	index	market share
Household type			
Married couples, total	$111.45	136	71.3%
Married couple only	117.37	143	30.6
Married couple with children	102.26	125	33.8
Oldest child under age 6	75.03	92	4.9
Oldest child aged 6 to 17	101.03	123	17.5
Oldest child aged 18 or older	124.17	151	11.3
Single parent with children under 18	35.58	43	2.8
Single person	48.18	59	16.6
Region			
Northeast	55.01	67	13.4
Midwest	89.43	109	27.4
South	76.83	94	31.9
West	107.30	131	27.3

Note: The average spending figures are extremely low because both purchasers and non-purchasers are included in the calculation. While the average spending figures do not show how much buyers of gasoline for out-of-town trips spend, the patterns revealed by the index and market share figures do show who is most likely to spend on gasoline on trips and how much spending is controlled by each demographic segment.
Source: Bureau of Labor Statistics, 1995 Consumer Expenditure Survey; calculations by New Strategist

Spending on Intercity Bus Fares

Bus travel accounts for a tiny share of all pleasure trips in the United States. This mode of transportation is dominated by older Americans taking bus tours to shows and sites of interest in neighboring cities and states. Many older Americans are reluctant to fly, while others are unwilling to pay the high cost of flying. Yet this age group has the time and money for travel, making them the best customers for the bus industry.

As the well-educated and sophisticated baby-boom generation ages into the prime traveling age groups, however, bus travel will have to change. Already, buses are becoming more luxurious to attract upscale travelers. Seats have become wider and windows bigger. Many buses have on-board video for in-transit movies. Some buses even provide customized seating. By offering more-luxurious accommodations at reasonable prices, bus companies may be able to appeal to affluent, educated boomers who are wary of flying and tired of driving.

The biggest spenders on intercity bus travel are householders aged 65 or older, spending 66 percent more than the average household on bus trips. This age group accounts for fully 35 percent of all spending on bus travel. Householders aged 55 to 64 also spend more than average on bus travel, while younger householders spend less.

The biggest spenders on bus travel are also the biggest spenders in most travel categories—the most-affluent householders. Households with incomes of $70,000 or more spent well over twice as much as the average household on bus fares and control 33 percent of the market.

Married couples without children at home spend more than twice as much as the average household on bus travel and control over half the spending in this market. Spending is below average for all other household types.

Householders in the West spend more than average on bus travel, while those in the South spend less than average on bus fares.

Spending on Intercity Bus Fares, 1995

(average annual, indexed, and market share of spending by consumer units on intercity bus fares, by selected demographic characteristics, 1995; index definition: 100 is the average; an index of 132 means that spending by consumer units in the segment is 32 percent above average; an index of 68 means spending by consumer units in the segment is 32 percent below average)

	average	index	market share
Total	**$14.09**	**100**	**100.0%**
Age			
Under age 25	5.32	38	2.6
Aged 25 to 34	8.64	61	11.6
Aged 35 to 44	11.24	80	18.2
Aged 45 to 54	13.86	98	17.8
Aged 55 to 64	17.06	121	14.8
Aged 65 or older	23.36	166	35.0
Income			
Under $20,000	6.53	45	16.6
$20,000 to $29,999	9.54	65	9.9
$30,000 to $39,999	14.73	101	12.9
$40,000 to $49,999	12.09	83	8.1
$50,000 to $69,999	22.65	155	19.3
$70,000 or more	38.20	261	33.2
Race			
White and "other"	14.83	105	93.3
Black	8.26	59	6.6
Hispanic origin			
Non-Hispanic	14.55	103	95.2
Hispanic	8.67	62	4.8
Education			
Not a high school graduate	5.37	38	8.0
High school graduate only	11.69	83	26.6
Some college	14.48	103	23.5
College graduate	24.39	173	42.0

(continued)

(continued from previous page)

	average	index	market share
Household type			
Married couples, total	$19.86	141	73.9%
Married couple only	33.48	238	50.8
Married couple with children	9.77	69	18.8
Oldest child under age 6	5.62	40	2.1
Oldest child aged 6 to 17	9.76	69	9.9
Oldest child aged 18 or older	12.79	91	6.8
Single parent with children under 18	7.58	54	3.5
Single person	7.52	53	15.1
Region			
Northeast	14.14	100	20.1
Midwest	13.12	93	23.4
South	9.51	67	23.0
West	22.67	161	33.5

Note: The average spending figures are extremely low because both purchasers and non-purchasers are included in the calculation. While the average spending figures do not show how much buyers of intercity bus fares spend, the patterns revealed by the index and market share figures do show who is most likely to spend on bus tickets and how much spending is controlled by each demographic segment.
Source: Bureau of Labor Statistics, 1995 Consumer Expenditure Survey; *calculations by New Strategist*

Spending on Intercity Train Fares

Trains were once the fastest way to get from one end of the country to the other. Now airplanes are the most efficient way to travel. Unlike air travel, however, trains hold a certain romance. Rail enthusiasts gather at conventions, publish their own magazines, and still ride the trains.

For the rest of the public, train travel has become a novelty. Today's travelers have little time, and they cannot afford to spend days getting to their destination. But as baby boomers enter the prime traveling age groups, and as their free time expands in retirement, train travel may surge. Unlike airplanes, trains allow travelers to see and experience the countryside. Air-rail vacations, in which travelers take a train one way and a plane the other, offer both sightseeing opportunities and time savings.

Perhaps the biggest danger to train travel in the U.S. is that Amtrak—the government-subsidized passenger train system—is dependent on Congressional appropriations. In a time of budget cutbacks, Amtrak could be left behind at the station.

The biggest spenders on intercity train travel are householders aged 55 to 64, who spend 55 percent more than the average household on train fares. Householders aged 45 to 54 also spend well above average on train travel. But householders aged 35 to 44 control the largest share of spending on train travel (25 percent) simply because they are more numerous. As the large baby-boom generation enters the older age groups, the market share controlled by older householders will surpass that controlled by younger Americans.

Spending on train travel is three times greater than average among the most-affluent householders, who control 39 percent of all spending in this market. But even householders with incomes as low as $30,000 spend more than the average household on train fares.

College graduates spend twice as much as the average household on train travel and control over half the spending in this market. Those with at least some college experience also spend more than the average household, while less-educated householders spend less than average on train fares.

Married couples with children aged 18 or older at home spend 74 percent more than the average household on train fares. Those without children at home spend 72 percent more than average. These two household types control half the spending on train fares.

Households in the Northeast spend 19 percent more than the average household on intercity train fares. Much of this spending may be for commuter rail travel from one city to another, such as from New York City to surrounding suburbs. Households in the Midwest and South spend slightly more than average on train travel, while households in the South spend less than average.

Spending on Intercity Train Fares, 1995

(average annual, indexed, and market share of spending by consumer units on intercity train fares, by selected demographic characteristics, 1995; index definition: 100 is the average; an index of 132 means that spending by consumer units in the segment is 32 percent above average; an index of 68 means spending by consumer units in the segment is 32 percent below average)

	average	index	market share
Total	**$18.41**	**100**	**100.0%**
Age			
Under age 25	4.03	22	1.5
Aged 25 to 34	11.49	62	11.8
Aged 35 to 44	20.05	109	24.8
Aged 45 to 54	23.06	125	22.7
Aged 55 to 64	28.52	155	19.0
Aged 65 or older	17.69	96	20.3
Income			
Under $20,000	4.26	22	8.3
$20,000 to $29,999	5.62	30	4.5
$30,000 to $39,999	20.25	107	13.6
$40,000 to $49,999	22.02	116	11.4
$50,000 to $69,999	35.49	187	23.2
$70,000 or more	58.33	307	38.9
Race			
White and "other"	19.83	108	95.5
Black	7.32	40	4.5
Hispanic origin			
Non-Hispanic	19.13	104	95.8
Hispanic	9.90	54	4.2
Education			
Not a high school graduate	5.91	32	6.7
High school graduate only	9.25	50	16.1
Some college	19.46	106	24.1
College graduate	40.28	219	53.1

(continued)

(continued from previous page)

	average	index	market share
Household type			
Married couples, total	$26.95	146	76.7%
Married couple only	31.61	172	36.7
Married couple with children	22.65	123	33.4
Oldest child under age 6	14.23	77	4.2
Oldest child aged 6 to 17	20.88	113	16.1
Oldest child aged 18 or older	32.07	174	13.0
Single parent with children under 18	4.38	24	1.5
Single person	9.73	53	14.9
Region			
Northeast	21.98	119	23.9
Midwest	19.59	106	26.7
South	14.92	81	27.6
West	19.28	105	21.8

Note: The average spending figures are extremely low because both purchasers and non-purchasers are included in the calculation. While the average spending figures do not show how much buyers of intercity train fares spend, the patterns revealed by the index and market share figures do show who is most likely to spend on train fares and how much spending is controlled by each demographic segment.
Source: Bureau of Labor Statistics, 1995 Consumer Expenditure Survey; calculations by New Strategist

Spending on Lodging While on Out-of-Town Trips

The lodging industry is becoming increasingly specialized as hotels and motels compete against one another for the growing ranks of travelers. Today, some hotels cater to business travelers, others are designed for families, and still others for couples without children. "Niche" travelers—such as eco-tourists, adventure sports enthusiasts, and travelers with special needs—will drive this specialization even further.

With older, affluent travelers becoming more important to the travel market, the lodging industry is moving upscale. As hotels and motels are renovated, they are losing their public spaces in favor of the larger private rooms that appeal to today's travelers. Even historic landmarks like Mohonk Mountain House in New Paltz, New York, are going upscale. For years, Mohonk offered hotel rooms without private bathrooms—but no more.

Spending on lodging while on out-of-town trips rises with age, peaking in the 55-to-64 age group at 43 percent above average. Householders aged 45 to 54 also spend more than average on lodging while on trips. Householders aged 35 to 44 spend only an average amount on lodging, but they control a larger share of the market (23 percent) than do those aged 55 to 64 (18 percent) simply because they are more numerous. As the large baby-boom generation enters the 55-to-64 age group, the share of the lodging market controlled by older householders will surpass the share controlled by younger Americans.

Spending on lodging while on trips rises sharply with income. The most-affluent households spend nearly three times as much as the average household on lodging and control 36 percent of all spending in the market.

Married couples without children at home spend more on lodging than other household types, 74 percent more than the average household. Many of these couples are empty nesters, and they control over one-third of all spending on lodging.

Spending on lodging is significantly above average in the West and below average in the South.

Spending on Lodging While on Out-of-Town Trips, 1995

(average annual, indexed, and market share of spending by consumer units on lodging while on out-of-town trips, by selected demographic characteristics, 1995; index definition: 100 is the average; an index of 132 means that spending by consumer units in the segment is 32 percent above average; an index of 68 means spending by consumer units in the segment is 32 percent below average)

	average	index	market share
Total	**$209.59**	**100**	**100.0%**
Age			
Under age 25	47.02	22	1.5
Aged 25 to 34	155.81	74	14.1
Aged 35 to 44	211.39	101	22.9
Aged 45 to 54	278.08	133	24.0
Aged 55 to 64	299.35	143	17.5
Aged 65 or older	197.90	94	20.0
Income			
Under $20,000	75.45	36	13.4
$20,000 to $29,999	99.92	48	7.2
$30,000 to $39,999	187.40	89	11.4
$40,000 to $49,999	249.38	119	11.7
$50,000 to $69,999	340.56	163	20.3
$70,000 or more	591.64	283	35.9
Race			
White and "other"	225.58	108	95.4
Black	84.33	40	4.6
Hispanic origin			
Non-Hispanic	220.80	105	97.2
Hispanic	76.53	37	2.8
Education			
Not a high school graduate	53.74	26	5.4
High school graduate only	140.02	67	21.4
Some college	224.95	107	24.5
College graduate	421.12	201	48.7

(continued)

(continued from previous page)

	average	index	market share
Household type			
Married couples, total	$304.55	145	76.2%
Married couple only	364.15	174	37.2
Married couple with children	265.86	127	34.4
Oldest child under age 6	177.42	85	4.6
Oldest child aged 6 to 17	280.84	134	19.1
Oldest child aged 18 or older	300.97	144	10.8
Single parent with children under 18	70.33	34	2.2
Single person	115.56	55	15.6
Region			
Northeast	226.84	108	21.7
Midwest	204.92	98	24.5
South	173.76	83	28.2
West	257.18	123	25.6

Note: The average spending figures are extremely low because both purchasers and non-purchasers are included in the calculation. While the average spending figures do not show how much buyers of lodging while on out-of-town trips spend, the patterns revealed by the index and market share figures do show who is most likely to spend on lodging and how much spending is controlled by each demographic segment.
Source: Bureau of Labor Statistics, 1995 Consumer Expenditure Survey; *calculations by New Strategist*

Spending on Ship Fares

The average age of passengers on cruise ships is 49, according to the Cruise Line Industry Association's (CLIA) 1996 market profile study. This age has been dropping, according to Bernadette Harding, account executive at Diana M. Orban Associates, which handles public relations for CLIA. "Younger people are realizing that cruising offers a lot," she explains. By including adventure land excursions with cruise vacations, the cruise industry is appealing to younger customers. "You can be adventurous. You can go hiking in a rain forest or sightseeing in Hawaii. There's no need to be confined to the boat," she says.

The number of cruisers is on the rise, Harding says, and the female share of cruisers is down to 53 percent. CLIA projects a total of 5 million cruisers in 1997, a figure that should increase by another 2 million by 2000.

The average age of cruisers may be declining because boomers are entering the younger end of the age groups most likely to spend on a cruise vacation. Spending on ship fares first rises above average in the 45-to-54 age group. It peaks at 69 percent above average in the 55-to-64 age group and remains well above average among householders aged 65 or older. Overall, householders aged 45 or older control 70 percent of all spending on ship fares.

While the most-affluent households spend the most on ship fares, spending on this item is above average in households with incomes as low as $30,000. Behind this spending pattern is that older Americans—many of them retirees with modest incomes—are the biggest spenders on ship fares.

Married couples without children at home spend more than twice as much as the average household on ship fares—controlling 57 percent of all spending in this market.

Households in the Northeast spend the most on ship fares—31 percent more than the average household. Households in the West also spend well above average on ship fares, while those in the Midwest and South spend less.

Spending on Ship Fares, 1995

(average annual, indexed, and market share of spending by consumer units on ship fares, by selected demographic characteristics, 1995; index definition: 100 is the average; an index of 132 means that spending by consumer units in the segment is 32 percent above average; an index of 68 means spending by consumer units in the segment is 32 percent below average)

	average	index	market share
Total	$27.31	100	100.0%
Age			
Under age 25	9.48	35	2.4
Aged 25 to 34	16.44	60	11.4
Aged 35 to 44	18.51	68	15.4
Aged 45 to 54	33.70	123	22.3
Aged 55 to 64	46.11	169	20.7
Aged 65 or older	35.93	132	27.8
Income			
Under $20,000	7.63	28	10.9
$20,000 to $29,999	2.09	8	1.2
$30,000 to $39,999	29.37	114	14.5
$40,000 to $49,999	32.35	125	12.3
$50,000 to $69,999	52.25	202	25.2
$70,000 or more	73.17	283	35.9
Race			
White and "other"	29.61	108	96.1
Black	9.30	34	3.9
Hispanic origin			
Non-Hispanic	29.31	107	99.0
Hispanic	3.59	13	1.0
Education			
Not a high school graduate	3.97	15	3.0
High school graduate only	18.70	68	21.9
Some college	25.22	92	21.1
College graduate	60.72	222	53.9

(continued)

(continued from previous page)

	average	index	market share
Household type			
Married couples, total	$41.31	151	79.3%
Married couple only	73.13	268	57.3
Married couple with children	18.62	68	18.5
Oldest child under age 6	6.23	23	1.2
Oldest child aged 6 to 17	26.51	97	13.8
Oldest child aged 18 or older	12.53	46	3.4
Single parent with children under 18	5.41	20	1.3
Single person	13.21	48	13.7
Region			
Northeast	35.80	131	26.2
Midwest	22.23	81	20.4
South	22.04	81	27.5
West	33.87	124	25.9

Note: The average spending figures are extremely low because both purchasers and non-purchasers are included in the calculation. While the average spending figures do not show how much buyers of ship fares spend, the patterns revealed by the index and market share figures do show who is most likely to spend on ship fares and how much spending is controlled by each demographic segment.
Source: Bureau of Labor Statistics, 1995 Consumer Expenditure Survey; calculations by New Strategist

Spending on Recreational Activities While on Out-of-Town Trips

Recreation has always been an important part of travel. Of the travelers in 1995, 16 percent visited historic sites or museums, 10 percent attended cultural events and festivals, and 9 percent went to amusement parks. Many of these activities have a cost—sometimes a hefty one.

The biggest spenders on recreational activities while on trips are householders aged 45 to 54, spending 37 percent more than average on recreational expenses. But householders ranging in age from 35 to 64 spend more than average on recreational activities while on trips. The largest share of the market is controlled by householders aged 35 to 44 (28 percent) simply because there are so many households in this age group. As boomers enter the 45-plus age groups, the market share controlled by older Americans will surpass that held by younger householders.

The most-affluent householders spend nearly three times as much as the average household on recreational activities while on trips. But even householders with incomes as low as $30,000 spend more than average on this item. Whites and non-Hispanics spend slightly more than average on recreational activities while on trips. In contrast, blacks and Hispanics spend well below average.

Householders with at least some college experience spend more than average on recreational activities while on trips. Married couples with children aged 18 or older at home are the biggest consumers of this item, spending 66 percent more than the average household. The large size of these households accounts for this high level of spending. Households with children aged 6 to 17 and couples without children at home are also above-average spenders on recreational activities while on trips.

Householders in the West are the only ones who spend significantly more than average on recreational activities while on trips.

Recreational Activities of Travelers, 1995

(percent of person-trips that include selected recreational activities, 1995)

Shopping	33%
Enjoying the outdoors	18
Visiting historical sites and museums	16
Visiting beaches	11
Visiting national and state parks	10
Attending cultural events and festivals	10
Visiting theme and amusement parks	9
Enjoying nightlife and dancing	7
Gambling	7
Attending sports events	5
Golfing, playing tennis, and skiing	4
Other	5

Note: Figures will not sum to 100 because more than one activity could be cited. A person-trip is one person traveling at least 100 miles one-way from home.
Source: Tourism Works for America, Washington, D.C.

Spending on Recreational Expenses While on Out-of-Town Trips, 1995

(average annual, indexed, and market share of spending by consumer units on recreational expenses while on out-of-town trips, by selected demographic characteristics, 1995; index definition: 100 is the average; an index of 132 means that spending by consumer units in the segment is 32 percent above average; an index of 68 means spending by consumer units in the segment is 32 percent below average)

	average	index	market share
Total	$21.21	100	100.0%
Age			
Under age 25	6.98	33	2.3
Aged 25 to 34	17.82	84	15.9
Aged 35 to 44	25.62	121	27.5
Aged 45 to 54	28.98	137	24.7
Aged 55 to 64	25.49	120	14.7
Aged 65 or older	14.97	71	14.9
Income			
Under $20,000	8.29	37	13.6
$20,000 to $29,999	11.28	50	7.6
$30,000 to $39,999	23.72	105	13.4
$40,000 to $49,999	23.28	103	10.1
$50,000 to $69,999	37.37	165	20.6
$70,000 or more	61.84	274	34.7
Race			
White and "other"	22.58	106	94.4
Black	10.47	49	5.6
Hispanic origin			
Non-Hispanic	22.15	104	96.3
Hispanic	10.05	47	3.7
Education			
Not a high school graduate	6.08	29	6.0
High school graduate only	14.50	68	21.9
Some college	24.25	114	26.1
College graduate	40.23	190	46.0

(continued)

(continued from previous page)

	average	index	market share
Household type			
Married couples, total	$29.35	138	72.5%
Married couple only	28.01	132	28.2
Married couple with children	29.11	137	37.2
Oldest child under age 6	16.34	77	4.1
Oldest child aged 6 to 17	30.79	145	20.7
Oldest child aged 18 or older	35.11	166	12.4
Single parent with children under 18	7.99	38	2.5
Single person	12.92	61	17.2
Region			
Northeast	21.28	100	20.1
Midwest	23.02	109	27.2
South	16.08	76	25.8
West	27.33	129	26.9

Note: The average spending figures are extremely low because both purchasers and non-purchasers are included in the calculation. While the average spending figures do not show how much buyers of recreational activities while on out-of-town trips spend, the patterns revealed by the index and market share figures do show who is most likely to spend on recreational activities while traveling and how much spending is controlled by each demographic segment.
Source: Bureau of Labor Statistics, 1995 Consumer Expenditure Survey; calculations by New Strategist

Camping

Camping is an economical means to get away from it all while providing the opportunity to be outdoors. There is more interest in camping today because people "want to get away from their pagers, cell phones, and faxes, and spend quality time with their family," says Phil Ingrassia, communications director for the Recreational Vehicles Dealers Association.

Because not everyone relishes the idea of sleeping on the ground, recreational vehicles (RVs) are a popular alternative to tent camping. The variety of RVs available ranges from bare bones to super deluxe with all the amenities. The more basic the RV, the lower the median age of the owner, says Ingrassia. The typical RV owner is 48 years old, married, has a household income of $39,000 and no children at home.

One trend in RV camping is luxury accommodations, says Ingrassia. Some RV parks are beginning to feature Olympic-sized swimming pools, golf courses, and organized activities—resorts without the hotel.

Many people camp with tents rather than RVs. Some do so because of the cost (the least expensive towable RV costs about $10,000). Others do so for aesthetic reasons. Some tent campers are vehemently opposed to RVs. But for both tent campers and RVers, the story is the same: Fees and regulations are increasing, and campgrounds are becoming more crowded.

About one in four Americans aged 16 or older went camping at least once in the past 12 months. The largest share of people (21 percent) camp in developed areas, while 14 percent camp in primitive areas.

Those most likely to camp are people under age 40. At least one-third of adults aged 16 to 39 went camping in the past 12 months. Campers in primitive areas are much younger than those in developed area.

Camping is an activity most popular among middle-income Americans. Only 27 percent of people in households with incomes of $100,000 or more went camping in the past 12 months, versus about one-third of those in households with incomes between $25,000 and $74,999. The most-affluent householders can afford to stay in hotels on vacation trips, and so are less likely to camp. This pattern holds true for camping in both developed and primitive areas.

Men are more likely to camp than women—31 versus 22 percent. Women are almost as likely as men to camp in developed areas, but men are twice as likely as women to camp in primitive areas—19 versus 9 percent.

Camping is much more popular among whites than among blacks. While 30 percent of whites have been camping in the past 12 months, only 9 percent of blacks have done so. People of "other" race (primarily Asians and Hispanics) are almost as likely as whites to camp.

The propensity to camp does not vary much by education, but the activity is much more popular among people living in large households and those with pre-schoolers in the home. Camping is an economical way for families with children to travel.

Participation in Camping

(percent of persons aged 16 or older who went camping at least once in the past year, by selected demographic characteristics, 1994-95)

	total	camping in developed area	primitive area
Total	**26.8%**	**20.7%**	**14.0%**
Age			
Aged 16 to 24	37.7	27.6	22.7
Aged 25 to 29	33.3	25.5	19.9
Aged 30 to 39	33.5	26.0	16.6
Aged 40 to 49	28.7	22.6	13.8
Aged 50 to 59	19.8	15.6	9.2
Aged 60 or older	10.7	9.0	4.3
Income			
Under $15,000	18.8	14.8	10.1
$15,000 to $24,999	23.2	17.3	12.9
$25,000 to $49,999	31.5	24.4	16.3
$50,000 to $74,999	32.8	25.7	16.6
$75,000 to $99,999	29.3	22.8	14.9
$100,000 or more	26.7	19.6	14.1
Sex			
Men	31.4	22.9	19.0
Women	22.1	18.7	9.4
Race and Hispanic origin			
White	29.6	22.9	15.5
Black	8.6	6.3	4.2
Other, including Hispanic	23.8	18.2	12.3
Education			
Not a high school graduate	25.7	19.6	14.7
High school graduate	26.0	19.7	14.0
Some college	29.3	22.9	14.8
College graduate	26.2	20.4	13.0
Number of persons in household			
One	18.1	13.3	10.2
Two	23.6	18.4	12.4
Three	30.6	23.8	16.2
Four	31.7	24.8	15.6
Five or more	34.7	26.6	18.0

(continued)

(continued from previous page)

| | total | camping in | |
		developed area	primitive area
Number of persons aged			
16 or older in household			
One	20.9%	15.9%	11.3%
Two	28.0	21.9	14.1
Three or more	30.6	23.1	16.7
Number of persons under			
age 6 in household			
None	25.7	19.8	13.6
One or more	31.4	24.3	15.8

Source: USDA Forest Service, 1994-95 National Survey on Recreation and the Environment

Sightseeing

Sightseeing is one of America's most-popular recreational activities, with over half the people aged 16 or older having been sightseeing in the past year. Sightseeing is likely to grow in the future as travel companies offer more specialized excursions and experiences. Participation in sightseeing peaks in the 40-to-49 age group at 64 percent. But most people, regardless of age, have been sightseeing at least once in the past 12 months. The only exception are the oldest Americans: Only 45 percent of people aged 60 or older have been sightseeing in the past year.

Participation in sightseeing rises with income. Among people with household incomes of $75,000 or more, over 70 percent have been sightseeing in the past year. Fewer than half the people with household incomes below $25,000 have been sightseeing. Many people living in low-income households do not sightsee because they do not have cars to go to the sights.

Whites are somewhat more likely than blacks or "others" (primarily Asians and Hispanics) to go sightseeing. Sixty percent of whites have done so in the past 12 months versus fewer than half the blacks and "others."

People with at least some college experience are much more likely to sightsee than those who did not graduate from high school. Fully 69 percent of college graduates have been sightseeing in the past year, versus only 35 percent of people who did not graduate from high school. Many of those lacking a high school diploma are elderly and not able to get out to sightsee.

Sightseeing is most popular in households with two adults. Many are married couples whose children are grown. With more free time on their hands, they spend it seeing the sights.

Participation in Sightseeing

(percent of persons aged 16 or older who participated in sightseeing at least once in the past year, by selected demographic characteristics, 1994-95)

Total	**56.6%**
Age	
Aged 16 to 24	52.0
Aged 25 to 29	60.4
Aged 30 to 39	63.4
Aged 40 to 49	64.4
Aged 50 to 59	59.6
Aged 60 or older	44.5
Income	
Under $15,000	37.0
$15,000 to $24,999	48.6
$25,000 to $49,999	62.6
$50,000 to $74,999	68.6
$75,000 to $99,999	70.3
$100,000 or more	70.4
Sex	
Men	57.8
Women	55.7
Race and Hispanic origin	
White	59.5
Black	41.9
Other, including Hispanic	47.6
Education	
Not a high school graduate	35.2
High school graduate	50.2
Some college	61.2
College graduate	69.1
Number of persons in household	
One	47.9
Two	59.2
Three	58.8
Four	59.9
Five or more	55.4

(continued)

(continued from previous page)

**Number of persons aged
16 or older in household**

One	49.1%
Two	60.6
Three or more	56.2

**Number of persons under
age 6 in household**

None	56.5
One or more	57.6

Source: USDA Forest Service, 1994-95 National Survey on Recreation and the Environment

Visiting a Beach or Water Side

Visiting a beach or water side is one of America's most-popular recreational activities. Nearly two in three people aged 16 or older went to a beach or water side at least once in the past 12 months. The enormous popularity of this activity has itself become a problem for many recreational areas, with crowds of people disturbing the often-delicate shoreline environment. In addition, beach erosion, agricultural and industrial pollution, and growing coastal populations are also putting pressure on shorelines. The very popularity of visiting the beach insures, however, that the public will force a compromise between the crowds and preservation of the beach environment.

As with most outdoor recreational activities, those most likely to visit a beach or water side are young adults. More than 70 percent of adults under age 40 visited a beach or water side in the past 12 months. The proportion remains above 50 percent to age 60, then drops to 41 percent among people aged 60 or older.

Visiting a beach is a popular activity regardless of income. Nevertheless, the higher the income, the more likely people are to visit a beach—largely because those with higher incomes can better afford to travel to beaches and water sides. Among people with household incomes of $100,000 or more, 79 percent have been to a beach in the past 12 months. The proportion visiting a beach is below 40 percent only for those with household incomes under $15,000.

Men are somewhat more likely to visit a beach or water side than women, and whites are more likely than blacks and "others" (primarily Asians and Hispanics). But over half the women and "others" have been to a beach or water side in the past year. Among blacks, 46 percent have done so.

College graduates are more likely to visit a beach or water side than people with less education, in part because the college educated have more money to spend on travel to recreational areas. Visiting a beach or water side is more popular among people living in large households because larger households include the age groups most likely to go to the beach.

Visiting a Beach or Water Side

(percent of persons aged 16 or older who visited a beach or water side at least once in the past year, by selected demographic characteristics, 1994-95)

Total	**62.1%**
Age	
Aged 16 to 24	70.2
Aged 25 to 29	71.6
Aged 30 to 39	71.3
Aged 40 to 49	66.9
Aged 50 to 59	57.1
Aged 60 or older	40.9
Income	
Under $15,000	39.3
$15,000 to $24,999	56.1
$25,000 to $49,999	66.7
$50,000 to $74,999	74.5
$75,000 to $99,999	79.2
$100,000 or more	78.6
Sex	
Men	64.9
Women	59.6
Race and Hispanic origin	
White	64.8
Black	46.0
Other, including Hispanic	56.9
Education	
Not a high school graduate	45.0
High school graduate	56.0
Some college	67.0
College graduate	72.0
Number of persons in household	
One	50.2
Two	60.0
Three	67.3
Four	69.1
Five or more	66.6

(continued)

(continued from previous page)

Number of persons aged 16 or older in household	
One	53.1%
Two	64.7
Three or more	66.0
Number of persons under age 6 in household	
None	60.4
One or more	68.8

Source: USDA Forest Service, 1994-95 National Survey on Recreation and the Environment

Visiting Historic and Prehistoric Sites

Visiting historic sites is a popular recreational activity among Americans. Nearly half (44 percent) the people aged 16 or older have visited a historic site in the past 12 months. Visiting prehistoric sites is much less popular, in part because these sites are less common. Only 17 percent of Americans aged 16 or older have visited a prehistoric site in the past year.

In the future, the popularity of visiting historic and prehistoric sites will depend on how much the public insists on the preservation of these areas. Preservation can be made more difficult by environmental, corporate, and sometimes constitutional challenges to designating historic landmarks. And the public's interest in these sites may be waning. A 1994 survey by the National Endowment for the Arts found that a smaller share of Americans visited historic sites than in the past.

But that may change. Visiting historic and prehistoric sites is most popular among educated Americans. Fully 58 percent of college graduates visited an historic site in the past year, and 23 percent visited a prehistoric site. As the well-educated baby-boom generation enters its 40s and 50s, the popularity of historic and prehistoric sites could grow. Demands for preservation of historic and prehistoric sites are certain to arise more frequently in communities across the country in the decades ahead.

Visiting an Historic Site

(percent of persons aged 16 or older who visited an historic site at least once in the past year, by selected demographic characteristics, 1994-95)

Total	**44.1%**
Age	
Aged 16 to 24	44.6
Aged 25 to 29	48.7
Aged 30 to 39	49.8
Aged 40 to 49	50.4
Aged 50 to 59	45.4
Aged 60 or older	30.8
Income	
Under $15,000	26.3
$15,000 to $24,999	35.5
$25,000 to $49,999	48.2
$50,000 to $74,999	56.3
$75,000 to $99,999	56.5
$100,000 or more	60.3
Sex	
Men	46.1
Women	42.5
Race and Hispanic origin	
White	46.6
Black	31.1
Other, including Hispanic	36.8
Education	
Not a high school graduate	27.3
High school graduate	35.0
Some college	47.9
College graduate	58.1
Number of persons in household	
One	35.0
Two	45.0
Three	47.1
Four	48.6
Five or more	45.0

(continued)

(continued from previous page)

Number of persons aged	
16 or older in household	
One	36.5%
Two	47.4
Three or more	45.2
Number of persons under	
age 6 in household	
None	44.3
One or more	44.0

Source: USDA Forest Service, 1994-95 National Survey on Recreation and the Environment

Visiting a Prehistoric Site

(percent of persons aged 16 or older who visited a prehistoric site at least once in the past year, by selected demographic characteristics, 1994-95)

Total	**17.4%**
Age	
Aged 16 to 24	18.5
Aged 25 to 29	20.0
Aged 30 to 39	19.3
Aged 40 to 49	19.8
Aged 50 to 59	17.3
Aged 60 or older	11.8
Income	
Under $15,000	10.8
$15,000 to $24,999	14.2
$25,000 to $49,999	18.9
$50,000 to $74,999	21.6
$75,000 to $99,999	21.0
$100,000 or more	24.6
Sex	
Men	19.5
Women	15.6
Race and Hispanic origin	
White	18.0
Black	13.3
Other, including Hispanic	18.1
Education	
Not a high school graduate	11.3
High school graduate	13.5
Some college	19.5
College graduate	22.5
Number of persons in household	
One	12.8
Two	17.1
Three	19.2
Four	20.3
Five or more	18.5

(continued)

(continued from previous page)

Number of persons aged 16 or older in household	
One	14.0%
Two	18.3
Three or more	19.2
Number of persons under age 6 in household	
None	17.3
One or more	18.2

Source: USDA Forest Service, 1994-95 National Survey on Recreation and the Environment

Visiting a Nature Center

Nature centers are a good first stop for people developing an interest in the outdoors. Wildlife observers—especially birders—often affiliate with nature centers. Thus, it is troubling to see the results of the United States Fish and Wildlife Service's 1996 National Survey of Fishing, Hunting, and Wildlife-Associated Recreation, which showed that the number of people observing, feeding, or photographing wildlife declined 17 percent between 1991 and 1996. On a brighter note, the same survey found that expenditures on wildlife observation were up 27 percent.

Nearly half (46 percent) the Americans aged 16 or older have been to a nature center in the past 12 months. Those most likely to visit nature centers are people aged 25 to 49, with over half doing so in the past year. Nature centers were visited by 44 percent of people in their 50s, and by just 31 percent of those aged 60 or older.

As with most outdoor activities, the propensity to visit nature centers rises with income. Nearly 60 percent of people with household incomes of $50,000 or more have visited a nature center in the past 12 months, versus fewer than 40 percent of adults with incomes under $25,000.

Men and women are about equally likely to visit nature centers. Whites are more likely to visit nature centers than blacks and "others" (primarily Asians and Hispanics).

The propensity to visit a nature center rises steeply with education. Most people with at least some college experience have visited a nature center in the past 12 months, versus only 38 percent of people who went no further than finishing high school and just 29 percent of those without a high school diploma.

Nature center visits are most common among people in households with two adults, suggesting that it is an activity enjoyed most by empty nesters. As more baby boomers enter the empty-nest lifestage in the years ahead, the popularity of nature centers may grow. But these facilities will have to adapt to boomer interests, providing the in-depth information and sophisticated presentations boomers demand.

Visiting a Nature Center

(percent of persons aged 16 or older who visited a nature center at least once in the past year, by selected demographic characteristics, 1994-95)

Total	**46.4%**
Age	
Aged 16 to 24	44.2
Aged 25 to 29	54.9
Aged 30 to 39	56.6
Aged 40 to 49	52.4
Aged 50 to 59	44.2
Aged 60 or older	30.5
Income	
Under $15,000	28.8
$15,000 to $24,999	38.3
$25,000 to $49,999	51.6
$50,000 to $74,999	58.7
$75,000 to $99,999	61.5
$100,000 or more	59.4
Sex	
Men	46.3
Women	46.7
Race and Hispanic origin	
White	48.7
Black	33.2
Other, including Hispanic	42.0
Education	
Not a high school graduate	28.9
High school graduate	38.2
Some college	50.6
College graduate	59.2
Number of persons in household	
One	35.2
Two	45.1
Three	49.1
Four	53.9
Five or more	51.4

(continued)

(continued from previous page)

Number of persons aged 16 or older in household	
One	38.5%
Two	51.1
Three or more	44.7
Number of persons under age 6 in household	
None	43.9
One or more	45.6

Source: USDA Forest Service, 1994-95 National Survey on Recreation and the Environment

Appendix

Contact Information for
Sport and Recreational Organizations

Below is a list of Internet addresses (or telephone numbers for those without Internet sites) for a variety of sport and recreational information resources. They are listed in alphabetical order by activity. This list is by no means complete, but is meant to offer a starting point for readers who would like more information about outdoor sports and recreation.

The links listed below are provided as a convenience and are for reference only. The author and New Strategist do not warrant the accuracy or completeness of the information, text, graphics, or any other items provided on the referenced Internet pages. The citation of the links is not meant to be an endorsement of or recommendation for any product or service, including the links themselves. The owner of each Internet site is solely responsible for the material contained therein.

Backpacking

- Adventure Sports On-Line: http://www.adventuresports.com
- *Backpacker* magazine: http://www.rodalepress.com
- Colorado Outward Bound: telephone (303) 837-0880
- Great Outdoors Recreation Pages: http://www.gorp.com

Baseball

- Nando Baseball Server: http://www.nando.net/baseball
- The Sporting Goods Manufacturers Association's Baseball and Softball Council: http://www.sportlink.com/sport
- Total Baseball: http://www.totalbaseball.com
- USA Baseball (national governing body): http://www.usabaseball.com

Basketball

- American Basketball League: http://www.ableague.com
- National Basketball Association: http://www.nba.com
- USA Basketball (national governing body): telephone (719) 590-4800
- Women's National Basketball Association: http://www.wnba.com

Bicycling

- Bicycle Transit Authority: http://www. bikeinfo.com
- *Bicycling* magazine: on America Online, keyword "bicycling"
- League of American Bicyclists: http://www. bikeleague.org
- U.S. Cycling Federation: http://www. usacycling.com

Birding

- The American Birding Association: http://www.americanbirding.org
- The Aviary: http://theaviary.com
- *Audubon* magazine: http://audubon.org/audubon
- *Bird Watcher's Digest:* P.O. Box 110, Marietta, OH 45750
- Birder.com: http://www.birder.com
- *Birding* magazine: http://www.americanbirding.org
- Birding FAQ: http://www.birdwatching.com/birdingfaq.html
- EyrieUSA—the Birder's Home Page: http://www.eyrieusa.com

Boating

- Boat Owners Association of the U.S.: http://www.boatus.com
- BoatFacts: http://www.boatfacts.com
- Boat/U.S.: http://www.boatus.com
- Internet Waterway: http://www.iwol.com
- Soundings: http://www.soundingspub.com
- U.S. Power Squadrons: http://www.usps.org

Camping

- American Camping Association (summer camps): http://www.aca-camp.org
- Appalachian Mountain Club: http://www.lehigh.edu/ludas/public/www-data/amc.htm
- Great Outdoors Recreation Pages (GORP): http://www.gorp.com
- Recreational Vehicle Dealers Association: 3930 University Dr., Fairfax, VA 22030; telephone (703) 591-7130

Canoeing

- American Canoe Association: http://www.aca-paddler.org
- *Canoe & Kayak* magazine: http://www.canoekayak.com

Caving

- National Caves Association: http://www.cavern.com
- National Speleogical Society: http://www.caves.org/~nss
- United States Show Cave Directory: http://www.goodearth.com/showcave.htm

Consumer Expenditure Survey

Bureau of Labor Statistics: http://www.BLS.gov

Cross-Country Skiing

See Skiing

Cruising

Cruise Line Industry Association: 500 FifthAve., Ste. 1407, New York, NY 10110; telephone (212) 921-0066

Downhill Skiing

See Skiing

Fishing

See Hunting and Fishing

Football

- ESPN SportsZone NFL: http://espnet.sportzone.com/nfl
- Fox Sports–Football Newsroom: http://www.foxsports.com/sports/news/newsroom/nfl.index.html
- National Football League: http://www.nfl.com
- National Touch Flag Football League: http://www.ntfl.com

Golf

- Family Golf Assocation: http://www.familygolf.org
- *Golf* magazine: telephone (212) 779-5522
- *Golf Illustrated* magazine: Kachina Publications, Ste. 250, 5050 N. Fortieth St., Phoenix, AZ 85018; telephone (612) 955-0611
- *The Golfer* magazine: Heather and Pine Publishing, 42 West 38th Street, New York,

NY 10024; telephone (212) 768-8360

- Golf.com: http://golf.com
- GolfWeb: http://www.golfweb.com
- National Golf Foundation: http://www.ngf.org

Hiking

- *American Hiker* magazine: American Hiker Society, P.O. Box 20160, Washington, DC, 20041; telephone (310) 565-6704
- Hiking through the Web: http://www.autonomy.com/hiking.htm
- Outdoor Enthusiast: http://www.cyberbrokers.com/outdoors-enthusiast

Hockey

National Hockey League: http://www.nhl.com

Horseback Riding

- *The Equine Image* magazine: P.O. Box 916, 1003 Central Ave., Fort Dodge, IA 50501; telephone (800) 247-2000.
- Great Outdoor Recreation Pages: http://www.gorp.com
- *Horse and Horseman* magazine: 34249 Camino Capistrano, Capistrano Beach, CA 92629; telephone (714) 493-2101
- *Horse Illustrated* magazine: P.O. Box 6050, Mission Viejo, CA 92690; telephone (714) 855-8822

Hunting and Fishing

- *American Angler* magazine: Northland Press, P.O. Box 280, Route 16, Intervale, NH 03845; telephone (603) 356-9425
- *Bassin* magazine: telephone (918) 366-4441
- *Field and Stream* magazine: http://www.fieldandstream.com
- The Fishing Network: http://www.the-fishing-network.com
- Hunters.com: http://www.hunters.com
- *Fly Fisherman* magazine: Box 8200, 2245 Kohn Rd., Harrisburg, PA 17105; telephone (717) 657-9555
- *The In-Fisherman* magazine: 651 Edgewood Dr., Brainerd, MN 56401-9681; telephone (218) 829-1648
- International Hunting and Fishing Museum: http://www.ihfm.org
- *Outdoor Life* magazine: Times Mirror Magazines, Inc., 2 Park Ave., New York, NY 10016; telephone (212) 779-5000
- Outdoors Network Online: http://www.outdoors.net

- Outdoors On-line: http://www.ool.com
- Responsive Management: P.O. Box 389, Harrisonburg, VA 22801; telephone (540) 432-1888
- *Sports Afield* magazine: http://www.sportsafield.com
- United States Fish and Wildlife Service: http://www.fws.gov
- United States Forest Service: http://www.fs.fed.us
- Wildlife Legislative Fund: http://www.wlfa.org

Ice Skating

See Winter Sports

In-Line Skating

- *In-Line Skating* magazine: http://www.xcscx.com/skater
- International In-Line Skating Association: http://www.inlineskate.com

Kayaking

- Adventure Sports On-Line: http://www.adventuresports.com
- American Whitewater Affiliation: http://www.awa.org
- *Canoe and Kayak* magazine: http://www.canoekayak.com
- Great Outdoors Recreation Pages: http://www.gorp.com

Mountain Climbing and Rock Climbing

- 1997 About Climbing: http://www.aboutclimbing.com
- Access Fund: http://www.outdoorlink.com/accessfund
- American Mountain Guides Association: http://www.climbnet.com/amga/index.html
- Appalachian Mountain Club: http://www.lehigh.edu/ludas/public/www-data/amc.htm
- *Climbing* magazine: http://www.climbing.com
- Great Outdoors Recreation Pages: http://www.gorp.com
- Mountain On-Line: http://dialspace.dial.pipex.com/ikhaya/mountain.htm
- National Recreation and Parks Association: http://www.nrpa.org

National Collegiate Athletic Association

http://www.ncaa.org

National Federation of State High School Associations

11724 N.W. Plaza Circle, P.O. Box 20626, Kansas City, MO 64195; telephone (816) 464-5400

National Survey of Recreation and the Environment

http://www.orca.org

Orienteering

- Rogaineing: http://www2.aos.princeton.edu/rdslater/orienteering/definitions/rogaining.htm
- United States Orienteering Federation: P.O. Box 1444, Forest Park, Georgia 30051; telephone (404) 363-2110

Outdoors On-Line (outdoors web site)

http://www.ool.com

Personal Water Craft

- Jet Ski Net: http://www.geocities.com/yosemite/6229/main.html
- *Personal Watercraft Illustrated*: http://www.watercraft.com
- Personal Watercraft Zone Internet magazine: http://www.caleb.com/~pwczone
- PWC Club USA: http://www.pwcclubusa.com
- Sea-Doo (manufacturer): http://www.sea-doo.com

Rafting

- Adventure Sports On-Line: http://www.adventuresports.com
- American Whitewater Affiliation: http://www.awa.org
- Great Outdoors Recreation Pages: http://www.gorp.com

Responsive Management

P.O. Box 389, Harrisonburg, VA 22801; telephone (540) 432-1888

Rock climbing

See Mountain Climbing

Rowing

- Row as One: http://www.tiac.net/users/rowasone/index.html
- Rower.com: http://www.rower.com
- The Rower's Resource: http://www.rowersresource.com
- US Rowing: 800-314-4-ROW

Running

- Dead Runners Society: http://storm.cadcam.iupui.edu/drs/drs.html
- *Runner's World*: Rodale Press, 33 East Minor St., Emmasus, PA 18098; telephone (610) 967-5171; Rodale's Internet site: http://www.rodalepress.com
- Running Network: http://www.runningnetwork.com

Sailing

- *Cruising World*: http://www.cruisingworld.com
- DownWind Online: http://www.downwind.com
- *Sailing* magazine: http://www.sailnet.com
- The Sailing Index: http://www.sailingindex.com
- *Sailing World* magazine: http://www.sailingworld.com
- World Wide Sail: http://www.onramp.net

Skiing (*see also* Winter Sports)

- Cross Country Ski Information Center: http://www.xski.com
- *Cross Country Skier* magazine: http://www.crosscountryskier.com
- National Ski Areas Association: http://www.travelbase.com/skiareas
- Ski Web: http://www.skiweb.com
- Skinet (a collaboration between *Ski* and *Skiing* magazines): http://www.skinet.com
- United States Skiing Association: http://www.ussa.org

Sledding

See Winter Sports

Snorkeling

- *Freediving and Snorkeling* magazine: http://www.freediving-mag.com
- Oceans: http://www.oceans.net
- Scuba! on-line interactive magazine: http://www.scubaon-line.com
- Underwater Society of America: e-mail, USAFIN@aol.com

Snowmobiling (*see also* Winter Sports)

- American Council of Snowmobile Associations: telephone (517) 351-4362
- *American Snowmobiling* magazine: http://www.amsnow.com
- Snowmobile homepage: http://www.sledding.com

Snowboarding (*see also* Winter Sports)

- International Snowboard Federation: http://www.isf.ch
- United States Amateur Snowboarding Association: http://wwride.com/usasa/index.htm

Soccer

- FIFA Online (Fédération Internationale de Football Association, in Zurich, Switzerland—international governing body): http://www.fifa.com
- Soccer America On-Line: http://www.socceramerica.com
- Soccer Industry Council of America: http://www.sportlink.com/soccer
- *Soccer Now* (the official publication of American Youth Soccer Organization): 5403 W. 138th St., Hawthorne, CA 90250; telephone (310) 643-5455
- U.S. Soccer (national governing body): telephone (312) 808-1300

Softball

Amateur Softball Association: http://www.softball.org

Sporting Goods Manufacturers Association

http://www.sportlink.com

Surfing

- Adventure Surf: http://www.advensurf.com
- Ocean Surfer: http://www.southcoast.com
- Surf and Sun: http://www.surf-sun.com
- Surflink: http://www.surflink.com

Swimming

- Swim Info: http://www.swiminfo.com
- Swim News Online: http://www.swimnews.com
- World of Masters Swimming: http://www.hk.super.net

Tennis

- Tennis Industry Association: http://www.sportlink.com/sport
- *Tennis Week*: Tennis News, Inc., 341 Madison Ave., 6th Fl., New York, NY 10017; telephone (212) 808-4750.
- *Racquet* magazine: Heather and Pine Publishing, 42 W. 38th St., #1202, New York, NY 10024; telephone (212) 768-8360.

Tourism Works for America Council

telephone (202) 408-2183

Travel Industry Association of America

http://www.tia.org

Volleyball

- USA Volleyball: http://volleyball.org
- *Volleyball* magazine: Avcom Publishing, Ltd., 21700 Oxnard St., Ste. 1600, Woodland Hills, CA 91367; telephone (818) 593-3900
- Volleyball Worldwide: http://www.volleyball.org
- Volleyball.com: http://www.volleyball.com

Walking

- American Volkssport Association: http://www.ava.org
- National Organization of Mall Walkers: P.O. Box 256, Hermann, MO 65041; send self- addressed stamped envelope for more information
- PedNet: http://www.flora.org/pednet
- *Walking* magazine: 9-11 Harcourt St., Boston, MA 02116; telephone (617) 266-3322
- Wellness Walking: http://www.racewalk.com

Water Skiing

- *Behind the Boat* magazine: http://www.behindtheboat.com
- USA Water Ski (national governing body): http://www.usawaterski.org
- Waterski World: http://www.deerfield.com/waterski
- *Waterskier* magazine: http://waterski.net/awsa/waterskier.html

Wildlife Observation

- Great Outdoor Recreation Pages: http://www.gorp.com
- Watchable Wildlife in the National Parks: http://www.aqd.nps.gov/natnet/wr/watchwl.htm

Windsurfing

- *American Windsurfer* magazine: http://www.american.windsurfer.com
- Windsurfer web page: http://www.windsurfer.com
- American Windsurfing Industry Association: http://www.gorge.net/windsurf/awia

Winter Sports

- Ice Castle: http://www.ice-castle.com
- Snowsports Industries America: http://www.snowlink.com
- Winter Sports Foundation: http://www.wintersports.org

Glossary

age The age of the reference person, also called the householder or head of household.

baby boomers Americans born between 1946 and 1964.

consumer unit For convenience, called households in the text of this book. Defined as follows:
• All members of a household who are related by blood, marriage, adoption, or other legal arrangements.
• A person living alone or sharing a household with others or living as a roomer in a private home or lodging house or in permanent living quarters in a hotel or motel, but who is financially independent.
• Two persons or more living together who pool their income to make joint expenditure decisions. Financial independence is determined by the three major expense categories: housing, food, and other living expenses. To be considered financially independent, at least two of the three major expense categories have to be provided by the respondent.

education The highest degree attained by the survey respondent or householder.

expenditure The transaction cost including excise and sales taxes of goods and services acquired during the survey period. The full cost of each purchase is recorded even though full payment may not have been made at the date of purchase. Average expenditure figures may be artificially low because figures are calculated using all consumer units within a demographic segment rather than just purchasers. Expenditure estimates include money spent on gifts for others.

Generation X Americans born between 1965 and 1976, also known as the baby bust.

Hispanics Persons or householders who identify their origin as Mexican, Puerto Rican, Central or South American, or some other Hispanic origin. Persons of Hispanic origin may be of any race. In other words, there are black Hispanics, white Hispanics, and Asian Hispanics.

household According to the Census Bureau, all the persons who occupy a household. A group of unrelated people who share a housing unit as roommates or unmarried partners is also counted as a household. Households do not include group quarters such as college dormitories, prisons, or nursing homes. A household may contain more than one consumer unit. The terms "household" and "consumer unit" are used interchangeably in this book.

household, race/ethnicity of Households are categorized according to the race or ethnicity of the householder only.

income Money received in the preceding calendar year by each person aged 15 or older. In this book, income is shown for households.

non-Hispanics People who do not identify themselves as Hispanic. Non-Hispanics may be of any race.

race Race is self-reported and appears in three categories in this book: white, black, and "other" (primarily Asian).

region Consumer units are classified according to their address at the time of their participation in the survey. The four major census regions of the United States are the following state groupings:

• *Northeast* Connecticut, Maine, Massachusetts, New Hampshire, New Jersey, New York, Pennsylvania, Rhode Island, and Vermont.

• *Midwest* Illinois, Indiana, Iowa, Kansas, Michigan, Minnesota, Missouri, Nebraska, North Dakota, Ohio, South Dakota, and Wisconsin.

• *South* Alabama, Arkansas, Delaware, District of Columbia, Florida, Georgia, Kentucky, Louisiana, Maryland, Mississippi, North Carolina, Oklahoma, South Carolina, Tennessee, Texas, Virginia, and West Virginia.

• *West* Alaska, Arizona, California, Colorado, Hawaii, Idaho, Montana, Nevada, New Mexico, Oregon, Utah, Washington, and Wyoming.

Index

Motorboating, Kayaking, Personal watercraft riding, Rowing, Sailing.
  number participating, 3-4, 11-12
  percent participating, 12, 187
  spending on, 237-241

Bowling, in high school, 282

Bus fares, intercity, spending on, 313-315

Canoeing
  in high school, 282
  number participating, 12
  percent participating, 12, 187-191
    by age, 14-19, 188, 190-191
    by education, 42, 189-190
    by household type, 190-191
    by income, 20-24, 188, 190
    by race and Hispanic origin, 30-37, 188, 190
    by sex, 25-29, 188, 190

Camping
  number participating, 3-4, 11-12
  percent participating, 12, 330-333
    by age, 14-19, 330, 332
    by education, 42, 331-332
    by household type, 331-333
    by income, 20-24, 330, 332
    by race and Hispanic origin, 30-37, 331-332
    by sex, 25-29, 331-332

Caving
  number participating, 12
  percent participating, 12, 83, 95-98
    by age, 14-19, 95-97
    by education, 42, 95, 97
    by household type, 96-98
    by income, 20-24, 95, 97
    by race and Hispanic origin, 30-37, 95, 97
    by sex, 25-29, 95, 97

College sports
  number participating, by sex, 288-293
  percent participating, by sex, 288-297

Competitive spirit squads, in high school, 282

Crew. See Rowing.

Cross-country
  running, See Running.
  skiing see Skiing

Decathalon, in high school, 282

Disabled, 7

Downhill skiing. See Skiing.

Entertainment, spending on, 44-46

Equestrian, in high school, 282. See also Horseback riding.

Fan Cost Index™, 62-63

Fencing
  in high school, 282
  National College Athletic Association, 290-297

Field hockey, in high school, 282

Fish viewing
  number participating, 11-12
  percent participating, 12, 143, 149-152
    by age, 149, 151
    by education, 149, 151
    by household type, 150-152
    by income, 150-151
    by race and Hispanic origin, 150-151
    by sex, 150-151

Fishing
  number participating, 3-4, 11-12
  percent participating, 12, 69-74
    by age, 14-19, 70, 73
    by education, 42, 71, 73
    by income, 20-24, 70, 73
    by household type, 71, 73-74
    by race and Hispanic origin, 30-37, 71, 73
    by sex, 25-29, 71, 73
  spending on, 80-82

Floating, rafting
  number participating, 12
  percent participating, 12, 187, 192-195
    by age, 14-19, 192, 194-195
    by education, 42, 192, 194
    by household type, 194-195
    by income, 20-24, 192, 194
    by race and Hispanic origin, 30-37, 192, 194
    by sex, 25-29, 194

Football
  in high school, 282-284
  National College Athletic Association, 290-295
  National Football League, 2, 168
    Fan Cost Index™, 62-63
  number participating, 12

percent participating, 12, 153, 167-170
  by age, 14-19, 167, 169
  by education, 42, 167-169
  by household type, 167, 169-170
  by income, 20-24, 167, 169
  by race and Hispanic origin, 30-37, 167-169
  by sex, 25-29, 167-169

Gasoline on out-of-town trips, spending on,
  310-312

Gathering with friends and family outdoors
  percent participating, 65-68
  by age, 65, 67
  by education, 65, 67
  by household type, 65, 67-68
  by income, 65, 67
  by race and Hispanic origin, 65, 67
  by sex, 65, 67

Golf
  in high school, 282-284
  National College Athletic Association, 290-297
  number participating, 3, 12
  percent participating, 12, 83, 99-105, 327
  by age, 14-19, 99-100, 102
  by education, 42, 99-102
  by household type, 102-103
  by income, 20-24, 99-100,102
  by race and Hispanic origin, 30-37, 99, 102
  by sex, 25-29, 99-100, 102
  spectators at PGA events, 100-101, 104-105

Gymnastics
  in high school, 282
  National College Athletic Association, 290-297

Heptathlon, in high school, 282

High school sports
  number participating, 277-287
  by sex, 279-284
  by sport, 281-284
  by state, 285-287
  percent participating, 279-282
  by sex, 279-282
  by sport, 281-282

Hiking
  number participating, 3-4, 12
  percent participating, 12, 83, 106-109
  by age, 14-19, 106-108
  by education, 42, 106, 108
  by household type, 106-109

by income, 20-24, 106, 108
  by race and Hispanic origin, 30-37, 106, 108
  by sex, 25-29, 106, 108

Historic sites, visiting. *See also* Prehistoric sites.
  percent participating, 340-342
  by age, 341
  by education, 340-341
  by household type, 341-342
  by income, 341
  by race and Hispanic origin, 341
  by sex, 341

Hockey
  field, in high school, 282
  National Hockey League, 2, 4, 172
  Fan Cost Index™, 62-63
  ice
    in high school, 282
    National College Athletic Association, 290-297
    number participating, 173
    percent participating, 153, 171-173
  roller
    number participating, 173
    percent participating, 153, 171-173

Horseback riding
  in high school, 282
  number participating, 3, 11-12
  percent participating, 12, 83, 110-113
  by age, 14-19, 110-112
  by education, 42, 110, 112
  by household type, 110-113
  by income, 20-24, 110-112
  by race and Hispanic origin, 30-37, 110, 112
  by sex, 25-29, 110, 112

Hotels. *See* Lodging while on out-of-town trips.

Hunting
  number participating, 3, 12
  percent participating, 12, 69, 75, 78-79
  by age, 14-19, 78
  by education, 42, 78
  by household type, 78-79
  by income, 20-24, 75, 78
  by race and Hispanic origin, 30-37, 78
  by sex, 25-29, 78
  spending on, 80-82

Hybrid sports, 6, 115, 266

Ice hockey. *See* Hockey.

Ice skating
  number participating, 3, 12
  percent participating, 12, 245, 257-260
    by age, 14-19, 257, 259-260
    by education, 42, 259
    by household type, 257, 259-260
    by income, 20-24, 257, 259
    by race and Hispanic origin, 30-37, 257, 259
    by sex, 25-29, 257, 259

In-line skating
  as a hybrid sport, 6, 115
  number participating, 114, 116
  percent participating, 83, 114-116
    by age, 114-116
    by sex, 114, 116

Jogging. *See* Running.

Judo, in high school, 282

Kayaking
  number participating, 11-12
  percent participating, 12, 187, 196-199
    by age, 14-19, 196, 198-199
    by education, 42, 196, 198
    by household type, 198-199
    by income, 20-24, 196, 198
    by race and Hispanic origin, 30-37, 196, 198
    by sex, 25-29, 196, 198

Lacrosse
  in high school, 282
  National College Athletic Association, 290-297

Lodging while on out-of-town trips, spending on,
    320-322

Major League Baseball
  Fan Cost Index™, 62-63
  number attending games, 2

Motels. *See* Lodging while on out-of-town trips.

Motorboating. *See also* Boating.
  number participating, 3-4, 12
  percent participating, 12, 187, 200-203
    by age, 14-19, 200, 202-203
    by education, 42, 201-202
    by household type, 202-203
    by income, 20-24, 200, 202
    by race and Hispanic origin, 30-37, 201-202
    by sex, 25-29, 200, 202
  spending on, 237-239

Mountain climbing. *See also* Rock climbing.
  number participating, 12
  percent participating, 12, 83, 117-120
    by age, 14-19, 117, 119
    by education, 42, 119
    by household type, 118-120
    by income, 20-24, 117, 119
    by race and Hispanic origin, 30-37, 117, 119
    by sex, 25-29, 117, 119

National Basketball Association
  Fan Cost Index™, 62-63
  number attending games, 2

National Collegiate Athletic Association
  attendance at games, 2
  participation in sports, by sex, 288-297

National Football League
  Fan Cost Index™, 62-63
  number attending games, 2

National Hockey League
  Fan Cost Index™, 62-63
  number attending games, 2

Nature center, visiting
  percent participating, 345-347
    by age, 345-346
    by education, 345-346
    by household type, 345-347
    by income, 345-346
    by race and Hispanic origin, 345-346
    by sex, 345-346

Off-road driving, 3, 12

Olympics, 7-8, 122

Orienteering
  number participating, 12, 121
  percent participating, 12, 83, 121-124
    by age, 14-19, 121-123
    by education, 42, 121-123
    by household type, 122-124
    by income, 20-24, 121, 123
    by race and Hispanic origin, 30-37, 121, 123
    by sex, 25-29, 121, 123

Participant sports, spending on, 47-49

Pentathalon, in high school, 282

Personal watercraft riding
number participating, 11-12
percent participating, 12, 187, 205-207
by age, 14-19, 204, 206-207
by education, 42, 205-206
by household type, 206-207
by income, 20-24, 204, 206
by race and Hispanic origin, 30-37, 204, 206
by sex, 25-29, 204, 206
regulation of, 7

Picnicking
number participating, 3-4, 11-12
percent participating, 12, 65-68
by age, 14-19, 65, 67
by education, 42, 65, 67
by household type, 65, 67-68
by income, 20-24, 65, 67
by race and Hispanic origin, 30-37, 65, 67
by sex, 25-29, 65, 67

Prehistoric sites, visiting. *See also* Historic sites.
percent participating, 340, 343-344
by age, 340, 343
by education, 340, 343
by household type, 343-344
by income, 343
by race and Hispanic origin, 343
by sex, 343

Recreational
activities while on out-of-town trips, 327
spending on, 326, 328-329
lessons, spending on, 9, 50-52
travel, 299-302
characteristics of, 302
number participating, 301
percent participating, 301-302

Riflery
high school, 282
National College Athletic Association, 290-291,
294-295

Rock climbing. *See also* Mountain climbing.
number participating, 12, 125
percent participating, 12, 83, 125-128
by age, 14-19, 125, 127
by education, 42, 125, 127
by household type, 126-128
by income, 20-24, 125, 127
by race and Hispanic origin, 30-37, 125, 127
by sex, 25-29, 125, 127

Rowing
National College Athletic Association, 209,
290-297
number participating, 12
percent participating, 12, 187, 208-211
by age, 14-19, 208, 210-211
by education, 42, 208, 210
by household type, 210-211
by income, 20-24, 208, 210
by race and Hispanic origin, 30-37, 208, 210
by sex, 25-29, 210

Running
cross-country,
high school, 282-284
National College Athletic Association, 290-297
number participating, 3-4, 12
percent participating, 12, 83, 129-132
by age, 14-19, 129, 131
by education, 42, 131
by household type, 130-132
by income, 20-24, 129, 131
by race and Hispanic origin, 30-37, 129, 131
by sex, 25-29, 129, 131

Sailing
National College Athletic Association, 294-295
number participating, 3, 12
percent participating, 12, 187, 212-215
by age, 14-19, 212, 214-215
by education, 42, 213-214
by household type, 213-215
by income, 20-24, 212, 214
by race and Hispanic origin, 30-37, 212, 214
by sex, 25-29, 212, 214

Ship fares, spending on, 323-325

Sightseeing
number participating, 3-4, 11-12
percent participating, 12, 334-336
by age, 334-335
by education, 334-335
by household type, 334-336
by income, 334-335
by race and Hispanic origin, 334-335
by sex, 334-335

Skating. *See* Ice skating, In-line skating.